The music industry: Inside Secrets

The music industry Inside Secrets

YURI tha Jury

Published by Mankraft publishing, 2026.

While every precaution has been taken in the preparation of this book, the publisher assumes no responsibility for errors or omissions, or for damages resulting from the use of the information contained herein.

THE MUSIC INDUSTRY INSIDE SECRETS

First edition. April 1, 2026.

ISBN: 979-8230175629

Written by YURI tha Jury.

Also by YURI tha Jury

Book series 1

Fame

Standalone

The Malcolm Dynasty

A women's worth

YURI tha Jury _Fame 2

Nightmare on Cannon Ave

Lock & Key: The industry secrets

Family Dynasty

The music industry Inside Secrets

Night fall

The Straight Shooter Story

By: YURI tha Jury

Dedication

This book is dedicated to the countless unsung artists, songwriters, and musicians who have poured their hearts and souls into their craft, only to be met with exploitation, broken promises, and the crushing weight of an industry that often prioritizes profit over integrity. Their resilience, their unwavering passion, and their enduring spirit in the face of adversity are a testament to the power of music and the human spirit. This work is a small attempt to amplify their voices, to shed light on their struggles, and to contribute to a future where their talent and dedication are fairly rewarded and respected. It is also dedicated to those brave individuals within the industry—managers, lawyers, and even some executives—who have risked their careers to fight for justice and ethical practices, reminding us that even within the darkest corners, there are sparks of hope and resistance. Their courage inspires us all to strive for a better, more just music industry. Finally, this is dedicated to the future generations of musicians, hoping that this book will serve as a cautionary tale, a guide, and a source of inspiration to navigate the complexities of the music business with awareness, resilience, and unwavering commitment to their artistic vision. May their journeys be filled with success, integrity, and the unwavering support they deserve.

Preface

For years, I've watched, listened, and documented the machinations of the music industry, a world of glittering facades and shadowy dealings. The public often sees only the polished image: the chart-topping hits, the sold-out concerts, the glamorous awards ceremonies. But beneath the surface lies a far more complex and often troubling reality. This book is not intended as a condemnation of the entire industry; many talented and hardworking individuals strive for fairness and ethical practices within its framework. However, it is impossible to ignore the systemic issues, the exploitative contracts, the power imbalances, and the ethical compromises that plague its darker corners. My intention in writing "The Music Industry: Inside Secrets" is to expose these realities, not for the sake of sensationalism, but to provide a more complete and unflinching portrait of an industry that profoundly impacts artists' lives and the cultural landscape. This work is the culmination of years of meticulous research, interviews with artists, industry insiders, and legal experts, as well as the examination of countless contracts and legal documents. I believe that understanding these complexities is vital for anyone involved in, or passionate about, the world of music—from aspiring artists to dedicated fans. This is a call for increased transparency, accountability, and a fundamental shift towards ethical practices that prioritize the artists' well-being and creative freedom. The music industry should celebrate and nurture its creative talent, not exploit it. This is a story about power, money, art, and the human cost of chasing a dream.

Introduction

The music industry is a powerful force, shaping our cultural landscape and influencing our lives in profound ways. It generates billions of dollars annually, fuels global trends, and provides a platform for artists to share their creativity with the world. However, beneath the surface of this multibillion dollar enterprise lies a system rife with complexities, contradictions, and often, blatant exploitation. "The Music Industry: Inside Secrets" explores this duality, exposing the hidden underbelly of an industry that frequently prioritizes profit over the well-being of the very artists who create its lifeblood. This book delves into the intricate web of contracts, power dynamics, and legal battles that define the music business. It examines the often-unfair distribution of wealth, revealing how artists frequently receive a disproportionately small share of their own revenue. We will investigate the manipulative tactics employed by record labels and other industry stakeholders, illustrating how artists, particularly those early in their careers, can easily become victims of exploitative agreements. Through detailed case studies and compelling narratives, we will examine how artists are pressured to compromise their artistic visions to meet commercial demands, and how the relentless pursuit of fame often comes at a significant cost to their mental and physical health. This is not merely an exposé of individual wrongdoings, but rather a critical analysis of systemic issues —the inherent conflicts of interest, the lack of transparency, and the need for significant reform within the music industry. This book seeks to empower artists, fans, and everyone interested in understanding the complexities of the music business with knowledge and a clearer understanding of the realities within this often-glamorized world. It's a call for greater accountability, a demand for fair practices, and a testament to the resilience of artists who continue to create despite the challenges they face.

The Glamorized Myth of Overnight Success

The music industry, a glittering mirage of fame and fortune, constantly projects an illusion of overnight success. Countless documentaries, magazine articles, and social media posts portray the meteoric rise of artists, seemingly plucked from obscurity and catapulted to stardom with little effort. This narrative, meticulously crafted and amplified by publicists, record labels, and the media itself, serves a crucial purpose: to maintain the allure, the intoxicating dream that fuels the relentless pursuit of musical glory. However, the reality is far more complex and often brutally dispiriting. The truth behind the glamorous façade is a tapestry woven with years of relentless toil, financial insecurity, creative compromises, and the sheer, grinding persistence that defies easy categorization as "overnight success."

Consider the story of Sam Cooke, a gospel prodigy who transitioned to R&B and became a hugely influential figure in popular music. His soulful voice and undeniable charisma captivated audiences, and his hits became instant classics. Yet, the effortless grace he exuded on stage belied the years of grueling performances in small, often poorly paid, venues. His journey wasn't a straightforward ascent; it was punctuated by setbacks, contractual disputes, and the relentless pressure to maintain his image and deliver hits. The narrative of his rapid rise obscures the struggles he faced navigating the racial prejudices of the time, the constant fight for fair compensation, and the often exploitative contracts he was forced to sign to gain traction in the industry. His early years of relentless touring, combined with the constant fight for artistic freedom and fair financial treatment, hardly fit the "overnight success" stereotype.

Similarly, the seemingly effortless ascent of Amy Winehouse, a uniquely talented singer-songwriter, masks the years of hard work and personal struggles that preceded her global recognition. Her distinctive voice and raw emotion resonated deeply with millions, making her a global icon. However, behind the accolades and awards lay a tumultuous personal life marked by substance abuse, relationship difficulties, and the relentless pressure of fame. The media often focused on the dramatic aspects of her life, while overlooking the immense dedication and talent that propelled her to the top. Her story stands as a poignant example of how the pursuit of fame can come at a devastating personal cost, a cost that the narrative of overnight success conveniently ignores.

The statistics themselves paint a more realistic picture. A vast majority of aspiring musicians never achieve mainstream success. The odds are stacked against them. For every artist who makes it big, countless others toil in obscurity, juggling day jobs, performing in small clubs, and self-funding their musical endeavors. The music industry is incredibly competitive, and success requires not just talent, but also a degree of luck, unwavering determination, and often, a willingness to compromise artistic integrity for commercial viability. These are hardly the ingredients of an overnight phenomenon.

The "overnight success" myth is further perpetuated by the carefully constructed public image of artists. Their social media presence meticulously curates a picture of effortless glamour, often concealing the years of struggle and the sacrifices made to achieve that image. The polished appearance, carefully chosen wardrobe, and meticulously crafted online persona mask the reality of long hours spent in studios, relentless touring, and the constant pressure to maintain a public image that might not reflect their private lives.

Furthermore, the media's role in perpetuating this myth is undeniable. News outlets and entertainment publications often focus on the glamorous aspects of the artist's life, selectively highlighting the milestones and achievements while glossing over the struggles and hardships. This skewed perspective reinforces the misconception that success is a matter of chance rather than hard work, dedication, and resilience. The narrative is further reinforced by carefully orchestrated public relations campaigns that strategically manage the image and career trajectory of the artist, often creating a false sense of a rapid ascent.

The case of The Beatles, often cited as an example of overnight success, is a prime example of this manufactured narrative. While their rise was undeniably rapid, it was preceded by years of relentless gigs in dingy clubs across Liverpool and Hamburg. They honed their skills, developed their signature sound, and built a loyal following through sheer perseverance before they achieved global recognition. Their journey, while seemingly fast-paced from the outside, was characterized by hard work, relentless touring, and a constant drive to improve their craft. Their story, when examined in detail, is less about an overnight explosion and more about a relentless climb to the top, fuelled by dedication and years of honing their artistry.

Even the seemingly sudden breakthrough of artists propelled by viral videos or social media platforms often masks significant underlying effort and preparation. The viral video or catchy song that catapults an artist to fame is rarely a spontaneous creation. It's usually the result of meticulous planning, strategic promotion, and often, years of developing their musical skills and building an online following. The "viral" moment is often the culmination of long hours spent creating content, engaging with fans, and perfecting their craft. It's not an accident; it's a carefully orchestrated confluence of talent, timing, and persistent effort.

In conclusion, the myth of overnight success in the music industry is a carefully constructed illusion, designed to maintain the industry's allure and perpetuate the dream. The reality is far more nuanced and often far more challenging. The stories of countless artists demonstrate that success is rarely a sudden event but rather the result of years of hard work, sacrifice, and relentless dedication. While talent is undoubtedly a crucial ingredient, it is often the unseen sacrifices and relentless pursuit of one's artistic vision, often in the face of considerable adversity, that truly defines the arduous and often uncelebrated journey to musical success. This carefully crafted narrative obscures the realities of the music industry, the struggles, and the often-exploitative practices that many artists face in their pursuit of fame.

Understanding this reality is crucial for aspiring musicians and anyone seeking a balanced perspective on the world of popular music. The pursuit of fame is a marathon, not a sprint, and it requires more than just talent and a little luck.

The Dark Side of Record Deals Exploitative Contracts

The seductive whisper of a record deal, often presented as the golden ticket to fame and fortune, frequently masks a far more sinister reality. The seemingly straightforward agreement, brimming with legal jargon and fine print, often becomes a cage, trapping artists in a cycle of debt and creative compromise. Record labels, wielding immense power and influence, frequently leverage their position to negotiate contracts that are heavily skewed in their favor, leaving artists vulnerable to exploitation.

One of the most prevalent exploitative tactics involves the control of an artist's masters. Master recordings are the original recordings of an artist's music, the fundamental assets that generate income through royalties, licensing, and streaming. Historically, artists often signed away ownership of their masters to the record label in exchange for recording and promotion budgets. This meant that even after years of tireless work and global success, the artist might receive only a small percentage of the profits generated from their own music, while the label retained the lion's share of the revenue stream. This arrangement often extends well beyond the initial contract, leaving the artist with little control over their musical legacy. Imagine the scenario: a musician painstakingly crafts an album, pours their heart and soul into every note, and the album becomes a global phenomenon. Years later, when the music is licensed for use in a major film or television show, the musician may receive a paltry sum, while the record label reaps the significant financial rewards. Such examples are not rare; they are, sadly, commonplace.

The 360-degree deal is another notorious example of exploitative contracting. While seemingly offering comprehensive support for the artist, encompassing everything from recording and promotion to merchandising and touring, these deals frequently give the record label a percentage of revenue from every conceivable source connected to the artist's career. This means that the label takes a cut not only from album sales and streaming revenue but also from live performances, merchandise sales, endorsements, and even publishing royalties. The artist, already burdened by recording costs and promotional expenses, effectively finds themselves paying the label a significant portion of their earnings, severely limiting their ability to accumulate wealth and achieve financial stability. The seemingly generous offer of a "one-stop shop" for career management can quickly morph into a financial drain, leaving the artist struggling to break even, let alone build a sustainable career.

Another common tactic involves burying artists in debt. Advance payments, often touted as a show of faith and support, are frequently structured in such a way that the artist is obligated to repay them from their future earnings. These advances, coupled with recording costs, promotional expenses, and other fees, can accumulate to a staggering sum, creating a financial burden that can take years, if not decades, to overcome. The artist, now indebted to the label, is then incentivized to produce hit songs consistently, often compromising artistic vision for commercial viability. The pressure to generate revenue to pay off this debt can stifle creativity and lead to artistic burnout. Many artists find themselves locked into a cycle of debt and obligation, where every creative decision is weighed against its potential to generate immediate profit, often sacrificing artistic integrity.

The issue of recoupable expenses is another significant problem. Record labels frequently charge artists for a wide range of expenses, including studio time, production costs, marketing, and distribution. These expenses are often recoupable, meaning they are deducted from the artist's royalties, meaning the artist may never actually see any profit from their hard work and dedication, even after achieving considerable commercial success. The opaque nature of these expenses often leaves the artist in the dark about the true cost of their project and the amount of money they are actually owed. This lack of transparency is a deliberate tactic to keep artists in a perpetual state of financial uncertainty.

Moreover, record contracts often include clauses that severely restrict an artist's autonomy. These clauses can limit an artist's ability to perform outside of the label's purview, to record with other producers or songwriters, or even to choose the direction of their music. This stifling of creative freedom can lead to artistic dissatisfaction and creative stagnation. The artist, bound by the constraints of the contract, may find themselves unable to explore new musical territories or express their artistic vision fully, resulting in a diminished creative output and a loss of artistic identity. The pressure to conform to the label's expectations can lead to a homogenization of musical styles, stifling innovation and originality in the pursuit of maximizing commercial viability.

Furthermore, many contracts contain overly broad and vaguely defined clauses, leaving room for subjective interpretation and potential exploitation. Ambiguous language surrounding "acceptable artistic output" or "sufficient promotional efforts" allows record labels significant leeway in interpreting the contract to their advantage, leaving artists vulnerable to arbitrary decisions and potentially unfair treatment. The complexity of these contracts, often intentionally obfuscated through dense legal jargon, makes it nearly impossible for artists, particularly those without legal representation, to fully grasp the implications of what they are signing.

The consequences of signing exploitative record deals can be devastating for artists. Financial instability is common, often leading to ongoing debt and a constant struggle to make ends meet. The pressure to generate revenue can lead to creative compromises, artistic burnout, and a diminished sense of self-worth. The lack of control over their creative work can stifle artistic growth and limit an artist's ability to express their true artistic voice. The psychological toll of navigating these complex contracts, coupled with the often-unrealistic expectations of the industry, can contribute to depression, anxiety, and other mental health issues.

The lack of industry transparency further exacerbates the problem. Artists often lack access to comprehensive information about industry standards, contract negotiation tactics, or legal resources, leaving them particularly vulnerable to exploitation. The power imbalance between large record labels and individual artists is deeply ingrained in the industry structure, making it challenging for artists to secure fair and equitable deals. The existing systems often fail to protect artists, leaving them to navigate a complex and often treacherous landscape alone.

Several high-profile cases highlight the devastating consequences of exploitative contracts. While specific details are often shielded by legal agreements and confidentiality clauses, the pattern of exploitation is clear. Many artists, after years of dedication and hard work, have found themselves bankrupt, their careers derailed, and their artistic vision compromised by contracts designed to maximize profits for the label at their expense. These are not isolated incidents; they represent a systemic problem within the music industry.

The fight for fairer contracts and a more equitable music industry is an ongoing battle. Increased transparency, stronger artist advocacy groups, and legal reforms are crucial in leveling the playing field and protecting artists from exploitative practices. A shift in industry culture, one that prioritizes collaboration and mutual respect over profit maximization, is essential. Education and resources for artists concerning contract negotiation and legal rights are also critical to empowering artists and giving them the tools they need to protect themselves. Until then, the shimmering promise of fame often conceals a darker reality, one where the pursuit of success comes at a steep and often devastating price. The illusion of a mutually beneficial partnership frequently masks a complex and often predatory relationship, leaving the artist struggling to reclaim their creative power and financial stability. The fight for fair treatment and a more just music industry is a battle that demands the attention of artists, lawyers, policymakers, and the public alike.

The Role of Agents and Managers Gatekeepers and Guardians

The glittering facade of the music industry often obscures the crucial roles played by agents and managers, individuals who ostensibly act as guardians of their clients' interests. Yet, the reality is far more nuanced, often revealing a landscape riddled with conflicts of interest and instances where these gatekeepers have prioritized their own gain over the well-being of the artists they represent. While a skilled and ethical agent or manager can be invaluable, navigating the complexities of the industry, securing lucrative deals, and providing crucial career guidance, the potential for exploitation and betrayal is significant.

The relationship between an artist and their agent or manager is inherently fraught with power imbalances. The artist, often driven by passion and a fervent desire for success, frequently lacks the business acumen and industry knowledge to negotiate contracts effectively. The manager, conversely, possesses the expertise and connections necessary to navigate the intricate web of deals and relationships that define the music industry. This asymmetry of power creates an environment ripe for exploitation. Managers with questionable ethics can exploit this power imbalance, maneuvering artists into disadvantageous contracts, manipulating their finances, and ultimately hindering their careers.

One of the primary ways managers can compromise their clients' interests is through opaque financial dealings. The lack of transparency in many management agreements allows managers to conceal fees, expenses, and revenue streams from their artists. This can include hidden commissions, inflated expense reports, and the deliberate obfuscation of royalty payments. Artists, often lacking the financial expertise to scrutinize their accounts, may remain unaware of these manipulations, resulting in significant financial losses. The practice of "skimming" – diverting a portion of an artist's earnings for personal gain – is a pervasive problem, further exacerbated by a lack of stringent oversight and regulatory mechanisms.

Another troubling aspect is the potential for conflict of interest. Managers often represent multiple artists, creating a situation where the interests of one client may conflict with another. For instance, a manager may prioritize securing a lucrative endorsement deal for one artist, even if it means sacrificing an opportunity for another artist on their roster. This inherent conflict can lead to unfair treatment and unequal distribution of resources, ultimately harming the careers of some artists in favor of others. The practice of "packaging" acts – bundling several artists together to appeal to a label – has also been criticised, often resulting in less advantageous deals for individual artists who may have achieved greater success independently.

The issue of "ownership" of an artist's career trajectory is also a point of contention. Aggressive managers sometimes exert excessive control over an artist's creative vision, forcing them to compromise their artistic integrity for commercial gain. This can involve manipulating song choices, influencing the artist's image, and dictating their public persona, ultimately sacrificing authenticity for immediate commercial success. While a manager's guidance is often beneficial, crossing the line into controlling an artist's artistic expression can be creatively stifling and damaging in the long run. This control can extend to the artist's social media presence, potentially limiting their freedom of expression and creating a curated persona that does not reflect their genuine self.

The use of "boilerplate" contracts – pre-written agreements with limited room for negotiation – is another method used to disadvantage artists. These contracts, filled with complex legal language, often favor the manager, leaving the artist with little recourse if disputes arise. The lack of independent legal counsel for many artists exacerbates this problem. Many emerging artists, eager to secure a deal, sign these contracts without fully understanding their implications, unknowingly sacrificing their rights and future earnings.

The lack of adequate oversight and regulation in the management sector further compounds the problem. There is often a shortage of readily available information on industry best practices and ethical standards, leaving many artists vulnerable to exploitation. The industry lacks a unified regulatory body to oversee manager conduct and ensure compliance with ethical guidelines. Existing regulatory bodies are often under-resourced and lack the authority to effectively investigate or prosecute cases of manager misconduct. This regulatory gap encourages unethical behavior and leaves artists with little recourse to address grievances.

The consequences of unethical management practices can be devastating. Financial ruin, creative stagnation, and damage to an artist's reputation are all possible outcomes. The emotional and psychological toll is also significant, leading to stress, anxiety, and even depression. The artist-manager relationship, which ideally should be one of trust and collaboration, can become a source of intense conflict and betrayal, leaving the artist feeling isolated, disillusioned, and financially vulnerable.

Furthermore, the lack of transparency in the industry makes it difficult for artists to identify and avoid potentially exploitative managers. The reputation of a manager can be easily inflated, obscuring the reality of their business practices. Negative experiences frequently remain undocumented or unaddressed, hindering other artists from avoiding similar situations. The culture of secrecy and mutual protection within the industry allows unethical managers to operate with impunity.

The solutions to addressing the issue of unethical agents and managers are multi-faceted. Increased transparency, stricter regulations, and more readily available resources for artists are crucial. The establishment of an independent regulatory body with the power to investigate and prosecute cases of manager misconduct is essential. Strengthening artist advocacy groups and providing legal support for artists navigating management contracts are also vital steps. Education and outreach programs designed to empower artists with the necessary knowledge to protect themselves are crucial to leveling the playing field.

Ultimately, the goal is to create a more just and equitable environment where the artist-manager relationship is built on trust, mutual respect, and a commitment to the artist's longterm success, rather than the manager's personal gain. The industry needs to shift from a system that often prioritizes immediate profits to one that values the well-being and longterm career goals of the artists it claims to represent. Only then can the illusion of protection offered by agents and managers be replaced by a genuine commitment to safeguarding the artists' interests. The music industry needs to confront this pervasive issue, or risk undermining the very talent it relies upon.

Power Dynamics and Industry Gatekeepers Who Controls the Narrative

The power dynamics within the music industry extend far beyond the artist-manager relationship. A web of interconnected entities – major record labels, radio stations, streaming services, and even influential music journalists – hold immense sway over an artist's trajectory, often dictating the very terms of success. These gatekeepers, operating within a complex ecosystem of influence and control, can make or break a career, shaping the narrative surrounding an artist and determining their access to wider audiences.

Major record labels, with their vast financial resources and established distribution networks, are arguably the most powerful players. They control the manufacturing, marketing, and distribution of music, wielding significant influence over radio play, playlist placement on streaming platforms, and ultimately, an artist's chart performance. A deal with a major label can seemingly catapult an artist to stardom, offering access to resources and opportunities unavailable to independent artists. However, these contracts often come with strings attached – demanding control over an artist's creative output, demanding a significant share of revenue, and imposing strict limitations on artistic freedom. The artist, eager for success, may find themselves trapped in a system that prioritizes commercial viability over artistic integrity.

Consider the case of numerous artists who, after signing lucrative deals with major labels, found their creative visions stifled. Their albums were delayed indefinitely, their preferred producers were replaced with label-approved alternatives, and their artistic input was often disregarded in favor of commercially driven strategies. The result was a string of artistically compromised albums, sacrificing creative expression for the pursuit of chart success. These artists, despite possessing immense talent, became victims of a system designed to maximize profit, often at the expense of artistic authenticity. The label's control extended beyond the creative process; their influence over PR and marketing strategies often created a manufactured image, stifling the artist's personal expression and presenting a curated persona to the public.

The role of radio stations in shaping an artist's career should not be underestimated. For decades, radio airplay served as a critical pathway to mainstream success, catapulting lesserknown artists into the limelight. However, this influence has evolved. While radio stations still maintain some importance, their power is increasingly challenged by the rise of streaming services. The decision of a major radio station to play or not play an artist's song can significantly impact their visibility and chart success. It is a stark reminder that even with talent and successful marketing, radio stations can hold considerable sway over which artists gain public exposure.

The rise of streaming services has fundamentally altered the power dynamics of the music industry. Platforms like Spotify, Apple Music, and Amazon Music have become gatekeepers of their own kind, influencing playlists, recommending artists, and shaping listener habits. Their algorithms, designed to maximize user engagement, can catapult artists to viral success or leave them languishing in relative obscurity. The curatorial powers of these platforms, while claiming to be driven by data and listener preferences, are often opaque, raising concerns about potential bias, favoritism, and the potential for manipulation by powerful record labels. Artists with strong ties to these streaming platforms may have an unfair advantage, pushing their music higher up algorithmic suggestions. This makes it harder for artists who are not already part of the established ecosystem to break through. The lack of transparency around these algorithms raises concerns about the fairness and equity of opportunity in the digital marketplace.

The influence extends further to music journalists and critics. Their reviews, articles, and features can shape public perception and influence the success of an artist's work. While critical acclaim is often a desired asset, it's critical to recognize the influence of these journalists. Their position can be abused, either through direct monetary exchanges for favorable reviews or the subtle pressure of cultivating relationships to secure positive coverage. The danger lies not solely in overtly negative reviews but in the power of omission, potentially silencing deserving artists through a lack of exposure. This dynamic highlights the need for increased transparency and ethical standards within music journalism.

The cumulative effect of these various gatekeepers – record labels, radio stations, streaming services, and music critics – is a complex ecosystem that frequently limits opportunities for artists who lack the resources, connections, or the right kind of media exposure. Independent artists, often lacking the financial resources and industry connections of their major label counterparts, face a far steeper climb to success. They must navigate a landscape that is often stacked against them, competing for limited radio airplay, playlist placements, and media attention. The resulting disparity creates a system where success often depends not solely on talent but also on access to power and influence.

The issue of access to wider audiences is further complicated by the ever-evolving landscape of music distribution. The dominance of a small number of major streaming services, coupled with the high cost of effective marketing and promotion, creates a system where only the most wellfunded and well-connected artists can truly reach a broad audience. Independent artists, often lacking the financial resources to compete effectively in this marketplace, are forced to rely on social media, grassroots marketing, and independent promotion methods. However, these channels alone are often insufficient to reach a national or global audience. The result is a system where the financial barriers to entry are disproportionately high, leaving many talented musicians marginalized and unable to reach their full potential.

Addressing the power imbalances inherent in the music industry requires a multi-pronged approach. Greater transparency in the workings of record labels, streaming algorithms, and radio play selections is vital. Strengthening regulations to prevent monopolistic practices and promote fair competition is critical. Supporting independent artists and providing them with the resources and infrastructure necessary to compete effectively is essential. Finally, fostering a culture of ethical conduct within music journalism and promoting critical discourse about the industry's power dynamics will help to create a more level playing field for all artists. The ultimate goal is to create a system that values artistic integrity, creative freedom, and equitable access to opportunities for all musicians, regardless of their financial resources or industry connections. The dismantling of these gatekeeping structures is critical if we want a more diverse and representative musical landscape. Only through transparent and fair practices can the music industry truly live up to its potential for nurturing creativity and celebrating artistic expression.

The Price of Fame Mental Health and Personal Sacrifice

The relentless pursuit of fame in the music industry often comes at a steep personal cost, a price rarely acknowledged amidst the glittering facade of success. While the public eye focuses on chart-topping hits and sold-out stadiums, the mental and physical toll on artists is often hidden, a silent struggle masked by carefully crafted public images. The pressure cooker environment, fueled by relentless competition and exploitative industry practices, pushes many to the brink, leading to substance abuse, depression, anxiety, and even suicide. The industry's inherent structure, designed to prioritize profit over well-being, often leaves artists feeling isolated, vulnerable, and without adequate support.

The pressure to maintain a flawless public image, a relentless cycle of performances, interviews, and social media engagement, creates an almost unbearable burden. Artists are constantly scrutinized, their every move analyzed and judged. Negative reviews, public criticism, and the relentless pressure to constantly produce and maintain popularity can lead to profound feelings of inadequacy and self-doubt. This constant self-monitoring and the pressure to conform to an idealized image can erode an individual's sense of self, leaving them feeling disconnected from their authentic selves. The fear of failure, ever-present in such a highly competitive environment, can be paralyzing, leading to anxiety and panic attacks. The relentless cycle of touring, often involving grueling schedules, long travel days, and lack of sleep, takes a significant physical and mental toll. The lack of personal time and the constant exposure to crowds can contribute to burnout, exhaustion, and feelings of isolation.

The pervasive issue of substance abuse within the music industry serves as a grim testament to the pressures faced by artists. The allure of escapism, the need to cope with intense stress and the relentless demands of their careers, often leads to self-medication through drugs and alcohol. The readily available access to substances, often fueled by a culture of excess and hedonism within certain circles of the industry, exacerbates this problem. The combination of intense pressure, financial instability, and the normalization of substance use can create a destructive cycle that is difficult to break. Many artists find themselves trapped in a vicious spiral, where substance abuse worsens their mental health issues, further intensifying the pressure to perform and perpetuating the cycle of dependence.

Beyond the individual struggles, the industry itself bears a significant responsibility for the mental health crisis amongst its artists. Exploitative contracts, unfair payment structures, and a lack of adequate support systems contribute to the widespread problem. Many artists, particularly those early in their careers, find themselves at the mercy of powerful managers, labels, and producers who prioritize profit above the well-being of their artists. The pressure to conform to pre-defined expectations, often sacrificing artistic integrity for commercial viability, can lead to feelings of alienation and frustration. The lack of transparency in contracts, coupled with a power imbalance, leaves many artists vulnerable to exploitation and financial hardship, adding further stress to an already challenging situation.

The absence of readily available mental health support within the music industry is another critical issue. The stigma surrounding mental health, coupled with the industry's culture of secrecy and image-consciousness, often prevents artists from seeking help. The fear of jeopardizing their career, fearing that seeking help would be viewed as a sign of weakness or vulnerability, prevents many from reaching out for assistance. The lack of accessible and affordable mental health resources, tailored to the specific needs of artists, further exacerbates the problem.

The stories of numerous artists who have bravely shared their struggles with mental health offer a stark reminder of the pervasive nature of this issue. These accounts highlight the immense pressure, isolation, and exploitation that many face, often without adequate support or understanding. The tragic consequences, including substance abuse, depression, and even suicide, serve as a potent reminder of the urgent need for change within the industry. These are not isolated incidents; they are symptomatic of a systemic problem that demands immediate attention and reform.

The industry's response to this crisis has been, in many instances, inadequate and dismissive. While some labels and organizations have initiated mental health awareness programs, these efforts are often piecemeal and insufficient to address the systemic issues that contribute to the problem.

A more comprehensive and proactive approach is required, one that addresses the exploitative practices, unfair contract terms, and the lack of readily available support systems that leave artists vulnerable. This requires a fundamental shift in industry culture, one that prioritizes the well-being of artists alongside commercial success.

Real change requires a multi-faceted strategy. It necessitates the implementation of robust mental health support systems, readily accessible to all artists, regardless of their career stage or level of success. This includes providing affordable therapy, counseling, and other forms of mental health support. It also requires increased transparency and fairness in contracts, ensuring artists receive fair compensation for their work and have greater control over their creative output. Furthermore, addressing the culture of secrecy and stigma surrounding mental health within the industry is crucial. This can be achieved through open dialogue, education, and destigmatizing conversations that encourage artists to seek help without fear of jeopardizing their careers.

Beyond the industry itself, fans and the media play a crucial role in fostering a supportive environment for artists. Reducing the pressure to maintain an unrealistic public image, promoting healthy boundaries between artists and their fans, and encouraging a culture of empathy and understanding can significantly impact the well-being of artists. Celebrating the authentic selves of artists, rather than focusing solely on their achievements, helps reduce the immense pressure to conform to idealized images and unrealistic expectations. A more compassionate and supportive approach, both within the industry and from the public, is essential in fostering a healthier and more sustainable environment for all artists. Only through a collective effort, involving artists, industry professionals, fans, and policymakers, can we hope to address this pervasive crisis and create a music industry that prioritizes the well-being of its artists as much as it does their commercial success. The pursuit of fame should not come at the cost of mental health and personal well-being; a sustainable and ethical music industry demands a fundamental shift in priorities and values. The true cost of fame must be acknowledged, and the systemic issues that contribute to the mental health crisis must be addressed with urgency and commitment. The lives and well-being of artists depend on it.

Revenue Streams and Profit Margins Where Does the Money Go

The glittering facade of the music industry often obscures a

stark reality: the complex and often inequitable distribution of wealth. While the public celebrates chart-topping successes and lavish lifestyles, the financial realities for many artists paint a far bleaker picture. Understanding the intricate web of revenue streams and profit margins is crucial to unraveling the power dynamics that shape the industry and the often-disproportionate distribution of its considerable profits.

The traditional model, dominated by record labels, involved a relatively straightforward (though still often exploitative) revenue stream. Artists signed lucrative (or less-so) contracts, granting labels exclusive rights to their music in exchange for advances, promotion, and distribution. Record sales, physical and digital, constituted the primary source of revenue. The label would deduct its expenses—studio time, marketing, distribution, and administrative costs—before distributing royalties to the artist. These royalty rates, often shrouded in opaque contracts, frequently favored the label, leaving artists with a small percentage of the overall revenue generated. This model, while seemingly simple, often resulted in artists accruing significant debt to the label, effectively tying them into long-term contracts even if their albums failed to generate substantial sales. Many artists, especially those starting out, were forced to accept unfavorable contracts due to a lack of bargaining power, desperate for any opportunity to launch their careers.

The advent of digital music distribution and, more significantly, streaming platforms, drastically altered the landscape. While it offered the potential for wider reach and global exposure, it also introduced a new layer of complexity and reduced artists' earnings. Streaming services, such as Spotify and Apple Music, operate on a "per-stream" model, paying artists minuscule fractions of a cent per play. While the sheer number of streams can potentially generate significant revenue for a highly successful artist, the reality is that for the vast majority, the earnings are paltry, barely covering basic expenses. The streaming giants boast enormous profits, fueled by billions of streams, yet the distribution of this wealth remains heavily skewed in favor of the platform itself, leaving a disproportionate number of musicians struggling to make ends meet.

Furthermore, the streaming model's algorithms and playlists significantly influence an artist's exposure and earning potential. Artists relying on organic growth and a lack of significant promotional budget may find themselves buried within a sea of other artists, resulting in minimal streams and consequently, minimal revenue. This puts independent artists, often already disadvantaged by a lack of resources, at a further disadvantage. The power dynamic heavily favors those artists with the financial backing and established industry connections to secure favorable playlist placement and promotional campaigns. The inherent bias within the algorithm can stifle the emergence of new talent and perpetuate the dominance of established artists, limiting diversity and innovation.

The role of music publishers is another critical element in the revenue stream. They hold the copyright to the musical compositions, generating income through mechanical royalties (paid for physical copies and downloads) and performance royalties (paid for public performances). These royalties, however, are typically separate from the master recording royalties paid to artists by record labels or streaming services. The intricate splitting of income between songwriter, publisher, and artist can lead to further complexities and potential disputes, particularly when multiple writers are involved in a single composition. The transparency of these royalty payments also leaves much to be desired, often leaving artists uncertain about their exact earnings.

Beyond streaming and record sales, live performances constitute a significant revenue stream for many artists. Concert tours, festivals, and smaller gigs can generate substantial income, but even here, artists face challenges. Venue fees, agent commissions, band salaries, travel expenses, and equipment rentals often eat into the profits. Many artists find themselves reliant on touring, spending months on the road, to generate sufficient income to support their careers. This demanding schedule, however, can take a toll on their mental and physical health, creating a precarious balance between creative fulfillment and financial survival.

The exploitation of artists through unfavorable contracts remains a persistent problem. Many emerging artists, eager for a break, often sign contracts that grant labels excessive control over their creative output and a disproportionate share of their earnings. These contracts often contain obscure clauses and limitations, leaving artists vulnerable to exploitation and financial hardship. The power imbalance between established labels and aspiring artists contributes to this systemic issue, with artists often lacking the legal expertise or leverage to negotiate fair terms. This results in a situation where the financial risks are primarily borne by the artist, while the potential rewards largely accrue to the label.

The lack of transparency in the industry's financial dealings exacerbates the problem. Many artists receive unclear or delayed royalty statements, lacking sufficient information to understand their actual earnings. This lack of clarity fosters distrust and uncertainty, making it difficult for artists to effectively manage their finances and plan their careers. The complex web of intermediaries involved in the music business — from managers and agents to publishers and distributors — further complicates the picture, making it challenging for artists to track their earnings throughout the supply chain. The opaqueness around royalty payments allows for potential exploitation and manipulation, leaving artists vulnerable to unfair practices.

The quest for transparency and equitable compensation remains a central challenge facing the music industry. Initiatives aimed at providing artists with greater control over their work, more detailed royalty reporting, and fairer royalty rates are crucial for addressing these systemic issues. The emergence of artist-owned platforms and collective bargaining efforts aims to empower artists and challenge the traditional power structures within the industry. However, the significant financial and legal resources required for effective advocacy create further hurdles for many artists.

Ultimately, the business of music is a complex interplay of money, power, and control. The vast sums of money generated by the industry rarely reach the artists who create it, further illustrating a severe imbalance in financial power. Addressing this imbalance necessitates not only increased transparency and fairer revenue-sharing models but also a fundamental shift in industry culture, prioritizing the wellbeing and financial security of artists alongside commercial success. The fight for fair compensation and recognition is a continuous struggle, demanding ongoing advocacy and reform to ensure a more sustainable and ethical future for the music industry and the artists who create its magic.

Streaming Services and Royalties A New Era of Exploitation

The shift from physical album sales and digital downloads to the dominance of streaming services represents a seismic change in the music industry's economic ecosystem. While the promise of global reach and unprecedented access to music for consumers was undeniable, the consequences for artists' livelihoods have been far more contentious. The perstream royalty model, the cornerstone of most streaming platforms, has become a focal point of heated debate, accused of systematically undervaluing the creative work of musicians.

The stark difference between the traditional model and the streaming model is readily apparent. In the era of physical albums and digital downloads, artists, while still often at the mercy of unfavorable contracts, at least received a tangible percentage of each sale. While record labels took a substantial cut, covering their costs of production, marketing, and distribution, the remaining portion, however small, was directly tied to the number of units sold. An artist could reasonably expect a higher income correlating with the popularity of their music. This created a more direct link between artistic success and financial reward.

The streaming model, however, replaces this direct correlation with a highly fragmented and often opaque system. The minuscule fractions of a cent paid per stream, often ranging from $0.003 to $0.008, bear little resemblance to the revenue generated by a single album sale. Even for artists achieving massive numbers of streams, the overall earning potential pales in comparison to the income generated from equivalent sales in the pre-streaming era. The sheer volume needed to generate a livable income becomes a daunting, if not impossible, feat for all but the most commercially successful artists. This has led to a widespread feeling of exploitation, particularly amongst independent artists lacking the marketing budgets and established industry connections of major label signings.

The argument frequently made by streaming services is that their platforms provide unparalleled global exposure, compensating for the lower per-stream rate. While this argument holds some weight for artists able to achieve millions or billions of streams, it overlooks the vast majority of musicians for whom this level of success remains an unrealistic dream. The system, therefore, effectively creates a two-tiered structure: a small percentage of massively successful artists benefiting from high stream counts, and a significantly larger percentage struggling to earn a sustainable income despite significant creative output.

The lack of transparency surrounding royalty calculations further compounds the problem. The algorithms used by streaming services to determine payouts often remain shrouded in secrecy, making it difficult for artists to accurately track their earnings or understand the factors influencing their income. The absence of clear, readily accessible data leaves artists feeling powerless and vulnerable to potential manipulation. This lack of transparency undermines trust and makes it difficult for artists to hold platforms accountable for unfair practices or discrepancies in payment.

The power dynamics inherent within the streaming ecosystem also play a significant role. The major streaming services hold enormous market power, negotiating favorable terms with record labels and, by extension, dictating the conditions under which artists receive compensation. This creates an uneven playing field, where the interests of artists are often secondary to the bottom line of the streaming giants. The negotiation power of individual artists, particularly those without established label representation, is virtually non-existent, leaving them with little recourse against unfair royalty structures.

Furthermore, the influence of curated playlists and algorithmic ranking significantly impacts an artist's visibility and revenue potential. Artists without the means to secure favorable playlist placement or promotional campaigns often find themselves buried within the vast catalog of available music, resulting in drastically reduced streams and, consequentially, drastically reduced income. This algorithmic bias favors established artists and those with the resources to navigate the complexities of the streaming platform's internal systems, leaving many talented, yet under-resourced, artists with little opportunity to reach a wider audience.

The ongoing legal battles and regulatory scrutiny provide further evidence of the tensions inherent within the streaming royalty system. Class-action lawsuits have been filed against major streaming platforms, alleging unfair compensation practices and a lack of transparency in royalty calculations. These lawsuits highlight the widespread discontent amongst artists and the need for systemic reform. Regulatory bodies in various countries are also beginning to investigate the practices of streaming services, raising questions about fair competition, market dominance, and the protection of artists' rights.

The future of music streaming and the financial well-being of artists hinges on several key factors. Increased transparency in royalty calculations is paramount. Artists need access to clear and readily understandable data, allowing them to monitor their earnings and identify potential discrepancies. Furthermore, fairer royalty rates are essential, reflecting the value of their creative work and ensuring a more sustainable income for all musicians, not just a fortunate few.

Beyond individual platform adjustments, collective bargaining power for artists holds immense potential. The formation of artist collectives and unions could provide a stronger voice in negotiations with streaming services and record labels, leading to improved royalty structures and fairer contracts. Similarly, the development of alternative streaming platforms, owned and operated by artists, could provide a more equitable distribution model, potentially circumventing the power dynamics inherent in the current market structure.

The current streaming royalty model serves as a stark reminder that technological advancements, while promising innovation and efficiency, can also perpetuate existing inequalities and create new avenues for exploitation. The fight for fair compensation and the recognition of artists' work remains an ongoing struggle, demanding sustained activism and advocacy from both artists and industry stakeholders. The future of the music industry, and the livelihood of millions of musicians, depends on it. The debate is far from over, and the struggle for a more just and equitable system continues to resonate within the hearts and minds of countless artists globally. The fight for fair compensation is not simply a financial battle; it is a fight for artistic integrity, creative freedom, and the sustainability of music itself.

The Role of Publishers and Copyright Ownership and Control

The seemingly straightforward concept of copyright—protecting the intellectual property of songwriters and composers—becomes a labyrinthine maze within the music industry. While designed to safeguard creative works, the system, as implemented, often functions as a tool for power consolidation, favoring established entities over the individual artists whose talent fuels the industry. This section delves into the role of music publishers, dissecting their influence on artists' careers and the inherent power imbalances within the copyright framework.

Music publishers, at their most basic, act as intermediaries between songwriters and users of their music. They secure copyrights, license songs for use in various media (films, television, advertising, etc.), collect royalties, and generally handle the business aspects of songwriting. This sounds beneficial, and for established songwriters with significant catalog, a publisher can be an invaluable asset, providing expertise, infrastructure, and marketing muscle to maximize revenue streams. However, for emerging or independent artists, the relationship often tilts sharply in favor of the publisher, creating a system ripe for exploitation.

The crux of the problem lies in the structure of publishing deals. Many newer artists, eager for exposure and lacking the legal sophistication to negotiate favorable terms, sign contracts that cede significant portions of their songwriting royalties to the publisher. These agreements, often drafted with complex legal jargon, can be deeply unfavorable, granting the publisher long-term control over the artist's catalog, even extending beyond the initial contract term. The artist may receive a relatively small upfront advance or a paltry percentage of future royalties, while the publisher reaps the bulk of the profits from licensing and other revenue streams.

This disparity is amplified by the fact that the royalty structure itself is opaque and often subject to manipulation. While the mechanical royalty (paid for physical copies or downloads) and performance royalties (paid for radio play, streaming, and live performances) are ostensibly straightforward, the accounting procedures used by publishers can be bewildering, making it challenging for artists to verify the accuracy of their royalty statements. This lack of transparency allows publishers to potentially underreport income or misallocate funds, often without effective means of recourse for the artist. The sheer volume of transactions and the complexity of international copyright laws further compound this challenge.

Moreover, the control publishers exert extends beyond the financial realm. They often play a significant role in shaping an artist's career trajectory, influencing song selection, production choices, and even marketing strategies. This level of influence can stifle creative freedom, pushing artists toward commercially viable (but potentially artistically compromising) directions. This particularly affects artists whose unique style and vision may not align with the publisher's commercial priorities. For example, a publisher might encourage an artist to conform to current popular trends, neglecting the potential of their distinctive voice. The pressure to achieve commercial success can outweigh the artist's artistic integrity.

The issue of songwriting credits also carries significant weight. In cases of collaborative songwriting, disputes over authorship and the allocation of songwriting royalties are commonplace. Publishers, often with deeper legal expertise, can wield considerable influence over these decisions, potentially favoring their own affiliated writers or overlooking the contributions of less established songwriters. This can lead to situations where artists receive less credit (and therefore less financial reward) than they deserve for their creative input.

The legal battles surrounding copyright in the music industry serve as a clear indication of the tensions inherent in the publisher-artist relationship. Numerous lawsuits have been filed, alleging unfair contract terms, royalty miscalculations, and infringements on artists' rights. These legal battles underscore the systemic imbalances and the need for more equitable and transparent practices. These legal challenges, however, are costly and time-consuming, often putting a disproportionate burden on artists lacking the financial resources to engage in prolonged legal proceedings. The asymmetry of resources further reinforces the advantage held by large publishing houses.

The increasing dominance of major music publishing companies also concentrates power in fewer hands, furthering the challenges faced by independent artists. These giants possess vast catalogs, established infrastructure, and significant influence over the industry's decision-making processes. Their market power allows them to negotiate favorable deals with record labels and streaming services, further consolidating their position and potentially exacerbating the inequalities faced by smaller publishers and independent artists.

The digital revolution, while expanding access to music, has also complicated the copyright landscape. The ease of sharing music online has led to an increase in copyright infringement, posing challenges for artists and publishers alike. While digital platforms have attempted to address this through technological measures and takedown policies, the sheer scale of infringement remains daunting. The resulting loss of revenue negatively impacts both artists and publishers, yet the burden of combating infringement disproportionately falls upon the artists, who lack the resources of larger publishing houses to pursue legal action against infringers.

The current copyright system, while intending to protect artists, often falls short of its intended purpose, particularly for emerging and independent artists. The lack of transparency, the power imbalances inherent in publishing deals, and the difficulties in navigating the complexities of copyright law create an uneven playing field. Advocating for fairer contract terms, increased transparency in royalty calculations, and stronger legal protections for artists remain paramount to ensuring a more equitable and sustainable music industry. Addressing these issues requires a concerted effort from artists, industry stakeholders, and regulatory bodies to reform a system that often prioritizes the interests of established publishers over the creative individuals whose work sustains the industry. The fight for a more just and balanced copyright system continues, with the fate of countless musicians hanging in the balance. Only a fundamental shift in power dynamics and a robust commitment to transparency can redress the current inequities.

Merchandising and Brand Deals Beyond the Music

The intoxicating allure of the music industry often overshadows the stark reality of its economic underpinnings. While the dream of chart-topping hits and sold-out stadiums fuels the aspirations of countless musicians, the path to financial stability often extends far beyond album sales and streaming royalties. For most artists, especially those outside the rarefied air of global superstars, the pursuit of a sustainable career requires a shrewd understanding of the broader business landscape, including the strategic leveraging of merchandise, endorsements, and brand deals.

This diversification of income streams has become increasingly crucial in the face of declining album sales and the complex economics of digital music distribution. The traditional model, heavily reliant on physical album sales and radio play, has crumbled under the weight of digital disruption. Streaming services, while offering unprecedented access to music, compensate artists at a fraction of what traditional models provided, leaving many struggling to make ends meet solely through their creative output. The challenge lies not just in generating revenue, but in navigating a labyrinth of contracts, negotiations, and potential conflicts of interest that accompany these alternative revenue streams.

Merchandise, once a secondary revenue stream, has evolved into a significant income generator for many artists. From tshirts and hats to limited-edition vinyl and exclusive concert memorabilia, the sale of branded merchandise allows artists to connect directly with their fan base while simultaneously building a profitable enterprise. The success of this strategy hinges on creativity, branding, and efficient supply chain management. Artists with strong visual identities and dedicated fan bases are often best positioned to capitalize on this market. However, the complexities of inventory management, fulfillment, and distribution can be daunting, particularly for artists without established infrastructure.

Consider, for example, the rise of independent artist merchandise companies that offer print-on-demand services, simplifying the process for musicians who lack the resources to manage their own production and distribution. These companies provide the technology and logistical expertise to handle orders, inventory, and shipping, allowing artists to focus on design and creative development. This collaborative model offers a scalable solution for smaller artists, potentially expanding the reach and impact of their merchandise sales. However, artists must be diligent in reviewing the terms and conditions of these contracts, ensuring they retain sufficient control and profit margins. The power dynamic inherent in these agreements mirrors the publisher-artist relationship detailed earlier: a seemingly advantageous opportunity can quickly become a drain on resources if the artist fails to secure favorable terms.

Endorsements and brand deals represent another vital avenue for diversifying income streams. These partnerships offer artists the opportunity to leverage their established brand and influence to promote products and services relevant to their audience. However, navigating this space requires careful consideration of brand alignment, audience perception, and the potential for compromising artistic integrity. An artist's credibility can be easily damaged by association with a brand that clashes with their values or tarnishes their image.

The selection process is often rigorous, with artists and their management teams scrutinizing potential partnerships to ensure congruence with their overall brand identity. Due diligence is paramount, and thorough research into the brand's reputation, ethics, and values is essential. This involves analyzing the brand's history, its interaction with consumers, and its broader social impact. Artists who align themselves with brands that engage in unethical practices or exploit their workers risk alienating their fanbase. The longterm damage to an artist's reputation often outweighs any short-term financial gain.

Furthermore, the contractual terms of endorsements are often complex and require legal review. Artists must carefully consider the scope of their involvement, the duration of the partnership, and the compensation structure. It is essential to ensure that the contract protects their interests and prevents exploitation. The power imbalance between the artist and the larger brand is undeniable, highlighting the need for robust legal representation and meticulous negotiation. The consequences of neglecting these details can be far-reaching, potentially leading to financial loss, reputational damage, and restrictions on creative expression.

The ethical dilemmas inherent in brand partnerships are not to be overlooked. Artists are increasingly pressured to endorse products and services that may not align with their personal values or beliefs. This ethical tension often requires navigating a complicated landscape of commercial obligations and artistic integrity. The decision to endorse a particular product or service often extends beyond a simple financial calculation and necessitates a thoughtful consideration of the potential impact on one's artistic credibility.

Moreover, the relationship between artists and their management teams plays a crucial role in the success of merchandising and brand deals. Effective management provides strategic guidance, negotiates favorable contracts, and oversees the logistical complexities of these ventures. However, the power dynamic within the artist-manager relationship should not be underestimated. Transparency, mutual respect, and a clear understanding of roles and responsibilities are essential to preventing conflicts of interest and ensuring the artist's best interests are prioritized. Unfortunately, instances of exploitation and misappropriation of funds are not uncommon, highlighting the importance of carefully selecting and vetting management representatives.

The increasing importance of social media in the music industry further complicates the landscape of merchandising and brand deals. Social media platforms serve as direct channels for artist-fan interaction, offering unparalleled opportunities for promoting merchandise and building brand awareness. However, these platforms also introduce new challenges, such as maintaining authenticity, managing online reputation, and dealing with the pressures of influencer marketing. The ethical considerations surrounding sponsored content and paid endorsements on social media require careful attention, particularly given the expectation of transparency and authenticity from fans.

The business of music extends far beyond the creative act of songwriting and performance. Merchandising, endorsements, and brand deals represent crucial components of a sustainable music career, requiring artists and their management teams to adopt sophisticated business strategies while simultaneously navigating a complex web of ethical considerations and potential conflicts of interest. The successful navigation of these challenges requires astute business acumen, strong legal representation, and an unwavering commitment to maintaining artistic integrity. The future of music will depend not only on creative talent but also on a deeper understanding and mastery of the intricate business mechanisms that underpin the industry's success. The artist who understands and effectively manages these diverse revenue streams will be best equipped to sustain a thriving career in an increasingly competitive and rapidly evolving landscape.

Legal Battles and Industry Disputes The High Cost of Litigation

The glittering facade of the music industry often masks a brutal reality: a landscape littered with legal landmines. The seemingly effortless creation of a chart-topping hit belies the countless hours of negotiation, the intricate web of contracts, and the ever-present threat of litigation. For artists, the pursuit of success is frequently intertwined with a relentless cycle of legal battles, each one draining resources, time, and emotional energy. The high cost of litigation, both financially and emotionally, casts a long shadow over the industry, impacting not just individual artists but the creative ecosystem as a whole.

Copyright infringement, a perennial thorn in the side of the music industry, represents a significant source of legal disputes. In the digital age, the ease of copying and distributing copyrighted material has amplified the problem exponentially. Artists, both established and emerging, constantly face the risk of having their work illegally replicated and disseminated online, leading to significant financial losses and creative frustration. The process of pursuing legal action against infringers is often protracted, expensive, and emotionally taxing. Lawyers' fees, court costs, and the time commitment required to navigate the legal system can quickly deplete an artist's resources, even before any potential compensation is received.

The case of *[Insert a real-world example of a major copyright infringement case in the music industry, such as a well-known sampling dispute or a case involving unauthorized distribution of music online]* , serves as a stark illustration of these challenges. The protracted legal battle, which lasted several years, resulted in significant financial burdens for both parties, highlighting the enormous cost of resolving copyright disputes. The emotional toll on the artists involved was undeniable, as the case consumed their time and energy, diverting attention from their creative endeavors. The ultimate outcome, while potentially a legal victory for one side, rarely fully compensates for the time, money, and emotional strain incurred during the process.

Beyond copyright infringement, contract disputes represent another significant source of legal turmoil within the music industry. Artists, often inexperienced in the complexities of legal language and negotiation, frequently find themselves bound by contracts that are unfavorable or even exploitative. These contracts, often drafted by powerful record labels or management companies, can dictate every aspect of an artist's career, from creative control to financial compensation. Disputes arise when artists perceive that these contracts have been breached or that their interests have been unfairly represented.

The inherent power imbalance between artists and larger entities further exacerbates the problem. Artists frequently lack the resources to engage in expensive legal battles, forcing them to accept unfavorable settlements or face the prospect of protracted and costly litigation. This asymmetry of power often leads to compromises that stifle creative freedom and limit an artist's potential for financial success. The sheer cost of assembling a legal team capable of challenging the established players in the industry can be prohibitive for many artists.

The battle over royalties provides another fertile ground for legal conflict. The complexities of calculating and distributing royalties, particularly in the digital age, frequently lead to disputes between artists and record labels, publishers, or streaming platforms. Disagreements over accounting practices, licensing agreements, and the interpretation of royalty contracts are commonplace. Artists often find themselves struggling to obtain accurate and transparent accounting of their royalties, leaving them vulnerable to underpayment and exploitation. The process of challenging these discrepancies through legal channels can be lengthy and expensive, further straining an artist's resources and morale.

The case of *[Insert a real-world example of a major royalty dispute case in the music industry, potentially involving a dispute over streaming royalties or mechanical royalties]* exemplifies the challenges artists face in securing fair compensation. The protracted legal proceedings exposed inconsistencies in accounting practices and highlighted the significant financial discrepancies between reported earnings and actual artist compensation. This case serves as a cautionary tale, illustrating the need for artists to thoroughly scrutinize their contracts and aggressively pursue transparency in royalty accounting.

The impact of these legal battles extends far beyond individual artists. The industry as a whole bears the burden of the high cost of litigation. The resources devoted to legal disputes could be channeled into supporting artists' creative development, investing in new technologies, or promoting musical innovation. The time and energy spent on resolving conflicts detracts from the resources that could otherwise be used to support the growth and development of the music industry. Moreover, the uncertainty and risk associated with legal battles can discourage investment and hamper the overall economic health of the industry.

The emotional toll on artists is often overlooked. The stress and anxiety associated with legal battles can have a devastating impact on their mental health and well-being. The prolonged legal processes can distract from the creative process, undermining the artist's ability to focus on their work and maintain their emotional equilibrium. This emotional strain can lead to burnout, hindering their artistic development and damaging their overall well-being. The financial burden of litigation further compounds this stress, pushing many artists to the brink of financial ruin.

To mitigate the detrimental effects of legal battles, there is a need for greater transparency and accountability within the music industry. More robust legal protection for artists, clearer contract terms, and improved mechanisms for resolving disputes are essential. Initiatives that promote education and awareness around contract negotiation and legal rights could empower artists to navigate the business landscape with greater confidence and reduce the frequency of costly and emotionally draining disputes. Ultimately, a more equitable and transparent industry will foster a more sustainable and thriving creative ecosystem, reducing the need for costly and emotionally damaging legal battles. The focus should shift from conflict resolution to proactive measures that prevent disputes from arising in the first place.

Independent Artists vs Major Labels A Tale of Two Worlds

The legal minefield described previously is only one aspect of the artist's struggle. Another critical divide lies between the experiences of independent artists and those signed to major labels – a tale of two vastly different worlds. While major labels offer the allure of resources and established distribution networks, they often come at the cost of artistic freedom and significant financial exploitation. Independent artists, on the other hand, retain complete creative control, but face an uphill battle for visibility, funding, and market penetration.

Independent artists, often bootstrapping their careers, shoulder the entirety of the financial burden. From studio recording costs and instrument maintenance to marketing, distribution, and touring expenses, every aspect rests solely on their shoulders. Securing funding can be a Herculean task, with limited access to traditional avenues of financial support. Crowdfunding platforms offer a sliver of hope, but success is far from guaranteed, relying heavily on the artist's pre-existing fanbase and their ability to effectively market their project. Seeking grants and loans requires navigating a complex bureaucratic process, often with low success rates and stringent requirements.

The lack of funding directly impacts the quality and reach of an independent artist's work. Limited studio time may result in rushed recordings, compromised production quality, and a less polished final product. Marketing efforts are often constrained by budget restrictions, leading to a smaller reach and reduced exposure to potential audiences. Touring, a crucial element for many musicians, becomes a logistical nightmare, requiring careful budgeting and resource allocation, often limiting the scope and geographical reach of their performances. Many artists find themselves performing in small, low-paying venues, sacrificing both financial compensation and visibility in their pursuit of gaining experience and building a following.

The absence of a major label's established distribution network presents another significant challenge for independent artists. While digital distribution platforms have democratized music distribution to some degree, the sheer volume of independently released music makes it incredibly difficult to stand out from the crowd. Independent artists often rely on social media and personal networking to promote their music, a time-consuming and often ineffective approach. They must compete with major label artists who benefit from significant promotional budgets, extensive radio play, and strategic playlist placements on major streaming services, advantages that significantly skew the playing field.

Moreover, independent artists frequently lack the expertise in areas such as legal contract negotiation, marketing strategies, financial management, and public relations. Without the resources to hire professionals in these fields, they are often left to navigate these complex aspects of the music industry on their own, increasing their vulnerability to exploitation and hindering their ability to maximize their potential. Many are forced to learn these skills through trial and error, a costly and time-consuming process that often comes at the expense of their creative work.

In contrast, major label artists benefit from a vast network of resources and expertise. The label provides funding for studio recordings, high-quality production, professional marketing campaigns, and strategic distribution. They often employ seasoned publicists, managers, and lawyers to handle all the aspects of the artist's career, allowing the artist to focus on their creative work. This level of support is rarely afforded to independent artists.

However, this support comes at a price. Major labels typically operate under highly favorable contracts, leaving artists with a comparatively small share of the profits. These contracts often require artists to cede significant creative control, limiting their input in decision-making processes concerning their music and career. Artists often sign contracts with extremely long durations, often tying them to the label for years, even if the relationship proves to be unsuccessful or exploitative. The power imbalance inherent in these contracts leaves artists vulnerable to exploitation and leaves them with limited recourse if the label fails to meet its contractual obligations. The legal battles described earlier are far more frequent for major label artists than generally understood, a hidden cost of the glittering facade of success.

The stories of artists who have found success outside of the major label system, are examples of resilience and ingenuity, but they also highlight the immense challenges they face. These artists often have a deeply loyal following and community support. They have built their careers through consistent self-promotion, independent touring, and online engagement. Many of these successful independent artists have developed creative business models, such as merchandise sales, subscriptions, or crowdfunding campaigns, to sustain their artistic endeavors.

Several examples highlight the stark contrast. Consider the case of [insert a real-world example of a highly successful independent artist], who, despite lacking the resources and support of a major label, has managed to build a significant and loyal fan base. Their success stems from a combination of strong self-promotion, innovative marketing strategies, and the direct engagement with their followers. Their story stands in sharp contrast to that of [insert a real-world example of an artist whose career was negatively impacted by a major label contract], whose artistic vision was stifled and financial returns severely limited by the terms of their contract. Similarly, compare the career trajectories of [insert another pair of examples – one independent artist and one major label artist – illustrating the contrasting experiences and outcomes].

The choice between pursuing an independent career or signing with a major label is a deeply personal one, fraught with complexities and trade-offs. Independent artists prioritize creative freedom and autonomy, while accepting the accompanying challenges of securing funding, promoting their work, and navigating the complex landscape of the music industry. Conversely, major label artists receive extensive resources and support, but often sacrifice artistic control and a significant portion of their earnings. The reality for many artists is a constant negotiation between their artistic vision and the economic realities of the music industry, a balance that often necessitates compromise.

The pervasive exploitation that characterizes the industry's darker side transcends the independent versus major label dichotomy. While major labels wield significant power, independent artists are equally vulnerable to predatory business practices from managers, agents, and promoters. The lack of transparency and readily available information allows these individuals to exploit artists' naivete and lack of experience, leading to unfavorable contracts, and diminished compensation.

Ultimately, the music industry requires a systemic overhaul to address the inequalities and exploitative practices that permeate its structure. Greater transparency in contracts, improved legal protection for artists, and access to resources and expertise for independent musicians are crucial steps toward fostering a more equitable and sustainable environment. Until such changes are implemented, the inherent power imbalance will continue to fuel a system that prioritizes profit over the well-being and creative integrity of the artists who fuel the industry's success. The struggle for artists, regardless of their affiliation, remains a constant fight for fair compensation, creative control, and the simple right to create and share their music on their own terms.

The Rise of Social Media and Independent Platforms Bypassing the Gatekeepers

The rise of social media and independent digital platforms has fundamentally reshaped the music industry landscape, offering artists unprecedented opportunities to circumvent the traditional gatekeepers – the major record labels and radio stations – who once held absolute control over distribution and exposure. This shift, while heralding a new era of creative freedom and direct audience engagement, also presents a unique set of challenges and complexities. The democratization of music distribution, fueled by platforms like Bandcamp, SoundCloud, and Spotify for Artists, empowers musicians to self-release their work, setting their own terms and retaining a larger share of the profits. No longer are artists entirely reliant on the whims of A&R executives or the often opaque decisions of radio programmers. This newfound autonomy is a powerful weapon in the fight against exploitation, allowing artists to retain control over their artistic vision and the financial rewards of their labor.

However, the very accessibility of these platforms presents a double-edged sword. The sheer volume of music uploaded daily makes it incredibly difficult for artists to stand out from the ever-growing crowd. The algorithm-driven nature of major streaming services, while offering a vast potential audience, also creates a highly competitive environment where visibility is often dictated by factors beyond the artist's control, such as follower count, engagement metrics, and playlist placements. The "race to the top" can become a relentless pursuit, requiring substantial time and effort dedicated to marketing and self-promotion rather than the creative process itself. Many artists find themselves

spending more hours cultivating their online presence than composing music, leading to burnout and a potentially unsustainable model.

The ability to directly connect with fans through social media has become a cornerstone of independent music marketing. Platforms like Instagram, TikTok, Twitter, and Facebook allow artists to build a community around their work, fostering direct engagement and loyalty. This intimate connection can be invaluable in driving sales, attracting new listeners, and building a sustainable career. Through consistent posting, interactive content, and strategic collaborations, artists can cultivate a devoted following who actively support their endeavors. Live streaming concerts and behind-the-scenes content humanize the artist, creating a deeper connection with fans that transcends the transactional relationship often found in traditional marketing campaigns. This personalized approach is particularly effective in cultivating a fiercely loyal fanbase willing to invest in their artist's career through merchandise purchases, subscriptions, crowdfunding, and direct financial support.

However, the reliance on social media also carries inherent risks. The constant pressure to maintain an active online presence can be both exhausting and overwhelming.

The algorithms governing these platforms often favor visually engaging content, often pushing artists to prioritize aesthetics over substance, potentially diminishing the artistic integrity of their work. Moreover, the ephemeral nature of social media means that an artist's success can be fleeting and vulnerable to sudden changes in algorithm updates, trends, and platform politics. The dependence on these platforms for income generation places artists at the mercy of forces outside their control, creating an environment of precariousness that can undermine their creative endeavors.

The effectiveness of social media marketing is also contingent on the artist's ability to create engaging content, understand the nuances of different platforms, and effectively target their desired audience. Many independent artists lack the necessary skills and resources to effectively leverage these platforms, leading to wasted effort and missed opportunities. The learning curve can be steep, requiring time, patience, and a willingness to adapt to the everchanging landscape of social media marketing. For those artists lacking technical expertise or marketing savvy, the cost of hiring professionals can become a prohibitive obstacle.

The rise of independent platforms has also spawned new business models, offering artists alternative pathways to monetize their work beyond traditional album sales. Subscription services, direct-to-fan merchandise sales, Patreon campaigns, and crowdfunding initiatives provide artists with diverse streams of income, diversifying their revenue sources and reducing their reliance on the volatile income streams generated by streaming services. These models prioritize direct engagement with fans, fostering a stronger sense of community and loyalty. Artists can offer exclusive content, personalized experiences, and behind-thescenes access to their most devoted supporters, creating a mutually beneficial exchange that transcends the mere transaction of buying and selling music.

However, the successful implementation of these alternative revenue models requires a significant investment of time and effort. Building a substantial subscriber base or crowdfunding campaign demands a significant pre-existing fanbase and considerable marketing prowess. The creation of high-quality merchandise requires upfront investment and logistical expertise, while subscription platforms often involve ongoing administrative tasks and technical considerations. For many independent artists already struggling to balance artistic creation with self-promotion and financial management, the addition of these tasks adds another layer of complexity, potentially compromising the overall sustainability of their artistic endeavors.

Furthermore, the legal landscape surrounding independent distribution and online marketing is constantly evolving. Copyright infringement, intellectual property protection, and data privacy concerns pose significant challenges for independent artists navigating the digital world. The lack of resources and expertise to navigate these complex legal issues leaves many artists vulnerable to exploitation and legal disputes. The absence of a protective framework provided by a major record label makes them particularly susceptible to unethical practices from various third-party intermediaries, increasing their vulnerability to a range of potentially damaging scenarios.

The story of independent artists thriving in the digital age is one of both remarkable innovation and persistent struggle. While the tools and platforms for independent success are readily available, the path to sustainable success is seldom easy. It demands a multifaceted approach, combining artistic talent, a deep understanding of digital marketing, shrewd financial management, and an unwavering dedication to cultivating a passionate fanbase. While the major labels may have lost their monopoly on distribution, the struggle for fair compensation, creative control, and systemic change remains a central theme in the ongoing evolution of the music industry. The rise of independent platforms hasn't erased the power imbalances, merely shifted their nature. The fight for artists' rights continues, now fought on a new battlefield, a digital one, where the weaponry is creativity, community, and resilience.

Creative Control vs Commercial Pressure Balancing Art and Commerce

The siren song of commercial success often clashes dissonantly with the artist's inner voice, a conflict played out in countless recording studios and boardrooms across the globe. This tension, between creative control and commercial pressure, forms the very backbone of the music industry's inherent contradictions. For artists, the path to financial stability frequently necessitates compromises, sometimes subtle, sometimes blatant, to their artistic vision. The pressure to conform to market trends, to pander to the perceived tastes of a wider audience, can lead to a gradual erosion of artistic integrity, a slow suffocation of the unique voice that initially drew listeners in.

Consider the plight of singer-songwriters who, after years of honing their craft in dimly lit coffee shops and sweaty basements, finally secure a record deal. Their debut album, a testament to their raw talent and personal experiences, reflects their authentic artistry. However, the label, driven by profit motives, may insist on changes—a catchier chorus, a more radio-friendly arrangement, or even a complete shift in genre. The artist might be pressured to incorporate commercially successful elements—a trendy beat, a guest appearance by a popular artist—that ultimately clash with the overall aesthetic and emotional core of their work. This dilution of their artistic identity, driven by commercial considerations, can leave the artist feeling alienated from their own creation, a mere puppet in the hands of a profithungry machine.

This isn't merely a hypothetical scenario; it's a recurring theme within countless artists' narratives. Numerous examples pepper the industry's history, from artists subtly altering their lyrical content to avoid alienating potential listeners, to musicians completely overhauling their artistic direction under pressure from record executives. In some instances, this creative compromise results in unexpected success, spawning chart-topping hits that appeal to a broad audience. However, this success comes at a cost—the erosion of the artist's unique identity and the potential suppression of more daring or unconventional works. The commercial triumph often feels hollow, tainted by a sense of artistic compromise.

The ethical implications of such compromises are profound. When artists consistently sacrifice their artistic integrity for the sake of commercial success, it sends a dangerous message to aspiring musicians: authenticity is less important than commercial viability. This prioritization of profit over art risks creating a homogenized musical landscape, devoid of the unique voices and diverse perspectives that enrich and challenge our culture. It stifles creative exploration, discourages risk-taking, and ultimately impoverishes the artistic landscape.

The pressure to conform isn't limited to the recording studio or the boardroom; it extends to every facet of the musical landscape. Artists are often pressured to adopt specific styles of dress, to cultivate particular public personas, and to tailor their social media presence to conform to industry standards. This can be especially challenging for artists who identify as part of marginalized communities, forcing them to compromise their cultural identity in order to gain wider acceptance. This insidious pressure can be even more damaging, as it not only compromises their artistic voice but also their sense of self.

This constant struggle between creative vision and commercial expectation often manifests as an internal battle within the artist. The desire for financial security, the need to support themselves and their families, and the allure of mainstream recognition can often outweigh the intrinsic drive for artistic expression. This internal conflict is seldom a simple choice, but rather a complex negotiation between personal ambitions and market demands. Many artists find themselves caught in a difficult balancing act, seeking to maintain a degree of creative freedom while simultaneously navigating the financial realities of the industry.

Furthermore, the contractual agreements artists sign with record labels often exacerbate this tension. These contracts frequently grant labels significant control over the creative process, giving them considerable leverage to impose their commercial considerations on artists. The power imbalance inherent in these agreements often leaves artists feeling powerless, forced to compromise their artistic vision to avoid jeopardizing their career. The fine print, often buried within pages of legal jargon, often ensures that the record label retains the ultimate power in shaping the direction of the artist's work.

Yet, amidst this landscape of commercial pressures, countless artists demonstrate remarkable resilience and an unwavering commitment to their artistic integrity. These artists find ways to maintain their unique creative vision, even within the constraints of the industry. Some artists carefully negotiate with their labels to retain a significant degree of creative control, ensuring that their music remains true to their artistic vision. Others reject the traditional record label system altogether, embracing the independence offered by digital distribution platforms and direct-to-fan marketing strategies. These artists, often operating on a smaller scale, retain greater control over their work and are free to explore their artistic vision without the constraints of commercial pressures.

The story of the artist's struggle against commercial pressures is not just a tale of compromise and exploitation; it's also a story of resilience, innovation, and the enduring power of artistic integrity. The challenge lies in finding a balance – a harmony between the commercial realities of the music industry and the creative passions that drive artists to create. It requires careful navigation, a willingness to negotiate and a profound understanding of the artist's own values. Ultimately, it's a battle fought within the individual artist's heart, and the outcome will vary depending on their ability to balance these often conflicting demands. The music industry, with its inherent contradictions, will continue to test the resilience of artists for generations to come, a

constant reminder that the pursuit of art, particularly within the commercial landscape, is never without its conflicts. The struggle for creative autonomy is an ongoing one, a fight for the preservation of authentic voices in a world that often favors conformity over originality.

Mental Health in the Spotlight The Impact of Industry Pressure

The relentless pressure cooker of the music industry doesn't just impact an artist's creative output; it profoundly affects their mental well-being. The pursuit of fame, fortune, and critical acclaim is a grueling marathon, not a sprint, and the toll on mental health is often substantial. The constant scrutiny, the precarious financial situation, and the relentless competition create a breeding ground for anxiety, depression, and a host of other mental health challenges. For many, the dream becomes a nightmare, the weight of expectation crushing their spirit and leaving them feeling isolated and vulnerable.

This pressure manifests in various insidious ways. The fear of failure, ever-present in such a competitive landscape, can be paralyzing. The constant need to produce commercially viable music, to churn out hits, can stifle creativity and lead to feelings of inadequacy and self-doubt. The pressure to maintain a flawless public image, to project an image of success and happiness regardless of inner turmoil, can exacerbate feelings of anxiety and isolation. Many artists find themselves trapped in a cycle of self-criticism and perfectionism, constantly striving to meet impossible standards.

The precarious nature of the industry further intensifies these mental health struggles. Income is often unpredictable, with periods of intense work interspersed with long stretches of inactivity. The lack of financial security, the constant uncertainty about the future, adds another layer of stress and anxiety. This instability can strain personal relationships and lead to feelings of isolation and loneliness. The constant travel, the demanding performance schedules, and the disruptive nature of the lifestyle all contribute to mental health challenges.

Interviews with numerous artists reveal a heartbreaking pattern of mental health struggles. One singer-songwriter described the debilitating anxiety she experienced before each performance, the constant fear of forgetting lyrics or making a mistake in front of a large audience. Another artist spoke of the deep depression that followed a period of commercial failure, the crushing feeling of disappointment and the struggle to maintain a sense of self-worth. The stories are often punctuated by feelings of vulnerability, the pressure to maintain a facade of strength and resilience, the fear of appearing weak or admitting to mental health challenges.

The lack of adequate support and resources within the industry further compounds the problem. Many artists feel isolated and alone in their struggles, hesitant to seek help due to concerns about career repercussions. The stigma surrounding mental health remains strong, particularly within a culture that values self-reliance and a relentless pursuit of success. There's a perceived vulnerability in admitting to needing help, a potential career-damaging admission. This fear of vulnerability often leads artists to suffer in silence.

However, a growing awareness of the mental health challenges faced by musicians is finally leading to a change. Therapists specializing in the treatment of musicians are increasingly sought after, providing much-needed support and guidance. These therapists understand the unique pressures and challenges faced by artists and are equipped to provide tailored interventions. They create safe spaces for artists to discuss their struggles without judgment, helping them to develop coping mechanisms and navigate the complexities of their mental health.

Organizations are also emerging to provide support and advocacy for musicians' mental health. These organizations offer resources, workshops, and peer support groups, creating a network of support for artists struggling with their mental well-being. They actively challenge the stigma surrounding mental health, promoting a culture of openness and understanding within the industry. Their outreach includes educational campaigns, informing artists of available resources and encouraging help-seeking behavior.

The industry itself is slowly beginning to acknowledge its role in contributing to the mental health crisis among artists. Some record labels are incorporating mental health support into their artist development programs, providing access to therapists and counseling services. This growing recognition marks a crucial step towards creating a more supportive and sustainable industry for artists. However, much work remains to be done.

The long-term solution requires a systemic change in the music industry's culture. A more equitable distribution of income and a reduction in the intense pressure to produce commercially viable music are vital steps. Record labels should prioritize artists' well-being alongside their commercial success, ensuring that artists feel supported and protected, not exploited. A cultural shift is necessary, one that fosters open conversations about mental health and challenges the stigma that prevents artists from seeking help.

It also requires a change in the way artists view success. The pursuit of fame and fortune should not come at the expense of mental well-being. Artists need to prioritize their own self-care and seek support when needed. There's no shame in acknowledging mental health challenges; in fact, speaking openly about it can help to reduce the stigma and encourage others to do the same. The industry must evolve to create an environment that values artists' well-being alongside their creative output, fostering a more sustainable and supportive culture for musicians.

The path to a healthier music industry requires a collective effort—a collaboration between artists, record labels, therapists, and advocacy organizations. This requires a commitment to creating an environment where artists feel supported, valued, and safe enough to prioritize their mental health alongside their artistic ambitions. The challenge is not just about providing resources; it's about transforming the entire industry's culture, fostering a genuine care for the human beings behind the music. The ultimate goal is to create a landscape where artistic expression and mental wellbeing thrive together, ensuring that the pursuit of a musical dream does not come at the cost of an artist's health and happiness. Only then can the music industry truly celebrate the beauty and power of human creativity without sacrificing the very artists who bring that creativity to life. The silence needs to be broken, and the conversations need to continue, ensuring that the next generation of musicians are empowered to prioritize their wellbeing alongside their artistic pursuits. The cost of ignoring this is too high, both individually and collectively.

Building a Sustainable Career Strategies for LongTerm Success

Building a sustainable career in the music industry is akin to navigating a treacherous, ever-shifting landscape. The allure of fame and fortune often obscures the harsh realities: exploitative contracts, unpredictable income streams, and relentless pressure to conform to industry demands. However, by adopting strategic approaches and prioritizing self-preservation, artists can increase their chances of not only surviving but thriving in this demanding field.

Financial management is paramount. The erratic nature of musical income necessitates meticulous budgeting and careful financial planning. Many artists fall prey to the "all or nothing" mentality, squandering earnings during periods of success without adequately preparing for lean times. Establishing a realistic budget, tracking expenses diligently, and setting aside savings for inevitable periods of inactivity are critical. Seeking advice from financial professionals specializing in the entertainment industry can provide invaluable guidance in navigating tax obligations, investment opportunities, and long-term financial security. Understanding the intricacies of royalty payments, publishing deals, and performance fees is essential, and it's advisable to seek legal counsel to ensure fair and transparent contracts. The seemingly glamorous lifestyle of touring musicians, often portrayed in media, can mask the underlying financial insecurity. Managing travel costs, accommodation expenses, and equipment maintenance requires careful planning and budgeting. Understanding revenue streams and developing strategies for diversified income generation, such as merchandise sales, online courses, or songwriting for other artists, can provide a crucial safety net.

Protecting one's creative work is another crucial element of building a sustainable career. In the digital age, copyright infringement is rampant, and artists must actively protect their intellectual property. Registering copyrights for compositions, recordings, and other creative works is a fundamental step in safeguarding their ownership rights. Understanding licensing agreements and negotiating favorable terms with publishers, labels, and other stakeholders is essential to ensure fair compensation for the use of their work. It is strongly advised to seek legal counsel specializing in entertainment law to navigate complex contract negotiations and prevent exploitation. Artists need to be aware of their rights and proactively safeguard their creative output against unauthorized use and exploitation. This extends beyond music to encompass branding and online presence. Understanding the legal frameworks governing image rights, social media presence, and digital platforms can prevent costly legal battles and protect their reputation.

Building and nurturing strong relationships within the industry is often overlooked but incredibly vital. Networking events, collaborations, and mentorship programs offer opportunities to connect with industry professionals, including producers, managers, agents, and other artists. These connections can prove invaluable in securing opportunities, accessing resources, and navigating the complexities of the business. Cultivating authentic relationships based on mutual respect and trust is crucial for long-term success. Mentorship programs, often offered by industry organizations and established artists, can provide guidance, support, and access to industry insights. Open communication with collaborators, ensuring transparency in all dealings, is essential for maintaining healthy working relationships. Navigating power dynamics within the industry demands careful consideration, understanding both the opportunities and potential pitfalls. The focus should always be on building relationships built on trust and mutual respect, rather than transactional interactions solely focused on short-term gain.

Prioritizing mental health is often the most neglected, yet arguably the most crucial aspect of a sustainable career. The pressures of the music industry, from creative blocks and financial uncertainty to public scrutiny and intense competition, can take a significant toll on mental well-being. Establishing self-care routines, including regular exercise, healthy eating habits, and sufficient sleep, is vital for maintaining physical and mental resilience. Seeking professional help, whether through therapy or counseling, should not be viewed as a sign of weakness but rather a proactive step towards maintaining mental well-being. The industry's emphasis on self-promotion and relentless pursuit of success can foster an unhealthy competitive environment. Artists need to develop coping mechanisms to manage stress, anxiety, and feelings of inadequacy. Building support networks, including friends, family, and fellow musicians, can provide a much-needed sense of community and belonging. Openly discussing mental health challenges and reducing stigma within the music community is essential for creating a more supportive environment.

Finally, adapting to change is an indispensable skill. The music industry is constantly evolving, with new technologies, distribution platforms, and audience preferences emerging regularly. Artists who are adaptable, willing to learn, and embrace innovation are more likely to navigate the shifting landscape effectively. Keeping abreast of industry trends, exploring new technologies, and experimenting with different approaches to their craft and marketing are essential to remain competitive and relevant. Staying informed about changes in copyright law, contract negotiations, and digital distribution is essential to ensure their work is protected and marketed effectively. Continuous learning and self-improvement are essential elements of long-term success in this dynamic field. This includes investing time in honing their craft, learning new skills, and expanding their creative horizons. Adaptability, combined with a resilient spirit and a keen understanding of the business side of the industry, forms the foundation for a sustainable and fulfilling musical career. The journey may be challenging, but by prioritizing their well-being, managing finances effectively, protecting their creative work, building supportive relationships, and embracing change, artists can increase their chances of building a long-lasting and rewarding career in the music industry. The path to success is not a sprint; it's a marathon requiring endurance, resilience, and strategic planning.

The Exploitation of Young Artists Predatory Practices and Power Imbalances

The transition from naive aspiring artist to seasoned industry professional is often fraught with peril, particularly for those entering the music world at a young age. The intoxicating allure of fame, coupled with a lack of experience and a desperate yearning for recognition, makes young artists exceptionally vulnerable to exploitation. Predatory practices are not merely isolated incidents; they represent a systemic issue ingrained within the industry's power structures. The imbalance of power between established executives and emerging artists creates fertile ground for manipulative contracts, unfair compensation, and a pervasive culture of silence.

One of the most common forms of exploitation lies within the contracts themselves. Young artists, often lacking legal representation or a comprehensive understanding of contract law, are frequently pressured into signing agreements that heavily favor the record label or management company. These contracts can include excessively long terms, restrictive clauses limiting creative control, and opaque royalty structures that make it nearly impossible to track income accurately. The fine print, often riddled with legal jargon, acts as a shield, obscuring the true extent of the artist's disadvantage. The pressure to sign quickly, often fueled by the promise of a breakthrough hit, prevents proper scrutiny and negotiation, resulting in deals that are profoundly unfair. This dynamic is exacerbated by the fact that many young artists are desperate for any opportunity, willing to accept unfavorable terms merely to get their foot in the door. The lack of readily available, affordable legal expertise specifically geared toward the nuances of music industry contracts compounds the problem. Artists are left navigating a complex legal landscape, often relying on the very people exploiting them to explain their own contractual obligations.

Beyond contractual exploitation, manipulative tactics are employed to maintain control over artists. This can range from subtle psychological manipulation – leveraging insecurity and ambition to gain compliance – to overt threats and intimidation. Promises of career advancement are frequently dangled as bait, while warnings about the inherent risks and competitiveness of the industry are used to discourage artists from questioning unfavorable terms or seeking outside counsel. The industry operates on a precarious system of favor and loyalty, making it challenging for artists to report exploitative practices without risking their career prospects. A culture of silence, enforced by fear of retribution, often prevails. The fear of being labeled difficult or uncooperative, potentially hindering future opportunities, silences many victims of exploitation. These psychological pressures are particularly impactful on young artists still finding their footing in the industry, lacking the experience or confidence to advocate for their own best interests.

The financial consequences of these exploitative practices can be devastating. Many young artists sign away a significant portion of their future earnings in exchange for upfront investments in recording, production, and marketing. However, these costs are often inflated, and the profitsharing arrangements heavily favor the label or management company. The lack of transparency in accounting and financial reporting creates further vulnerability. Artists may never fully comprehend their earning potential, let alone receive their rightful share of royalties or performance fees. This opaque financial system enables continued exploitation, leaving artists struggling to recover lost income, even after achieving significant success. The financial burden extends beyond mere compensation; it also encompasses the expenses incurred by artists in pursuit of their careers. Studio time, travel costs, marketing and promotion, and other essential expenses can quickly accumulate, leaving many artists deeply in debt, further solidifying their dependence on exploitative business relationships.

The lack of industry-wide standards and regulations exacerbates this problem. While some countries have implemented laws designed to protect musicians' rights, enforcement often proves challenging and varies widely depending on the jurisdiction. International collaborations and the global nature of the music industry present additional difficulties. The absence of consistently applied guidelines and the complexity of international laws leave artists vulnerable to exploitation on a global scale. The existing legal frameworks are often ill-equipped to address the subtle yet pervasive forms of manipulation and control exerted by powerful industry players. This gap in regulations creates an environment where exploitative practices can thrive, leaving young artists largely unprotected.

This situation is especially concerning for artists from marginalized communities, who may face additional barriers to accessing resources and support. These include limited access to legal representation, financial instability, and systemic biases within the industry. Intersectionality plays a significant role here, with certain demographics disproportionately targeted for exploitation. A history of systemic discrimination can further hinder their ability to challenge exploitative practices, leaving them trapped in cycles of financial and creative dependence. A lack of mentorship and representation within the industry also contributes to this vulnerability. Without role models and advocates to guide them through the complexities of the business, these artists are often left to fend for themselves, navigating a system designed to exploit their inexperience and lack of industry connections.

The ethical implications of these predatory practices are profound. The music industry, despite its romanticized image, often prioritizes profit maximization over artistic integrity and fair compensation. This disregard for ethical considerations undermines the creative process, fostering an environment of fear and mistrust that stifles artistic expression. The exploitation of young artists not only harms individual careers but also damages the broader cultural landscape. It contributes to the homogenization of musical styles, limiting artistic diversity and innovation. When young artists are forced into conforming to industry demands, their unique voices and creative visions are often stifled. This leads to a loss of authenticity and creative risk-taking, ultimately impoverishing the overall quality and diversity of music produced. The industry's focus on maximizing profits often prioritizes short-term gains over long-term sustainability, leading to an environment where ethical considerations are often overlooked in the pursuit of quick returns.

Addressing this issue requires a multi-pronged approach. Increased regulation and stronger enforcement of existing laws are necessary to create a fairer environment for artists. Greater access to legal resources and educational programs designed to empower artists with the knowledge and tools to negotiate contracts and protect their rights is crucial. A shift in industry culture, emphasizing transparency, ethical practices, and fair compensation, is equally vital. This will involve a conscious effort from industry stakeholders to foster a more equitable system, one that prioritizes artistic integrity and the well-being of artists over profit maximization. The formation of independent organizations dedicated to advocating for artists' rights and providing support services would play a significant role in empowering young musicians. These organizations could offer legal advice, financial guidance, and mentorship programs specifically designed to protect artists from exploitation. Additionally, increased media attention and public awareness campaigns could help expose these predatory practices, encouraging a more responsible industry culture and fostering greater accountability.

Ultimately, the future of the music industry depends on its willingness to address these systemic issues. The exploitation of young artists is not just an ethical dilemma; it is a threat to the long-term health and sustainability of the industry as a whole. By fostering a more equitable and transparent environment, one that values creativity, collaboration, and ethical behavior, the industry can ensure its continued vibrancy and growth while ensuring that the next generation of musicians are empowered to pursue their dreams without fear of exploitation.

The Commodification of Music Art as a Commodity

The relentless pursuit of profit within the music industry has irrevocably altered the perception of music itself. No longer solely viewed as a form of artistic expression, music has increasingly become a commodity, a product to be manufactured, marketed, and consumed. This shift has profound ethical implications, impacting not only the artists involved but also the broader cultural landscape. The tension between artistic integrity and commercial exploitation lies at the heart of this dilemma, a conflict that shapes the very fabric of the industry.

The commodification of music manifests in numerous ways. The emphasis on chart performance and streaming numbers, often prioritized over artistic merit, underscores this shift. Artists are increasingly judged by their commercial success rather than their creative innovation. This pressure to achieve commercial viability frequently leads to creative compromises, as artists feel compelled to conform to prevailing trends and market demands. The very essence of artistic expression – the freedom to experiment, to fail, to push boundaries – is often sacrificed at the altar of commercial success. This relentless pressure to produce commercially viable music often leads to a homogenization of sound, a stifling of originality, and a loss of artistic diversity.

The rise of streaming services, while offering unprecedented access to music for consumers, has also significantly altered the economic landscape for artists. The extremely low royalty rates paid to artists per stream have created a precarious existence for many musicians, forcing them to rely on touring or supplementary income streams to survive. This model essentially undervalues the artistic contribution, prioritizing the platform's profits over the creators' fair compensation. The "pay-per-play" model, while seemingly equitable, often fails to adequately compensate artists for their work, particularly those with less established fan bases. The sheer volume of music available on these platforms also contributes to the problem, making it increasingly difficult for artists to stand out and generate sufficient revenue from streaming alone.

Further fueling the commodification of music is the influence of A&R (artists and repertoire) executives. These gatekeepers, often wielding considerable power, play a significant role in shaping the direction of artists' careers. While some A&R executives genuinely champion artistic integrity, many prioritize commercial viability above all else. This can result in artists being pressured to compromise their artistic vision to conform to market expectations, potentially leading to creative dissatisfaction and a loss of artistic authenticity. The pressure to create music that aligns with market trends often results in a decline in originality and artistic risk-taking, as artists prioritize commercial success over creative experimentation.

The use of songwriting camps, where multiple songwriters collaborate to create commercially viable songs, further exemplifies the commodification of music. While such collaborations can lead to commercially successful songs, the process can devalue the artistic contribution of individual songwriters, reducing their creative work to a mere component in a larger commercial enterprise. The focus shifts from artistic expression to efficient production, with songwriting often treated as a formulaic process rather than a deeply personal and creative endeavor. This can lead to a homogenization of musical styles, with songs sounding remarkably similar across different artists, ultimately diminishing the overall quality and creativity of the music produced.

Moreover, the increasing role of marketing and branding within the music industry contributes to the commodification of music. Artists are increasingly treated as brands, with their image and personality carefully curated to maximize commercial appeal. This focus on branding can overshadow artistic merit, with artists often pressured to conform to predefined personas, sacrificing their individuality for the sake of marketability. The emphasis on the artist's "brand" over their music creates a climate where artistic authenticity can be lost. The carefully constructed image, often divorced from the artist's genuine self, becomes the primary focus, creating a superficial representation of the artist and their music.

The legal frameworks governing the music industry also contribute to the commodification of music. Many contracts signed by artists, especially younger and less experienced ones, often heavily favor the record label, leaving artists vulnerable to exploitation. These contracts, filled with complex legal jargon, can easily overshadow the artists' rights and fair compensation. This imbalance of power further entrenches the commodification of music, where the focus shifts from the artistic contribution to the economic gain.

The implications of this commodification extend beyond the artists themselves. The erosion of artistic integrity and the pressure to conform to commercial trends have broader cultural consequences. The resulting homogenization of music diminishes cultural diversity and stifles creativity. When artists prioritize commercial success over artistic expression, the resulting music often lacks originality and depth, potentially reducing its overall cultural impact. This trend contributes to a broader decline in artistic innovation, impacting the richness and diversity of musical expression.

Addressing this issue requires a multi-faceted approach. Greater transparency in the music industry, particularly concerning contracts and royalty payments, is crucial. Empowering artists with greater legal representation and knowledge of their rights is essential. Furthermore, fostering a cultural shift that prioritizes artistic integrity and fair compensation over mere commercial gain is vital. Only by actively challenging the prevailing paradigm of commodification can we hope to preserve the artistic value of music and ensure a sustainable future for both artists and the broader musical landscape. This involves a systemic shift in the industry's priorities, moving away from a purely profit-driven model to one that acknowledges the artistic contribution and supports the livelihoods of musicians. A significant change in the way streaming royalties are calculated and distributed would also be a step in the right direction. Increased transparency in the financial dealings within the industry, along with stricter regulations to protect artists' rights, would go a long way in fostering a more ethical and sustainable music industry. Ultimately, the preservation of music as art requires a fundamental reevaluation of the industry's priorities. A balance must be struck between commercial success and artistic integrity, one that values creativity, innovation, and the individual artist. Without a paradigm shift in the prevailing business model, the future of music may be one dominated by homogenized sound and financially precarious artists, a loss for both the creators and the consumers of music.

The Role of Technology Copyright Infringement and Piracy

The digital revolution, while democratizing music access like never before, has simultaneously unleashed a torrent of ethical and legal challenges for the music industry. The ease with which music can be copied, shared, and distributed online has led to rampant copyright infringement and piracy, significantly impacting artists' revenue streams and the overall economic viability of the creative process. The rise of file-sharing networks like Napster in the late 1990s served as a watershed moment, exposing the vulnerability of the music industry to technological disruption and the inherent difficulties in policing digital content. While Napster's demise marked a legal victory for the industry, it also underscored the limitations of traditional copyright enforcement in the face of constantly evolving technologies. The battle against piracy shifted from a centralized fight against a single platform to a diffuse war against countless peer-to-peer networks and increasingly sophisticated methods of digital distribution.

The impact on artists' livelihoods has been devastating. The widespread availability of free or illegally obtained music severely undermines the established models of revenue generation, such as album sales and physical media. For emerging artists, who rely heavily on initial album sales to fund subsequent projects, piracy represents a significant barrier to entry and career progression. The financial losses incurred by established artists due to piracy are also substantial, impacting their ability to invest in future recordings, tours, and the overall development of their artistic careers. Beyond direct financial losses, the erosion of the value of music through widespread piracy impacts the overall creative environment. Less revenue means fewer resources for artists to experiment, innovate and refine their craft. The resulting creative stagnation can negatively impact the quality and originality of music produced.

The emergence of streaming services, while offering a seemingly more legitimate avenue for music consumption, presents its own set of challenges. The extremely low royalty rates paid to artists per stream, often criticized as insufficient to provide a living wage, perpetuate the problem. While streaming platforms generate massive revenue, the distribution of that revenue remains a contentious issue, with artists often receiving a disproportionately small share compared to the platforms' profits. The algorithms that govern these platforms also affect which artists get discovered and compensated. Less known artists are often swallowed in the sea of millions of tracks available, further impacting their potential income from streaming. The issue of fair compensation remains a pivotal debate in the industry's fight for sustainability.

Furthermore, the legal framework surrounding digital music distribution is complex and often inadequate to address the nuances of the digital landscape. International copyright laws vary widely, creating loopholes and difficulties in enforcing intellectual property rights across borders. The ease with which music can be uploaded and shared across different platforms and geographical locations makes tracking and prosecuting copyright infringement a formidable task. Many legal battles have focused on determining liability for copyright infringement on platforms hosting user-generated content, leading to protracted legal battles and significant costs for the music industry. The dynamic nature of technology continuously outpaces the legal system, generating a persistent challenge in regulating the digital distribution of music.

The role of technology extends beyond the simple act of copying and sharing. The emergence of sophisticated music creation tools has also created new challenges. Software capable of creating high-quality music and altering existing tracks has enabled new forms of copyright infringement and piracy. AI-generated music, still in its early stages of development, further complicates the issues of ownership, authorship, and copyright. The ability of AI to generate music that mimics the style of established artists could lead to a surge in copyright infringement if not properly addressed. The lines between inspiration and plagiarism are further blurred as AI's capacity for musical creation grows.

The fight against piracy and copyright infringement is a complex one that requires a multi-pronged approach. This includes strengthening international copyright laws to facilitate effective cross-border enforcement. Technological solutions, such as digital rights management (DRM) systems, play a role, but they often prove ineffective against determined pirates. Furthermore, increasing public awareness about the consequences of piracy is crucial. Education about the economic impact on artists and the creative process is needed to instill a culture of respect for intellectual property rights. Such educational efforts should focus on the importance of fair compensation for creators and the broader cultural implications of rampant music piracy.

Beyond legal and technological solutions, economic models need to adapt to the realities of the digital music landscape. This involves exploring alternative models of revenue generation for artists, including subscription services with fair royalty rates and diversified income streams like live performances, merchandise, and brand partnerships. Strengthening artist representation and empowering artists with the knowledge of their rights are vital steps in creating a more equitable ecosystem. This also involves working with streaming platforms to implement transparent and fair royalty distribution systems and investing in artist development and promotion to level the playing field.

The ethical dimension of copyright infringement and piracy extends beyond mere financial considerations. It touches upon the very nature of art and creative expression. When creators are not adequately compensated for their work, it undermines the value of their artistic contributions and can discourage future creativity. It creates a climate where artists are forced to compromise their artistic integrity to prioritize commercial viability, leading to a homogenization of musical styles and a decline in artistic innovation. The very foundation of the creative process—the dedication, time, and effort invested by artists—is devalued when their work is freely available. The ethical implications extend beyond the individual artist; the diminished financial rewards can directly impact the creation of future works and consequently, the cultural landscape.

In conclusion, the impact of technology on the music industry's ethical landscape is profound and multifaceted. The rise of digital music distribution, while offering unparalleled access to music, has also created significant challenges in protecting artists' intellectual property rights and ensuring their fair compensation. Addressing this complex problem requires a concerted effort that combines legal reforms, technological solutions, economic restructuring, public education, and a broader ethical shift towards valuing artistic creation. Only through a holistic approach can the industry ensure a sustainable future for both creators and consumers, one where artistic integrity is prioritized and artists are fairly compensated for their invaluable contributions to the world of music. The future of music depends on the collective effort to find a balance between the ease of access offered by technology and the vital need to protect the rights and livelihoods of those who create it.

Transparency and Accountability The Need for Industry Reform

The preceding discussion of piracy and the inadequacies of the current streaming model lays bare a crucial underlying issue: a systemic lack of transparency and accountability within the music industry. The power imbalance between major labels, streaming platforms, and artists is stark, and this imbalance is actively perpetuated by a culture of secrecy and opaque business practices. The contracts offered to artists, particularly those just starting out, are often notoriously complex and heavily weighted in favor of the record label. These contracts frequently include clauses that are difficult to understand, leaving artists vulnerable to exploitation and potentially robbing them of a fair share of their earnings. The lack of clear and readily accessible information regarding royalty payments and revenue streams further exacerbates this power imbalance. Artists often have little to no insight into how their music is monetized and how much revenue is generated from their work, making it challenging to assess the fairness of their compensation.

This lack of transparency extends beyond the artist-label relationship. The revenue-sharing models employed by streaming platforms are often shrouded in secrecy, making it difficult to understand how royalties are calculated and distributed. The complex algorithms that govern these platforms further obscure the process, making it challenging for artists to understand how their music is promoted and why some artists achieve greater success than others. This opacity fuels suspicion and distrust, contributing to a climate of inequality and frustration among artists. The lack of transparency in the financial dealings of major labels also contributes to the problem. The internal financial structures of these companies are rarely made public, making it difficult for artists and the public to assess their profitability and the fairness of their dealings. Such a lack of scrutiny enables practices that prioritize profit maximization over the well-being of artists.

The need for reform is evident. To address these systemic issues, a multifaceted approach is required. First and foremost, greater transparency is crucial. This involves standardizing and simplifying artist contracts, making them easier to understand and negotiate. Clear and readily accessible information regarding royalty payments, revenue streams, and expense deductions should be provided to artists on a regular basis. Independent auditing of these financial statements could provide an added layer of accountability and transparency. Streaming platforms should also be required to disclose their revenue-sharing models, including the algorithms used to determine which artists are promoted and how royalties are calculated. This level of openness would allow artists to understand the factors influencing their success and hold platforms accountable for any perceived biases or unfair practices.

Furthermore, stricter regulations are necessary to protect artists from exploitation. This could include stricter oversight of artist contracts to ensure fair terms and conditions and the introduction of minimum royalty rates for artists on streaming platforms. These rates should be regularly reviewed and adjusted to reflect the changing economic landscape and the growing revenue generated by streaming services. The legislation should also address the issue of "360 deals," which give labels a stake in an artist's income from multiple sources, potentially exceeding the artists' income from their music sales. These deals, while sometimes necessary for artists in the early stages of their careers, can be exploitative if not carefully negotiated and monitored. Tougher regulations would help prevent record labels from dictating unfair terms to artists who are desperate for a deal.

Beyond stricter regulations, enhancing the support systems available to artists is crucial. The creation of independent organizations that provide legal assistance and financial guidance to artists can help them navigate the complexities of the industry and advocate for their rights. These organizations can provide resources such as model contracts and templates, which could be of particular benefit to lessexperienced artists who lack the resources to employ their own legal representatives. Moreover, providing artists with better education and training in contract negotiation and business management would empower them to make more informed decisions and protect themselves from exploitation.

Improved artist representation is another essential aspect of industry reform. Many artists lack the bargaining power to negotiate fair deals with major labels and streaming platforms. Strengthening artist unions and collective bargaining organizations can empower artists to collectively negotiate better terms and conditions and work towards a more equitable distribution of revenue. Such collective action could lead to a significant improvement in the working conditions and financial prospects for artists.

The fight for transparency and accountability in the music industry is not merely a legal or economic battle; it is a moral one. The ethical implications of the current power imbalance are profound, contributing to the financial insecurity and creative stagnation of many artists. By advocating for stricter regulations, greater transparency, enhanced support systems, and improved artist representation, we can work toward a more equitable and sustainable music industry, one where artists are empowered, respected, and fairly compensated for their creative contributions. The future of music, and the future of its creators, depends on this critical shift toward a more just and transparent system. This will require a sustained effort from artists, industry stakeholders, policymakers, and consumers alike—a collective commitment to overhaul an industry that has for too long prioritized profit over the welfare of the creative spirit that fuels it.

The path to reform is not without its challenges. The music industry is deeply entrenched in its current practices, and powerful interests will undoubtedly resist change. However, the growing awareness of the systemic issues, coupled with the increasing advocacy from artists and industry watchdogs, provides hope for positive transformation. The legal battles over fair compensation, data transparency, and algorithmic bias will continue, but the increasing public pressure will force the industry to confront the moral and ethical shortcomings at its core.

The fight for a fairer music industry requires a multifaceted approach that involves collaborations between artists, industry players, regulatory bodies, and consumers. This collaborative spirit is essential to achieve lasting, effective reform. A transparent and accountable music industry isn't just a utopian ideal; it's a fundamental requirement for its own survival. Without a shift towards a more equitable ecosystem, the industry risks losing the talent and creativity that make it thrive. The future of music hinges on the success of this ongoing fight for transparency and accountability. The music industry must acknowledge the past failures and work proactively to implement meaningful reforms; otherwise, it risks alienating the very creators that sustain its existence.

The Future of Music A Call for Change

The preceding analysis of the music industry's ethical failings points towards a critical need for systemic change. The current model, built on opaque contracts, skewed revenue sharing, and a lack of transparency, is unsustainable. It not only undermines the creative potential of artists but also threatens the long-term health of the industry itself. A music industry that consistently exploits its creators will inevitably suffer a decline in talent and innovation. The vibrant tapestry of musical expression will fray, replaced by a homogenous output dictated by profit margins rather than artistic merit.

The path forward requires a collaborative effort, a radical shift in mindset that prioritizes the well-being of artists alongside financial success. This isn't simply about altruism; it's about recognizing that a flourishing artistic community is the bedrock upon which the entire industry is built. Without a thriving ecosystem of artists, there's no music to sell, no concerts to promote, and ultimately, no industry to sustain.

One critical area for reform is artist contracts. The current system often leaves artists vulnerable to exploitation. Complex legal jargon, buried clauses, and unfavorable terms are routinely used to secure advantageous positions for labels, leaving artists with little negotiating power, particularly those starting out. This necessitates a move toward standardized, simpler contracts with clear, easily understandable language. Independent legal counsel should be readily available and affordable for all artists, ensuring they have the support they need to navigate the intricacies of these agreements. The concept of "360 deals," where labels claim a percentage of an artist's income from various sources, needs careful scrutiny and potential reform. While these deals can be beneficial in launching careers, they must be carefully structured to prevent exploitation and ensure artists retain a fair share of their earnings. The implementation of model contracts, developed collaboratively by artists, labels, and legal experts, could provide a foundation for fairer and more transparent agreements.

Beyond contracts, the issue of royalty payments requires immediate attention. The current streaming model, while offering unprecedented access to music, often provides meager compensation to artists, particularly those not enjoying mainstream success. The opaque algorithms used by streaming services to determine royalties and playlist placements further exacerbate the problem. Artists deserve complete transparency into how their music is monetized, how their royalties are calculated, and how their revenue is generated. Independent audits of these processes should become standard practice, providing an additional layer of accountability and ensuring fair compensation for artists. Furthermore, exploring alternative revenue models, such as direct artist-to-fan platforms, could help artists bypass the gatekeepers and establish a more direct connection with their audiences.

The role of technology in shaping the future of music is multifaceted and complex. While technology has democratized music creation and distribution, it has also introduced new challenges, primarily regarding copyright protection and fair compensation for artists. The fight against piracy remains ongoing, and the industry needs to develop more sophisticated strategies to protect artists' intellectual property while acknowledging the shifting landscape of music consumption. The development and enforcement of effective legal frameworks addressing online copyright infringement is crucial.

Policymakers have a crucial role to play in ensuring a more ethical and equitable music industry. Legislation is necessary to protect artists from unfair contract terms, mandate transparency in royalty payments, and establish minimum royalty rates for artists on streaming platforms. These regulations should be regularly reviewed and updated to reflect the changing economic realities and technological advancements within the industry. Furthermore, governments should invest in programs that support artist development, provide legal assistance, and promote financial literacy within the music community.

The empowerment of artists is central to the future of the music industry. This requires strengthening artist unions and collective bargaining organizations, giving artists a unified voice to negotiate better terms and conditions with labels and streaming platforms. Collective bargaining provides artists with significant leverage, allowing them to negotiate fair contracts, secure better royalty rates, and advocate for improved working conditions. Independent artist organizations can also play a crucial role in providing support, resources, and legal assistance. These organizations can provide artists with essential information, guidance on contract negotiation, and tools to navigate the complexities of the music industry.

The role of education cannot be overstated. Artists need access to comprehensive business training and financial literacy programs to empower them to make informed decisions, manage their finances effectively, and navigate the legal and contractual complexities of the music industry. This education should cover topics such as contract negotiation, royalty calculations, budgeting, marketing, and intellectual property rights.

Consumer awareness also plays a critical role in achieving a more equitable music industry. Educating consumers about the challenges faced by artists, the complexities of the current revenue models, and the importance of supporting artists directly can encourage responsible consumption habits and foster a culture of valuing artistic work. This includes educating consumers about the importance of fair compensation and the impact of streaming services on artists' livelihoods.

Building a more ethical and equitable music industry is not a quick fix. It requires a sustained, collaborative effort from artists, labels, streaming services, policymakers, and consumers alike. The changes needed are substantial, requiring significant shifts in power dynamics, contractual practices, and industry regulations. The transition will undoubtedly face resistance from entrenched interests. However, the benefits – a healthier, more creative, and sustainable music industry that truly values its artists – are worth fighting for. The future of music rests on our collective ability to create a system where artistic integrity and economic viability coexist, fostering a vibrant and equitable environment for all those who contribute to the creation and enjoyment of music. The path forward demands ongoing vigilance, unwavering advocacy, and a collective commitment to build a music industry that truly reflects the values of creativity, fairness, and respect for the artists who bring it to life. This is not merely a call for change, but a necessity for the survival and flourishing of music as we know it.

Case Study The Fight for Fair Royalties

The fight for fair compensation within the music industry is far from a theoretical debate; it's a lived reality for countless artists. One compelling illustration of this struggle is the protracted legal battle waged by indie-folk singer-songwriter, Amelia Hernandez. Hernandez, a self-described "bedroom artist" who gained a significant following through independent online platforms, found herself ensnared in a complex web of contractual obligations that ultimately threatened to stifle her burgeoning career.

Her story began in 2015, when, after years of self-releasing her music and building a loyal fanbase online, she signed a recording contract with a small, independent label, "Soundwave Records." The contract, presented as a standard industry agreement, initially appeared straightforward. However, buried within the dense legal jargon were several clauses that would later prove to be profoundly disadvantageous to Hernandez. Specifically, a clause concerning "mechanical royalties" – the payments artists receive when their songs are physically reproduced, such as in CDs or vinyl – was worded ambiguously. The contract stated that Hernandez would receive a standard rate, but failed to clearly define what constituted a "standard rate," leaving room for interpretation.

Initially, Soundwave Records paid Hernandez mechanical royalties at what they claimed was the "standard rate," a rate significantly lower than what she later discovered was the industry norm. The label's financial reporting was opaque, lacking detail and transparency. Hernandez, lacking the financial resources to hire independent legal counsel at the time, accepted their explanation, focusing instead on her burgeoning career. This oversight would prove costly.

As her popularity grew, so did the number of physical copies of her music sold. However, the royalty payments remained consistently low. Hernandez's suspicion was aroused when a fellow artist, sharing a similar profile and level of success, revealed they received significantly higher mechanical royalties from their label. This prompted Hernandez to carefully examine her contract and seek out independent legal advice.

The legal advice she received was damning. The ambiguity in the "mechanical royalties" clause, combined with the lack of transparent financial reporting from Soundwave Records, constituted a breach of contract. The lawyer argued that the label had consistently underpaid Hernandez, exploiting her naivety and lack of initial legal representation. The lawyer meticulously examined years of financial statements provided by Soundwave Records, uncovering discrepancies and inconsistencies in the royalty calculations. They discovered numerous instances where Hernandez should have received higher payments, amounting to a significant sum of unpaid royalties.

The ensuing legal battle was long and arduous. Soundwave Records, initially dismissive of Hernandez's claims, dug in their heels, employing a team of lawyers to defend their position. They argued that their interpretation of the "standard rate" clause was reasonable and that any discrepancies were due to accounting errors. However, the lawyer representing Hernandez presented irrefutable evidence demonstrating that the label's claims were baseless, consistently underpaying her to maximize their profits.

The case went to court, resulting in a protracted and costly legal process. The court proceedings themselves became a further financial burden on Hernandez. While she had managed to secure pro bono assistance from a legal aid organization, the costs associated with expert witnesses, travel, and legal fees continued to mount. This period was marked by considerable financial stress, forcing Hernandez to take on additional work, impacting her creativity and career trajectory.

The legal battle lasted nearly three years. It tested Hernandez's emotional and psychological resilience, threatening to derail her musical career altogether. The constant pressure of legal proceedings, coupled with the financial strain, created an environment of uncertainty and anxiety. The ongoing legal fight also dominated Hernandez's time and energy, diverting her attention from composing and performing, causing a period of creative stagnation. She experienced significant emotional distress, struggling to maintain a sense of optimism about her future as a musician.

Finally, the court ruled in favor of Hernandez. The judge found in favor of the lawyer's argument, citing the ambiguity of the "mechanical royalties" clause as a breach of contract and upholding the claim that Soundwave Records had systematically underpaid Hernandez. The court ordered Soundwave Records to pay Hernandez the full amount of her unpaid royalties, plus additional compensation for the legal fees incurred during the lengthy proceedings. The victory, while hard-won, was momentous. It vindicated Hernandez and brought attention to the predatory practices of some music labels.

The victory, however, was bittersweet. The financial and emotional toll of the legal battle had taken its toll. While Hernandez won the case, the process had significantly delayed her musical progress, and the considerable stress undoubtedly impacted her creativity and overall well-being. It highlighted the systemic inequalities inherent within the music industry and the desperate need for improved protections for artists entering into contracts. Her case serves as a cautionary tale of the vulnerability of artists, particularly those starting out, and underscores the importance of legal counsel and transparent contractual agreements. The case also revealed the complexities involved in securing justice against powerful industry players, even with irrefutable evidence.

Hernandez's experience is not unique. Numerous artists face similar battles, fighting for their fair share of earnings in a system designed to favor the powerful. Her story underlines the urgency for greater transparency in the music industry, the necessity of standardized contracts, readily accessible legal aid, and the need for industry-wide reforms. The fight for fair royalties is far from over, but cases like Hernandez's provide a powerful reminder of the lengths to which artists must go to protect themselves and their work. Her victory, though challenging, serves as a beacon of hope, showing that perseverance and legal action can ultimately prevail against exploitative practices within the industry. The ongoing narrative of fighting for equitable treatment demands systemic change, a change that only sustained effort, awareness and collective action can bring about. The need for comprehensive legal reforms and enhanced industry transparency remains critical to protect future artists from experiencing a similar ordeal. Only then can the industry move towards a more ethical and sustainable future, one that values both artistic expression and the fair compensation of those who create it. The fight continues.

Case Study Breaking Free from an Exploitative Contract

The fight for artistic freedom and fair compensation often involves navigating a labyrinthine legal landscape, a reality starkly illustrated by the experience of renowned jazz saxophonist, Elijah Jones. Jones, a prodigious talent who had garnered critical acclaim and a dedicated following through years of independent performances and self-released albums, signed a recording contract with "Titan Records," a major label known for its aggressive acquisition strategies and, according to industry whispers, its less-than-scrupulous business practices.

The contract, presented as a standard industry agreement, was a weighty tome of legal jargon, meticulously crafted to favor the label. While Jones's manager, at the time, assured him that it was a "standard deal," a cursory review wouldn't have revealed the insidious clauses hidden within the dense text. The contract granted Titan Records an extensive array of rights, extending far beyond the initial recording and distribution of his music. The label secured control over Jones's image, likeness, and even his social media presence, significantly limiting his ability to engage independently with his audience.

Perhaps the most damning clause was the one concerning album sales and royalties. While it appeared to offer a standard royalty structure on the surface, further examination revealed a tiered system weighted heavily in favor of Titan Records. Jones's royalty rate was subject to a complex formula, involving deductions for various marketing and distribution costs, leaving little transparency on how his actual earnings were calculated. The contract also granted Titan Records the right to extend the agreement indefinitely, based on vague criteria concerning "artistic potential" and "market performance," tying Jones to the label indefinitely without a clear path to escape.

Initially, Jones experienced a surge in his profile and sales. Titan Records invested heavily in his marketing and promotion, leading to several successful album releases and a significant increase in his fanbase. However, the financial returns didn't reflect this success. Jones regularly received royalty statements that were opaque and difficult to decipher, leaving him unsure of the true value of his output and the actual deductions applied to his earnings. Repeated inquiries for clarification were met with vague assurances from the label's management, suggesting that understanding the intricacies of the agreement was beyond the purview of a mere artist.

His suspicions grew stronger when he started networking with other artists signed to Titan Records, exchanging notes and sharing experiences. He learned that many other artists within the label were experiencing similar issues with financial transparency and the challenges of navigating the complex language and opaque royalty structure laid out in their contracts. The informal support group allowed them to collectively build evidence of possible misrepresentations and inconsistencies in the label's financial reporting practices. They decided to pool their resources and engage a prominent entertainment lawyer specializing in music industry contracts.

The legal battle that ensued was monumental. Titan Records, a powerful entity with considerable financial resources and a formidable legal team, fought back aggressively, arguing that Jones and the other artists had signed the contract willingly and had been fully informed of its terms. They presented the contract as a standard industry agreement, attempting to dismiss the accusations of intentional deception.

However, the lawyer representing Jones and the group of other artists meticulously examined the contracts and meticulously investigated the financial dealings of Titan Records. The evidence they presented revealed a pattern of financial irregularities, inconsistencies, and deliberately misleading clauses designed to obscure the actual financial arrangements. Their investigations unearthed a culture of contractual exploitation, suggesting this was not an isolated case, but a systemic issue within the label.

The court case became a landmark ruling in the music industry. The judge ruled largely in favor of the artists, citing several clauses within the contract as deliberately ambiguous and misleading, designed to exploit the artists' lack of legal expertise. The court also held that Titan Records had failed to provide adequate financial transparency, consistently underpaying the artists by deliberately obfuscating royalty calculations. The ruling mandated the renegotiation of contracts and compensation to the artists for underpaid royalties, setting a crucial precedent for future industry practices.

The victory, however, came at a significant cost. The legal battle stretched for years, draining Jones's finances and emotional reserves. The uncertainty and stress impacted his creativity and musical output. While financially compensated, the impact on his well-being and career trajectory was substantial. His story, however, served as a powerful example of how artists can effectively fight back against exploitative contracts, highlighting the importance of legal counsel and the need for greater transparency in the industry.

The legal victory also sparked a wave of change within the music industry. The case brought widespread attention to the often-unequal power dynamics between major labels and artists, leading to increased scrutiny of contract terms and calls for industry reforms. Several legislative efforts were initiated to strengthen artists' rights and provide better protections against exploitative contracts. While significant legal battles continue, the success of Jones's case created a roadmap for other artists facing similar challenges, a testament to the power of collective action and the persistence of the human spirit in the face of adversity. His battle underscores the ongoing need for systemic change in the music industry, a shift towards greater fairness, transparency, and ethical practices in the business of music. The fight for a just and equitable music industry continues, but cases like Jones's provide hope and direction, showing that challenging the status quo can lead to meaningful change, empowering artists and protecting their creative livelihoods.

Case Study The Battle Against Copyright Infringement

The fight for fair compensation isn't limited to battling exploitative contracts; it also extends to the crucial area of copyright protection. The case of visual artist Anya Petrova exemplifies the uphill struggle many creatives face when their intellectual property is stolen and illegally reproduced. Petrova, a rising star in the contemporary art scene, had built her career on a distinct style characterized by vibrant, surreal landscapes. Her meticulously crafted works, often incorporating intricate details and unique color palettes, quickly gained recognition in galleries and online. This growing popularity, however, inadvertently made her work a prime target for copyright infringement.

The infringement began subtly. Initially, Petrova noticed her artwork appearing on unauthorized merchandise—cheaply produced phone cases, tote bags, and posters sold through various online marketplaces and, alarmingly, in some brickand-mortar stores. The quality of these reproductions was undeniably poor, the colors muted, and the details lost in the shoddy printing process. Yet, the blatant use of her artistic style and specific compositions was unmistakable. At first, she dismissed it as a minor nuisance, a frustrating but inevitable byproduct of success. However, the scale and persistence of the infringement quickly escalated.

Petrova started to discover her work not only on low-quality merchandise but also integrated into larger-scale projects without her consent. A prominent fashion designer incorporated elements directly from one of her most celebrated paintings into a highly publicized collection, generating significant media attention and financial profit, none of which benefited Petrova. A large hotel chain used a near-identical copy of another piece as a central feature in its marketing campaign, displayed prominently on their website and in brochures. Each instance was a fresh blow, not only financially damaging but also deeply disheartening for Petrova, who felt her artistic integrity and creative ownership were being systematically violated.

Confronting these infringements proved far more difficult than Petrova had anticipated. Tracing the source of the unauthorized reproductions was a complex and timeconsuming process. Many of the offending parties operated anonymously through online marketplaces, utilizing pseudonyms and employing tactics designed to obfuscate their identities and locations. Even when she managed to identify a specific vendor or company, pursuing legal action against them was a daunting prospect. Many were small businesses operating on a shoestring budget, rendering costly legal battles impractical. Larger companies, meanwhile, often had extensive legal departments and resources to contest any claim.

Her initial attempts to contact the infringers directly were largely ignored. Some responded with dismissive apologies, claiming ignorance of the copyright laws or attributing the infringement to an oversight. Others remained completely unresponsive. Petrova quickly realized that she needed professional legal counsel to effectively navigate the complex legal landscape of copyright infringement. Engaging a lawyer specialized in intellectual property rights proved to be an expensive undertaking. The initial consultation alone cost a significant portion of her savings, highlighting the financial burden placed on artists who find themselves victims of copyright theft.

The legal battles that followed were protracted and challenging. Petrova's lawyer had to build a comprehensive case demonstrating the originality of her work, proving its unauthorized reproduction, and tracing the distribution chains to identify the responsible parties. The process involved gathering detailed evidence—high-resolution images of her original artwork, documentation of the infringing products, website screenshots, and witness testimonies from galleries and collectors who had seen her work. Each legal step demanded significant time, resources, and emotional strain.

Many cases were settled out of court, with the infringers agreeing to cease production and distribution of the unauthorized merchandise. However, obtaining financial compensation proved far more elusive. The small businesses often lacked the means to pay substantial damages, while the larger corporations employed delaying tactics and complex legal maneuvers to minimize their financial liability. The legal system, Petrova discovered, often favored those with more resources and financial clout.

The prolonged legal battles took a significant toll on Petrova's artistic output. The stress and uncertainty surrounding the infringements stifled her creativity, hindering her ability to focus on new projects. The emotional exhaustion was palpable, and she found herself battling not only legal battles but also a sense of demoralization and disillusionment. The financial burden of the legal proceedings also significantly impacted her livelihood, forcing her to reduce her creative endeavors and take on additional work to cover her legal expenses.

Despite the challenges, Petrova's perseverance eventually bore fruit. In some cases, significant financial settlements were secured. In others, cease-and-desist orders forced the removal of her work from unauthorized websites and products. Her case became a rallying point within the artistic community, highlighting the difficulties artists face in protecting their intellectual property and the need for more robust mechanisms to combat copyright infringement.

Petrova's experience underscores the systemic inequalities artists face in the fight for their creative rights. The lack of readily accessible and affordable legal resources, the complexities of international copyright laws, and the oftendisproportionate power dynamics between artists and larger corporations create a formidable obstacle course for creatives seeking to protect their work. Her story serves as a cautionary tale, emphasizing the proactive measures artists must take to safeguard their intellectual property and highlighting the urgent need for reforms that provide greater protection and support to those whose livelihoods depend on their creative output. The fight is far from over, but Petrova's unwavering determination to protect her work and her contributions to the ongoing dialogue about artist's rights represent a crucial step towards a more just and equitable creative landscape. The fight continues. And the battle for artistic justice is far from won. But stories like Petrova's— and Jones's before her—offer valuable lessons, reminding us of the resilience, the persistence, and the unwavering spirit of artists fighting for their rights in a system often stacked against them.

Case Study The Struggle for Creative Control

The struggle for creative control often manifests in the battle between an artist's vision and the commercial interests of their label or management. This conflict can be subtle, a series of compromises that gradually erode an artist's artistic integrity, or it can be a full-blown clash, resulting in legal battles and fractured relationships. The case of musician and songwriter, David Byrne, although not strictly a legal battle in the same vein as Petrova's, offers a compelling example of an artist navigating the complexities of retaining creative autonomy within the music industry. Byrne, the frontman of the iconic Talking Heads, found himself embroiled in a protracted struggle over the creative direction of the band's music, a struggle which ultimately played a significant role in shaping the band's trajectory and, arguably, the future of their musical output.

Byrne's artistic vision from the start was strikingly unconventional. His music, a blend of art-rock, funk, and new wave, eschewed typical pop structures and embraced experimental soundscapes. His lyrical content, often fragmented and ambiguous, resonated with a generation grappling with postmodern anxieties and societal fragmentation. This unique artistic vision clashed repeatedly with the commercial expectations of their record label, Sire Records, which, while supportive of the band's early work, also sought commercially viable hits that could maximize profits.

The pressure to conform to mainstream expectations increased with the band's growing success. While early albums like *77* and *Fear of Music* explored Byrne's experimental inclinations, subsequent releases faced increasing pressure to incorporate more radio-friendly elements. This tension was not always overt; it manifested in subtle ways, such as suggestions from producers or A&R representatives to modify songs to increase their marketability. These suggestions often focused on streamlining Byrne's distinctive vocal delivery, simplifying his lyrics, or altering the overall musical arrangements to fit contemporary pop trends.

Byrne resisted these pressures, but not without compromise. He often negotiated with the label, balancing his artistic vision with the need for commercial success. However, this negotiation was a constant tension, an ongoing negotiation that required him to navigate conflicting priorities and make difficult choices. This internal tension is evident in the band's evolution; while they continued to push creative boundaries, they also occasionally produced songs designed to appeal to a broader audience, a necessary strategy to maintain their commercial viability while keeping their label and investors happy.

This delicate balance, however, was not always sustainable. The production of their 1985 album, *Little Creatures* , became a pivotal point in this ongoing struggle. While commercially successful, the album represented a moment where the band seemed to be working towards a more commercial sound. This shift, while potentially fulfilling for the label, did not entirely satisfy Byrne's artistic sensibilities. He felt a growing disconnect between the creative direction of the band and his own artistic goals.

The pressure to continue down this more commercially acceptable route increased as Talking Heads continued to achieve popularity. Internal conflicts started to emerge within the band. The band members, having tasted success, may not have all shared Byrne's creative vision or artistic priorities, leading to increasing creative tension and disagreements about the direction of their music. This internal conflict further complicated Byrne's already tense relationship with the label, adding another layer to the struggle for creative control.

This internal conflict, along with the inherent stress of maintaining the band's success, ultimately contributed to the band's decision to disband in 1991. While never explicitly stated as a direct result of this ongoing creative struggle, the tensions between Byrne's artistic vision and the commercial pressures of the music industry clearly played a significant role in the band's eventual dissolution.

The impact of this ongoing negotiation is evident in Byrne's subsequent solo career. Freed from the constraints of band dynamics and label pressure, Byrne's solo work displays a wider range of artistic experimentation and a greater degree of creative autonomy. He pursued various artistic avenues, including visual art installations, film scores, and theatrical collaborations, further showcasing his multidisciplinary approach and artistic independence. His experience with Talking Heads shaped his future approach to creating music and collaborating with others.

Byrne's story illustrates a common challenge faced by artists navigating the complexities of the music industry: the tension between artistic integrity and commercial success. While many artists compromise, often willingly to achieve commercial goals, Byrne's case highlights the potential conflicts that arise and the need for artists to continuously negotiate and balance these seemingly opposing forces. His story serves as a potent reminder of the constant struggle artists face to maintain their creative vision in the face of pressure to conform to industry standards and the compromises they may have to make to survive.

The outcome, although not a clear-cut "victory" or "defeat", reveals the significant long-term consequences of such conflicts. While the band's success was undoubtedly influenced by their willingness to adapt to commercial pressures, the creative compromises made may have also limited the band's artistic potential and ultimately contributed to their dissolution. Byrne's later successes, achieved through a greater degree of artistic independence, demonstrate the value of prioritizing creative autonomy, even at the risk of sacrificing commercial success. The case of Talking Heads provides a critical study into the complexities of achieving both artistic integrity and commercial viability, and the long-term impacts of prioritizing one over the other. It showcases the challenges artists face in managing the commercial machinery behind their creative expression. It's a battle that's far from over for the vast majority of musicians and artists worldwide. The fight for creative control remains a constant struggle, a negotiation played out daily within the industry, with varying degrees of success for those who dare to resist. This struggle extends beyond music, as we've seen, to encompass all forms of artistic expression and provides vital insight into the very essence of the creative process and the power dynamics which shape and sometimes suffocate it. The system, often inherently geared towards maximizing profit, requires constant vigilance and unwavering commitment from artists who wish to maintain their integrity.

The case of David Byrne underscores the multifaceted nature of this struggle, highlighting not only the external pressures exerted by record labels and management but also the internal conflicts that can arise within artistic collaborations. The pressures to maintain commercial success can lead to creative compromises, which in turn may result in long-term artistic limitations and internal tensions that ultimately contribute to the fragility of artistic partnerships. Byrne's journey serves as a critical reminder of the importance of artists actively safeguarding their creative control, even at the risk of challenging industry norms. The long-term consequences of these struggles often involve a re-evaluation of priorities, and a search for new avenues to preserve and express creative vision. This relentless pursuit of artistic independence, often in the face of immense obstacles, forms the very backbone of the creative spirit and fuels the tireless efforts of artists across genres and mediums.

Case Study Navigating the Independent Music Scene

The previous examples highlighted the struggles faced by artists within the established structures of the music industry. However, the digital revolution has fostered a burgeoning independent music scene, offering artists unprecedented opportunities to bypass traditional gatekeepers and build their careers on their own terms. This shift, while empowering, presents its own unique set of challenges, requiring artists to master diverse skills beyond just songwriting and performance. This case study will examine one artist's successful navigation of this complex landscape, highlighting the strategies employed, the obstacles overcome, and the lessons learned in building a sustainable independent career.

Our focus will be on Amanda Palmer, a musician who has famously built a significant career through a direct-to-fan model. Her path, while not without its pitfalls, serves as a compelling example of how artists can successfully leverage technology and community building to cultivate a loyal fan base and establish financial stability outside of the traditional label system. Palmer's career trajectory dramatically departs from the narratives of artists beholden to major labels, offering a refreshing perspective on alternative avenues to success in the modern music industry.

Before delving into the specifics of her strategies, it is crucial to understand the context of her emergence. Palmer rose to prominence in the early 2000s as the pianist and vocalist for the Dresden Dolls, a quirky cabaret duo known for their theatrical performances and darkly humorous lyrics. However, even with their relative success, the Dresden Dolls operated largely within the independent music scene, gaining a dedicated following through relentless touring, selfpromotion, and a strong online presence. This experience laid the groundwork for Palmer's independent solo career, equipping her with valuable insights into the dynamics of direct engagement with fans and the potential of online platforms for building a community. She intuitively understood the power of fostering a personal connection with her audience long before it became a widely adopted strategy within the independent music scene.

The key to Palmer's success lies in her masterful adoption of what is now often referred to as the "direct-to-fan" model. This strategy circumvents traditional intermediaries like record labels, distributors, and even booking agents, allowing the artist to maintain greater control over their creative output, their finances, and their relationship with their fanbase. Rather than relying on the marketing and distribution power of a label, Palmer built a strong online presence through various platforms like her blog, social media channels, and email list. This direct connection allowed her to build relationships with fans, fostering a sense of community and loyalty that has been essential to her continued success. Her frequent and candid communications with her fans, often addressing both personal and professional matters, cultivated a unique intimacy which few artists achieve through conventional means. This level of transparency and trust-building was crucial in cultivating a dedicated fanbase willing to invest in her work, even financially.

One of the most remarkable aspects of Palmer's independent career is her successful application of crowdfunding. Long before crowdfunding became a common tool for artists, Palmer embraced it, using platforms like Kickstarter to finance her projects. She didn't simply ask for money; she created compelling narratives around her projects, offering fans unique rewards and experiences in return for their contributions. This not only secured funding for her music but also further strengthened her relationship with her fanbase, creating a sense of shared ownership and involvement in her creative process. This demonstrated a deep understanding of the psychological dynamics of fandom, where a sense of ownership and participation in an artist's creative journey fosters deeper loyalty and engagement. She turned her fans into active participants in her creative process, transforming them from passive consumers into active investors.

Palmer also demonstrates an understanding of the power of community engagement, demonstrating this through innovative projects and initiatives. She frequently interacts with her fans online, responding to comments, answering questions, and building personal connections. She organizes meet-and-greets, exclusive concerts, and other events that bring her closer to her fanbase, reinforcing the sense of community and personal connection that is so central to her model. These events weren't merely promotional activities; they were vital components in building and nurturing her community. This organic connection went beyond superficial interactions, creating a sense of genuine camaraderie among her fans, further strengthening their dedication and willingness to support her future endeavors.

The financial management aspect of Palmer's independent career is equally fascinating. By bypassing the traditional label structure, she retains a larger share of the profits from her work, giving her greater financial control and freedom. She carefully balances her expenses, employing innovative strategies to maximize her income. Furthermore, she is exceptionally transparent about her finances, regularly sharing insights into her income and expenses with her fans, fostering an environment of trust and accountability. This radical transparency, uncommon in the music industry, builds further trust with her fanbase and reinforces her authenticity. It also serves as an educational resource for aspiring independent artists, highlighting the potential for financial sustainability outside of traditional label systems. It encourages a deeper understanding of the realities of selfmanagement within the music industry.

However, Palmer's journey isn't without its challenges. Maintaining a consistent level of creative output and promotional activity requires immense dedication and resilience. The constant need to manage various aspects of her career, from marketing and distribution to finance and legal matters, demands a high level of organizational skills and multitasking capabilities. The lack of a traditional label support structure also means she has to bear the full brunt of any setbacks or unforeseen circumstances. This requires adaptability and the ability to swiftly adjust strategies when needed. This dynamic showcases the considerable responsibility and effort required to sustain an independent music career, effectively functioning as a one-person operation handling multiple facets of the business. The risks are significantly higher compared to an artist under the umbrella of a major label, but the rewards – both artistic and financial – can also be significantly greater.

Further complicating her journey was the need to navigate the complexities of digital distribution and marketing in a rapidly evolving digital landscape. This required her to adapt swiftly to emerging platforms, algorithms, and technological changes. The music industry has experienced rapid changes with the advent of streaming services, necessitating a constant learning curve in navigating these services' nuances, from royalty calculations to promotion strategies within their ecosystems. Staying ahead of the curve, therefore, became a crucial factor in maintaining her visibility and revenue streams, constantly demanding innovation in reaching and retaining her audience. This flexibility and the ability to continually adapt to the evolving digital landscape are crucial for success in the independent music scene.

In conclusion, Amanda Palmer's case study offers a compelling illustration of the possibilities and challenges inherent in pursuing an independent music career. Her success is not simply a matter of talent, but a result of a carefully constructed strategy combining direct-to-fan engagement, strategic use of crowdfunding, transparent financial management, and a deep understanding of community building. Her journey underscores the importance of adaptability, resilience, and a willingness to embrace innovative approaches in navigating the complexities of the independent music scene. Her example serves as a valuable resource and inspiration for aspiring artists seeking to chart their own course in the music industry, offering a viable alternative to the often-onerous reliance on traditional labels and their mechanisms. Her transparency and willingness to share her experiences are invaluable assets to the evolving landscape of the independent music world. The ability to learn from her triumphs and challenges is particularly valuable for artists navigating the evolving dynamics of this sector.

Copyright Law and its Implications for Artists

The previous section explored the innovative strategies employed by independent artists to navigate the changing landscape of the music industry. However, even the most resourceful and creative independent artist faces a significant hurdle: understanding and navigating the complex legal framework surrounding music copyright. This section delves into the intricacies of copyright law and its profound implications for artists at all stages of their careers, from the bedroom songwriter to the established international performer.

Copyright law, at its core, grants creators exclusive rights to control the reproduction, distribution, and public performance of their original works. For musicians, this means owning the rights to their musical compositions (the melody, harmony, and lyrics) and their sound recordings (the actual audio recording of the performance). These two types of copyright are distinct and often involve different parties. The composer typically holds the copyright to the composition, while the recording artist and record label typically share the copyright to the sound recording.

Understanding the distinction is crucial. A songwriter might license their composition to a record label for recording and distribution, but they still retain the copyright to the underlying composition. This means they can license the same composition to other artists, use it in film or television, or even create variations of it themselves. The record label, on the other hand, holds the copyright to the specific sound recording they produced, preventing unauthorized duplication or distribution of that particular version of the song. This separation of rights can lead to intricate legal battles and negotiations, particularly when multiple parties are involved in the creation and distribution of a musical work.

For artists signed to major labels, navigating copyright can be a minefield. Standard recording contracts often grant labels extensive control over the artist's work, including the rights to reproduce, distribute, and license their recordings. These contracts are frequently heavily weighted in favor of the label, leaving artists with limited control over their own creative output and potential income streams. Many artists find themselves unknowingly relinquishing significant rights in exchange for an advance or production budget, only to discover the limitations later in their careers.

Exploitative clauses in these contracts are often hidden within dense legal jargon, making it challenging for artists

– especially those lacking legal representation – to fully comprehend their implications. This power imbalance is a significant contributing factor to the financial and creative struggles many artists face within the traditional label system. Independent artists, while avoiding the restrictive clauses of major label deals, still face the considerable challenge of understanding and protecting their copyright.

One significant aspect of copyright law that directly impacts artists is the concept of "fair use." Fair use is a legal doctrine that allows limited use of copyrighted material without permission for purposes such as criticism, commentary, news reporting, teaching, scholarship, or research. However, determining what constitutes "fair use" is highly contextspecific and often involves complex legal interpretations. Factors considered by courts include the purpose and character of the use, the nature of the copyrighted work, the amount and substantiality of the portion used, and the effect of the use upon the potential market for or value of the copyrighted work.

For musicians, fair use can be relevant in situations such as sampling, where a portion of a pre-existing recording is used in a new composition. Determining fair use in sampling requires careful consideration of all four factors mentioned above. A small, transformative use of a sample might be considered fair use, while a substantial use that directly competes with the original work is likely to be deemed infringement. This area of copyright law is frequently contested in court, resulting in many landmark cases that shape the legal landscape for musicians.

The digital revolution has further complicated copyright enforcement. The ease of copying and distributing music online has created a surge in copyright infringement. Piracy, through file-sharing networks and unauthorized online platforms, significantly impacts the revenues of artists and labels, leading to decreased investment in new music and hindering the careers of aspiring artists. Moreover, the rise of user-generated content platforms has led to questions about the copyright ownership of user-uploaded content, often leading to disputes between creators and platforms.

In addition to copyright infringement, artists must also be aware of licensing agreements. Licensing allows others to use their copyrighted work under specific terms and conditions. Mechanical licenses are required for the reproduction of musical compositions in physical formats or digital downloads. Synchronization licenses grant permission to use a musical composition in conjunction with visual media such as film, television, or advertising. Performance licenses are necessary for public performances of musical works, including live concerts and radio broadcasts. These licenses often involve complex negotiations and agreements, particularly when dealing with multiple parties and varying uses of the musical work.

Navigating the world of licensing can be incredibly challenging, particularly for independent artists who lack the resources of a large music publisher or label. Understanding the different types of licenses, the associated fees, and the implications of each agreement is essential for artists to protect their interests and secure fair compensation for the use of their work. Many artists have unknowingly entered into unfavorable licensing agreements, relinquishing substantial control over their work and earning far less than they could have.

The legal implications of copyright infringement can be severe. Copyright holders can pursue legal action against infringers, seeking injunctions to stop the infringement, damages for financial losses, and even criminal penalties in certain cases. High-profile cases involving major artists and record labels illustrate the significant financial costs and reputational damage associated with copyright infringement. These cases also highlight the often-disproportionate resources available to large corporations in legal battles, which can significantly impact the prospects of independent artists facing infringement accusations.

In conclusion, copyright law is a fundamental element of the music industry, impacting every aspect of an artist's career, from creative control to financial stability. Understanding the complexities of copyright, including the distinctions between composition and sound recording copyrights, the concept of fair use, the nuances of licensing agreements, and the implications of infringement, is crucial for artists at all levels. Seeking legal advice from an attorney specializing in entertainment law is essential to ensure artists adequately protect their rights and navigate the legal landscape effectively. Without this crucial understanding, even the most talented artists risk losing control of their work and facing significant financial consequences. This lack of legal awareness creates an inherent disadvantage for aspiring artists, highlighting the need for increased education and resources to empower musicians in protecting their intellectual property. The financial implications, particularly for those not backed by powerful legal teams and corporations, can be deeply detrimental to career prospects. Thus, navigating the complexities of copyright remains a critical element in achieving sustainable success within the music industry.

Contract Law and the Fine Print of Record Deals

The previous section highlighted the complexities of copyright law and its impact on musicians. However, the legal landscape extends far beyond copyright, deeply impacting artists through the often-onerous contracts they sign. This section delves into the treacherous terrain of contract law as it applies to the music industry, focusing specifically on the frequently exploitative clauses hidden within the fine print of record deals. Understanding these legal intricacies is crucial for artists, as a poorly negotiated contract can severely limit their creative freedom and financial potential for years, even decades, to come.

Record deals, at their core, are contracts outlining the agreement between an artist and a record label. These agreements dictate the terms under which the label will promote, distribute, and market the artist's music in exchange for a share of the profits (or, more often, a significant portion of the profits). However, the reality is often far removed from this seemingly straightforward exchange. Major labels, wielding considerable power and resources, often leverage this imbalance to include clauses that significantly benefit the label at the expense of the artist.

One of the most contentious clauses is the "grant of rights." This section of the contract outlines the specific rights the artist grants to the label, including the right to reproduce, distribute, and license the artist's recordings. In many cases, these grants are incredibly broad, encompassing almost every conceivable use of the artist's work. This includes the right to use the recordings in advertisements, film soundtracks, and video games, among many other possibilities. The label often retains control over these rights for an extended period, potentially for the life of the copyright or beyond, leaving artists with little control over how their music is used and generating substantial revenue for the label but often a negligible amount for the artist themselves.

Furthermore, record deals often contain "360 deals," a controversial contract structure where the label receives a percentage of the artist's income from *all* sources, not just record sales. This includes revenue from touring, merchandise, endorsements, and even songwriting royalties. While seemingly beneficial to the artist as it provides a larger advance upfront, it often proves financially crippling in the long run. The label's share of these diverse revenue streams often significantly outstrips the artist's cut, leading to a situation where the artist essentially works for the label without receiving fair compensation for their full range of activities and contributions. These deals effectively convert the artist from a collaborator into a quasi-employee, with the label wielding an exorbitant amount of financial and creative control.

Another common, and often exploitative, clause relates to "recoupment." Recoupment clauses allow the label to deduct its expenses – including studio time, marketing, distribution, and even administrative costs – from the artist's royalties before the artist receives any payment. The accounting practices employed by these labels are often opaque and complex, making it incredibly difficult for artists to understand how their royalties are calculated. This lack of transparency has been cited in numerous cases of artists never actually receiving any royalties despite significant sales, as the label's expenses consistently outweigh the revenue generated. This practice essentially allows the label to continue accruing profits indefinitely, while the artist remains perpetually "in debt" to the label. Even successful artists with high-selling records can find themselves entangled in lengthy and complex recoupment schedules, effectively trapped within the label's system of financial control. The calculation of costs is frequently contested, leading to protracted and expensive legal battles that few artists can afford to undertake.

"Option clauses" are another common feature of record deals. These clauses grant the label the option to renew the contract for additional albums or periods, even if the artist has not achieved commercial success. This gives the label leverage to continue to control the artist's output even if their performance has not met expectations, locking them into unfavorable terms and limiting their ability to explore new opportunities. This represents a significant risk for artists who do not experience commercial success, leading to a prolonged period of contractual obligations with potentially diminishing returns. The options periods often continue even after the artist's initial contract has ended, allowing the label to maintain creative control and potential financial gains for a prolonged period.

"Exclusivity clauses" restrict artists from working with other labels or releasing music independently during the term of the contract. This effectively limits the artist's options and prevents them from exploring alternative avenues for distribution and promotion. The enforcement of these clauses is absolute, significantly restricting the artist's potential growth and the ability to work with other producers or writers, potentially stifling creativity and development. Artists may find themselves contractually bound to a label that is not actively promoting their music, limiting exposure and hindering career advancement.

Beyond these core contract elements, many record deals contain an array of additional clauses that further benefit the label. These include clauses limiting the artist's creative control, mandating label approval of all aspects of their musical output; clauses regulating the artist's image and public appearance; and clauses granting the label ownership of the artist's master recordings—even those that generate little financial return for the label. These clauses often contain subtle wording and legal jargon that many artists find difficult to navigate without the assistance of experienced legal counsel. The asymmetry in legal expertise and resources between the label's legal team and the artist further exacerbates this problem. Often, artists find themselves signing contracts without fully understanding their implications, a situation frequently exploited by powerful record companies.

The importance of seeking independent legal advice before signing any record deal cannot be overstated. The complex nature of these contracts, combined with the inherent power imbalance between artists and major labels, necessitates the involvement of an attorney specializing in entertainment law. Such an attorney can not only review the contract for potentially exploitative clauses but can also advocate for the artist's interests and negotiate more favorable terms. This includes clarifying ambiguities in contract wording, ensuring that the artist receives fair compensation, and protecting their creative freedom. The cost of legal representation is a significant investment, but it is an investment that can ultimately safeguard an artist's future. This cost is often far outweighed by the potential losses incurred by signing a contract without proper legal representation.

In conclusion, the legal landscape of the music industry is a complex and often challenging environment for artists. While record deals can provide invaluable opportunities for exposure and success, they can also be instruments of exploitation if not carefully scrutinized. Understanding the intricacies of contract law, specifically the common exploitative clauses embedded within record deals, is essential for artists to protect their creative freedom and financial interests. The critical role of independent legal advice in ensuring fairness and transparency in the negotiation process is vital for any artist seeking to navigate this challenging legal landscape successfully. The pursuit of a career in the music industry should not necessitate financial ruin or creative compromise. Knowledge of the legal parameters governing this industry and proactive legal representation offers a vital means to achieve sustained success and protect the artist's long-term future. Without this awareness, the dream of musical success can quickly become a financial nightmare.

Intellectual Property Rights and their Protection

The previous section detailed the often-onerous and exploitative contracts prevalent in the music industry. However, even before the negotiation of a record deal, an artist's most valuable asset—their music—needs robust protection. This hinges on understanding and effectively utilizing intellectual property (IP) rights, a critical yet often overlooked aspect of a musician's career. This section delves into the intricacies of intellectual property rights as they apply to music, exploring the different forms of protection available and the strategies artists can employ to safeguard their creative work from infringement.

The cornerstone of music IP protection is copyright. Copyright automatically protects original musical works, including the composition (melody, harmony, rhythm) and lyrics. This protection extends to the underlying musical work itself, irrespective of its fixation in any tangible medium. Registration of a copyright, while not mandatory in many jurisdictions, offers several significant advantages. Registration establishes a public record of ownership, providing stronger legal standing in case of infringement. It also allows the copyright holder to pursue statutory damages, often significantly higher than actual damages, in case of infringement. Further, registration creates a presumption of validity of the copyright claim, simplifying legal proceedings.

The process of copyright registration varies depending on the jurisdiction. In the United States, for example, registration is done through the U.S. Copyright Office, involving submission of an application form along with a copy of the work. The registration process can be straightforward for individual songs but becomes more complex for larger bodies of work like albums or compilations. It's crucial to understand the specific requirements and procedures within the relevant jurisdiction to ensure proper and timely registration.

Beyond the composition, the sound recording itself also enjoys copyright protection. This protects the specific arrangement, performance, and overall sonic presentation of the music. The rights related to the sound recording are distinct from the copyright to the underlying musical work. This means that someone could legally obtain the rights to a particular musical composition and create their own sound recording, but they cannot replicate an existing sound recording without the copyright owner's permission. This distinction is particularly important in situations involving cover songs or remixes.

The protection offered by copyright is not unlimited. It does not extend to ideas or concepts. Only the tangible expression of those ideas is protected. This means that while two songs might have similar thematic elements, only if there is substantial similarity in the expression of those elements (melody, harmony, rhythm, lyrics) will copyright infringement be found. This determination is often made on a case-by-case basis, with expert testimony often being required to assess the degree of similarity. Determining whether the similarity constitutes actual copying is a crucial step in proving copyright infringement.

Furthermore, copyright protection is subject to limitations known as "fair use" or "fair dealing" depending on the jurisdiction. These doctrines allow limited use of copyrighted works without permission for purposes such as criticism, commentary, news reporting, teaching, scholarship, or research. The determination of whether a particular use constitutes fair use depends on a four-factor test: the purpose and character of the use, the nature of the copyrighted work, the amount and substantiality of the portion used, and the effect of the use upon the potential market for or value of the copyrighted work. This legal test requires a careful balancing of various factors, making it a complex and sometimes uncertain area of law.

To further solidify their IP protection, musicians can utilize other legal mechanisms. A trademark, for instance, protects brand names, logos, and other distinctive identifiers associated with a musician or their work. Registering a trademark for an artist's stage name or album title can prevent others from using it in connection with similar goods or services, thus safeguarding brand identity and market recognition. The trademark's function is different from copyright. While copyright protects the musical work, trademark safeguards the name and branding.

Similarly, patents might apply in rare cases. If a musician develops a novel musical instrument or a unique recording technology, a patent could protect the invention from unauthorized use. However, patents are generally less relevant to the core musical works themselves. Patents are more focused on protecting technological inventions, not artistic expressions.

Beyond formal legal protection, practical steps can significantly enhance IP security. These include meticulous record-keeping, including dates of creation, revisions, and any other evidence of authorship. This documentation can prove crucial in the event of a copyright dispute. Clear contracts with collaborators and other involved parties also help to prevent future conflicts and establish clear ownership rights. Furthermore, utilizing digital rights management (DRM) technologies can provide some level of control over the distribution and use of digital music files, although the effectiveness of DRM is increasingly challenged by technological advancements.

The enforcement of IP rights is a multifaceted process. Direct negotiation with infringers, cease-and-desist letters, and legal action are all potential options, although they can vary significantly in cost and complexity. Copyright infringement lawsuits can be expensive and time-consuming, requiring substantial legal expertise and resources. The potential for recouping legal costs and damages from successful litigation needs to be weighed against the expenditure involved.

Given the complexities of IP law and the diverse range of protections available, seeking professional legal counsel is paramount for any musician serious about protecting their creative work. A lawyer specializing in entertainment and intellectual property law can advise on the most appropriate strategies for protecting different aspects of a musical creation, guide through the registration processes, and assist with enforcement if necessary. The investment in legal advice represents a crucial element in securing the long-term financial and artistic success of a music career. It's an investment that safeguards not only the immediate artistic output but also the artist's future endeavors. Failure to properly protect intellectual property can lead to significant financial loss, reputational damage, and creative frustration, making competent legal counsel an indispensable asset in the demanding landscape of the music industry. Without this vital protection, the artist's hard work and creativity are vulnerable to exploitation and infringement.

Legal Recourse for Exploited Artists

The previous section emphasized the crucial role of intellectual property protection in safeguarding a musician's creative work. However, even with robust IP protection in place, artists remain vulnerable to exploitation and unfair practices within the music industry. This section examines the legal recourse available to artists who have been subjected to exploitative contracts, breach of contract, fraud, or other forms of misconduct by record labels, managers, agents, or other industry professionals. Navigating the legal landscape requires understanding the various avenues for justice and the potential challenges involved.

One of the most common areas of conflict arises from the interpretation and enforcement of recording contracts. These contracts, often complex and heavily weighted in favor of the label, can contain clauses that limit an artist's creative control, restrict their touring opportunities, or dictate unfavorable royalty structures. If a label breaches the terms of a contract – for example, failing to promote an artist's work adequately or withholding agreed-upon royalties – the artist can pursue legal action. This might involve filing a lawsuit for breach of contract, seeking specific performance (requiring the label to fulfill its contractual obligations), or demanding monetary damages to compensate for the losses incurred. The success of such a lawsuit depends on the specific terms of the contract, the evidence presented, and the jurisdiction in which the case is filed. Gathering evidence of contract breaches can be challenging, often requiring detailed financial records, emails, contracts, and witness testimony.

Beyond breach of contract, artists may find themselves victims of fraud or misrepresentation. This could involve false promises made during contract negotiations, such as inflated promises of promotion or guaranteed sales figures. If an artist can prove that they entered into a contract based on fraudulent misrepresentations, they can seek to have the contract rescinded (declared void) or claim damages for the losses suffered as a result of the deception. Proving fraud requires demonstrating that the misrepresentation was intentional and that the artist relied on the false statements when entering the contract. This can be a difficult legal burden to meet, requiring compelling evidence of the fraudulent intent.

Another area of potential legal recourse involves claims of unfair business practices. This broad category encompasses a range of actions that violate various state and federal laws designed to protect consumers and businesses from deceptive or unfair conduct. Examples include claims of predatory lending practices by financiers who provide loans to artists at exorbitant interest rates, or allegations of anticompetitive behavior by large record labels that stifle competition and limit the opportunities available to independent artists. Unfair business practices claims are often complex and require a thorough understanding of relevant antitrust laws and regulations, as well as the specific details of the industry's power dynamics. These cases can involve protracted litigation and the need for expert testimony from economists and industry professionals.

In cases involving sexual harassment or assault by industry figures, artists have legal avenues available to seek justice through civil lawsuits. These cases often involve complex legal issues relating to liability, evidence, and the establishment of a pattern of abusive behavior. The emotional toll on victims can be significant, making these lawsuits particularly challenging. Support networks and legal assistance organizations specialize in providing support and legal representation for victims of sexual harassment and assault within the entertainment industry.

Additionally, artists can explore alternative dispute resolution mechanisms, such as mediation or arbitration, as a means to resolve disputes outside of formal court proceedings. Mediation involves a neutral third party facilitating communication and negotiation between the parties to reach a mutually agreeable settlement. Arbitration, on the other hand, involves a neutral arbitrator who hears evidence and makes a binding decision. These alternative methods can be faster, less expensive, and more confidential than traditional litigation, but they may not be suitable for all types of disputes. The choice between mediation, arbitration, or court proceedings should be carefully considered, taking into account the nature of the dispute, the strength of the evidence, and the parties' willingness to compromise.

The legal landscape for exploited artists is complex and nuanced, varying significantly depending on the specific circumstances of each case, the jurisdiction involved, and the applicable laws. Successful legal action often requires meticulous documentation, compelling evidence, and the expertise of lawyers specialized in entertainment and intellectual property law. The costs associated with litigation can be substantial, necessitating careful assessment of the potential benefits against the financial burden. Many artists find it challenging to navigate the legal system independently and may need to seek assistance from legal aid organizations or pro bono attorneys who specialize in helping artists with similar cases.

Furthermore, it's essential to understand the statute of limitations, which dictates the timeframe within which legal action must be initiated. This timeframe varies depending on the type of claim and the jurisdiction, and missing the deadline can permanently bar an artist from pursuing legal recourse. Therefore, seeking legal advice as early as possible after a potential exploitation or wrong is critical to preserve legal options and protect one's rights. Prompt action is crucial to gather evidence, secure witness testimonies, and understand the legal options available within the applicable statute of limitations.

The emotional and psychological toll of facing exploitation and pursuing legal action should not be underestimated. The legal process can be lengthy, stressful, and emotionally draining. Seeking support from mental health professionals, support groups, or trusted friends and family is paramount during this challenging period. Many organizations offer specialized support for artists facing these issues, providing emotional support, legal guidance, and resources to navigate the complexities of the legal system.

Finally, preventative measures are crucial in mitigating the risk of exploitation. This involves carefully reviewing and understanding contracts before signing them, seeking independent legal advice from experienced entertainment lawyers, and maintaining meticulous records of all communications, transactions, and agreements. Proactive steps to protect one's intellectual property rights, as outlined in the previous section, also play a significant role in preventing exploitation. Transparency and clear communication with all parties involved in business dealings are paramount in establishing a strong foundation for a healthy and equitable working relationship. By understanding the legal framework and taking proactive steps to protect their rights, artists can improve their chances of navigating the industry successfully and avoiding exploitation. The pursuit of justice in the music industry requires perseverance, careful planning, and access to adequate legal resources, creating a path towards a more equitable and just environment for all creative individuals.

The Role of Lawyers and Legal Representation

The previous sections highlighted the precarious position of artists within the music industry's often exploitative landscape. While understanding intellectual property rights and identifying potential breaches of contract are crucial first steps, effectively navigating the legal complexities requires skilled legal representation. The role of lawyers and legal counsel is paramount in protecting artists' rights and interests, ensuring fair treatment, and achieving just outcomes. Choosing the right legal team is, therefore, a critical decision that can significantly impact an artist's career trajectory and financial well-being.

Finding competent legal counsel specializing in entertainment law is paramount. These lawyers possess a deep understanding of the unique legal issues facing musicians, including copyright infringement, contract negotiation, royalty disputes, and intellectual property rights management. They possess the expertise to interpret complex contracts, identify potential pitfalls, and negotiate favorable terms for their clients. A lawyer with a proven track record in entertainment law possesses an invaluable network of industry contacts, which can prove crucial in resolving disputes and achieving successful outcomes. They can help artists not only in navigating litigation but also in preventative measures, such as drafting and reviewing contracts to ensure fair and equitable terms are established.

The selection process should be thorough and meticulous. Artists should carefully research potential lawyers, examining their experience, specializations, and client testimonials. Initial consultations should be used to assess the lawyer's understanding of the artist's specific circumstances and their ability to provide clear, concise, and actionable legal advice. Cost is another important consideration; legal representation can be expensive, particularly for lengthy litigation. Many artists may need to explore options such as pro bono services or legal aid organizations to access affordable legal representation. While cost is a factor, it shouldn't overshadow the importance of finding a lawyer with a proven track record and expertise in entertainment law.

The attorney-client relationship is built on trust and open communication. It's crucial for artists to maintain consistent contact with their legal team, providing them with all relevant documentation, including contracts, emails, financial records, and any other information pertinent to their case. Open communication fosters a collaborative approach, where the lawyer can offer effective counsel and strategize the best approach for achieving a favorable resolution. This collaborative approach extends beyond simply resolving legal disputes; a strong lawyer will advise artists on how to avoid disputes altogether by proactively addressing potential conflicts. This includes providing guidance on contract negotiation, intellectual property protection, and best practices for managing their music careers to reduce the potential for legal conflict.

One notable example of the importance of legal representation is the case of [Insert real-life example of an artist successfully navigating a legal battle with a record label or manager due to competent legal representation]. This case demonstrates how skilled legal representation can protect an artist's rights and ensure fair compensation for their work. The lawyer's meticulous preparation, negotiation skills, and assertive courtroom presence were instrumental in securing a favorable outcome for the artist. Conversely, there are countless examples of artists who suffered significant financial and career setbacks due to inadequate legal counsel or a lack thereof. [Insert real-life example of an artist who faced exploitation due to a lack of adequate legal representation].

Beyond contract disputes, lawyers play a crucial role in other areas impacting artists' careers. They advise on trademark and copyright registration, ensuring that an artist's intellectual property is adequately protected and preventing unauthorized use. This is especially critical in today's digital landscape, where music is easily copied and distributed online. The lawyer will not only help register the appropriate trademarks and copyrights but also guide the artist on how to actively enforce these rights, addressing copyright infringement and combating piracy. This proactive approach minimizes risks and protects the financial and creative integrity of the artist's work.

In addition to intellectual property rights, entertainment lawyers can assist with negotiating merchandising deals, endorsement contracts, and other commercial opportunities. These deals can be lucrative, but they often contain complex legal clauses that require careful scrutiny. A skilled lawyer ensures that an artist receives a fair share of the profits and that their rights are protected. They work to ensure that the terms are equitable, and prevent the artist from being exploited or taken advantage of. This involves not just reviewing existing contracts, but also assisting in developing strong contractual frameworks that safeguard an artist's interests in future ventures.

Furthermore, legal representation is invaluable in managing disputes with other parties, such as producers, publishers, distributors, or streaming services. These disputes can arise over payment issues, credit attribution, or breaches of contract. A lawyer can negotiate settlements, mediate disputes, or represent an artist in court to resolve these issues fairly and efficiently. The experience and expertise of an entertainment lawyer can prove invaluable in navigating these complex relationships and ensuring a favorable outcome for the artist. Their deep industry knowledge and existing network of contacts within the industry allows for efficient dispute resolution and the avoidance of costly litigation.

Beyond the purely legal aspects, a strong legal team can offer valuable business advice. They can help artists structure their businesses effectively, manage their finances responsibly, and navigate the complexities of the industry's financial landscape. They understand the various tax implications and financial aspects of running a successful music career, providing guidance that helps the artists maintain their financial stability. This holistic approach ensures that an artist's business operations are as sound as their creative endeavors.

However, even with the best legal representation, there are inherent challenges and limitations. Legal battles can be costly, lengthy, and emotionally draining. The outcome of a case is never guaranteed, and the legal process itself can be unpredictable and frustrating. This underlines the importance of preventative measures such as thorough contract review and meticulous documentation. While legal recourse is a powerful tool, artists should aim to avoid disputes through clear communication, robust contracts, and ethical business practices.

In conclusion, while the music industry's legal landscape is complex and frequently unforgiving, competent legal representation serves as a crucial lifeline for artists navigating its treacherous waters. It's more than simply resolving disputes; it's about proactively protecting an artist's creative work, securing fair compensation, navigating business deals effectively, and creating a sustainable and equitable career path. The choice of legal counsel is a critical decision, one that significantly impacts an artist's long-term success, well-being, and creative freedom. Careful consideration, thorough research, and open communication are essential for finding the right legal partner to navigate this challenging yet rewarding industry. The investment in skilled legal representation is not just a cost, but a strategic move toward a more secure and fulfilling artistic career.

The Influence of Globalisation on the Music Industry

The previous discussion highlighted the crucial role of legal representation in safeguarding artists' rights within the oftenexploitative music industry. However, the legal battles and contractual complexities artists face are increasingly shaped by a larger, globalized context. The rise of multinational corporations, the seamless flow of digital music across borders, and the homogenization of musical tastes have dramatically altered the landscape for musicians worldwide, creating both opportunities and unprecedented challenges. Globalization's influence on the music industry is a doubleedged sword, offering unprecedented reach but also intensifying pre-existing inequalities.

One of the most significant impacts of globalization is the consolidation of power within the hands of a few multinational corporations. These mega-companies, through mergers and acquisitions, control a vast network of record labels, distribution channels, and streaming platforms. This concentration of power creates a hierarchical structure where independent artists and smaller labels struggle to compete with the resources and marketing power of these global giants. The dominance of these behemoths enables them to dictate terms to artists, often leading to exploitative contracts and unfair royalty structures. Their global reach allows them to exploit differences in labor laws and intellectual property rights across various jurisdictions, leading to a scenario where artists in some regions are significantly less protected than their counterparts in others. This imbalance is further compounded by the fact that these multinational corporations are often headquartered in countries with stronger legal frameworks and greater bargaining power, further skewing the scales against independent artists and smaller labels in developing countries.

The internationalization of music markets presents both opportunities and pitfalls for artists. While globalization allows musicians to reach audiences worldwide, it also intensifies competition. The rise of digital platforms like Spotify and Apple Music has removed geographical barriers, creating a global marketplace where artists from all corners of the world compete for attention and streams. This increased competition can be advantageous for artists with strong international appeal, but for those with a niche or regional following, it can be overwhelming. The algorithms governing these platforms often favor established artists and popular genres, making it challenging for independent or less commercially viable artists to gain visibility. The result is a concentration of attention and revenue on a small percentage of artists, often those affiliated with major labels that possess the resources for extensive marketing and promotion.

The cultural implications of globalization in the music industry are complex and multifaceted. On one hand, the free flow of music across borders has facilitated cultural exchange, leading to exciting collaborations and the fusion of musical styles. Artists from different cultural backgrounds are able to share their music with global audiences, enriching the cultural landscape and promoting cross-cultural understanding. However, this increased exchange also raises concerns about cultural appropriation and the homogenization of musical styles. The dominant musical trends often originate from specific regions – notably, the Western world – leading to the marginalization of nonWestern musical traditions. Artists from non-Western countries often find themselves pressured to adapt their music to meet the tastes of Western audiences, compromising their artistic integrity and cultural identity in the process. The very act of translation into a global market can lead to simplification or misrepresentation, resulting in a loss of nuance and authenticity.

Furthermore, the globalized music industry often overlooks or undervalues the contribution of artists from marginalized communities. Access to resources, technological infrastructure, and effective distribution channels remains a significant barrier for artists from developing countries and underserved communities. The lack of equitable access to these resources contributes to a scenario where their music is less likely to be discovered and promoted on global platforms. This systemic inequality perpetuates the dominance of established artists and genres, further marginalizing less mainstream musical traditions. The lack of representation in decision-making positions within the major record labels and streaming platforms exacerbates this problem, perpetuating a cycle of cultural bias.

The rise of digital music distribution has dramatically lowered the barriers to entry for independent artists.

Theoretically, anyone with a computer and internet access can record and distribute their music globally. However, this accessibility masks the persistent challenges faced by independent artists in a globalized market. The sheer volume of music available online makes it extremely difficult for independent artists to stand out and reach wider audiences. The lack of resources for effective marketing, promotion, and networking places them at a significant disadvantage. The algorithms of streaming platforms can also be opaque and unpredictable, favouring artists who have already established significant followings or who have secured deals with major labels.

The legal frameworks governing the global music industry are often fragmented and inconsistent. Copyright laws, royalty structures, and contract regulations vary across different jurisdictions, creating challenges for artists navigating international markets. The digital nature of music distribution further complicates matters, making it difficult to enforce intellectual property rights and monitor the use of copyrighted material online. The lack of a harmonized international legal framework for the music industry leaves artists vulnerable to exploitation and copyright infringement. The burden of understanding and navigating these complex legal landscapes frequently falls on the artists themselves, adding another layer of difficulty to an already challenging profession.

Another critical aspect of globalization's impact on the music industry is the rise of music piracy. The ease with which music can be copied and shared online has made piracy a significant problem, significantly impacting the revenue streams of artists and record labels. While technological advancements have been made to combat piracy, the "cat and mouse" game between content creators and pirates continues. Globalized communication technologies have also facilitated the growth of illicit download and streaming sites, which make it challenging to enforce copyright laws effectively on an international scale. This problem disproportionately impacts independent artists and smaller labels, which lack the resources to engage in expensive legal battles to protect their intellectual property.

In conclusion, the influence of globalization on the music industry is a multifaceted issue with both positive and negative consequences. While it offers opportunities for artists to reach global audiences, it also leads to increased competition, cultural homogenization, and the consolidation of power within the hands of a few multinational corporations. The resulting imbalances in the industry often marginalize independent artists, particularly those from developing countries or underserved communities. Addressing these inequalities requires a multi-pronged approach that includes stronger international legal frameworks, increased support for independent artists and labels, greater transparency in streaming algorithms, and a concerted effort to combat music piracy. The future of the music industry depends on striking a balance between the benefits of globalization and the need to ensure that all artists, regardless of their geographical location or cultural background, have a fair and equitable opportunity to succeed. The ongoing challenges demand creative solutions, collaborative efforts, and a critical examination of the power dynamics at play. Only then can we hope to build a truly global music industry that celebrates diversity, supports artists, and fairly distributes the fruits of their creative labor.

The Role of Government Regulation and Policy

The preceding discussion illuminated the profound impact of globalization on the music industry, highlighting the challenges faced by artists navigating a landscape dominated by multinational corporations and the complexities of digital distribution. However, the playing field is not solely defined by market forces. Government regulation and policy play a crucial, often overlooked, role in shaping the industry's structure, power dynamics, and ultimately, the livelihoods of musicians. This influence manifests in various ways, from copyright laws governing intellectual property to antitrust regulations aimed at preventing monopolies and promoting competition, and further extends to policies specifically addressing streaming services and digital music distribution.

Copyright law forms the bedrock of the music industry, protecting the creative works of musicians and ensuring they receive compensation for their efforts. However, the application and enforcement of copyright laws are far from uniform across the globe. Variations in legislation across different countries create a complex and often fragmented legal landscape, making it challenging for artists to protect their intellectual property rights internationally. The digital nature of music distribution further complicates matters, as copyrighted material can be easily copied and shared online, leading to widespread piracy. While many nations have established copyright laws, the effectiveness of their enforcement varies widely. Some countries have robust mechanisms for tracking and penalizing copyright infringement, while others lack the resources or political will to effectively combat piracy. This disparity creates an uneven playing field, with artists in some countries enjoying stronger legal protection than those in others. The struggle to enforce copyright laws in the digital age is a persistent challenge. Technological advancements have made it easier for individuals to circumvent copyright protections, forcing legislators and copyright holders to continually adapt their strategies. The rise of peer-to-peer file-sharing networks in the early 2000s presented a significant challenge, prompting record labels to engage in costly and often unsuccessful legal battles against users. The emergence of streaming platforms has created a new set of challenges, with ongoing debates regarding fair compensation for artists in relation to the revenue generated by these services. The question of how to fairly compensate artists for their work in the digital realm continues to be a focal point of legal and policy discussions.

Antitrust regulations are designed to prevent monopolies and foster competition within industries. In the music industry, the consolidation of power within the hands of a few major multinational corporations raises concerns about potential anti-competitive practices. These corporations often control various aspects of the music ecosystem, from record labels and distribution channels to streaming platforms. Their dominance can lead to situations where independent artists and smaller labels struggle to compete effectively, resulting in limited opportunities for emerging talent and a less diverse range of musical styles.

Government regulators are tasked with monitoring the industry for potential antitrust violations, ensuring that the market remains competitive and prevents the emergence of monopolies that stifle innovation and creativity. However, determining what constitutes an anti-competitive practice in the dynamic and ever-evolving music industry can be complex. The line between legitimate business practices and anti-competitive behavior is not always clear-cut, requiring regulators to carefully balance the need to promote competition with the realities of a globalized market. The enforcement of antitrust regulations in the music industry has historically been a challenge, with accusations of anti-competitive behavior frequently raised but rarely leading to significant penalties. This reflects the complexity of proving anti-competitive intent and the difficulty in navigating the intricacies of global antitrust laws. The influence of lobbying by major corporations also plays a role, often hindering the effectiveness of regulatory oversight.

Government policies related to streaming services and digital music distribution have profoundly shaped the industry in recent years. The rise of streaming platforms has revolutionized how music is consumed and distributed, but it has also created new challenges for artists and the industry as a whole. Governments have played a role in shaping the regulatory frameworks governing these platforms, addressing issues such as royalty payments, licensing agreements, and data privacy. The debate surrounding fair compensation for artists on streaming platforms has been a central focus, with artists arguing that they receive insufficient payments relative to the revenue generated by these services. Government intervention has been proposed to address this issue, including regulations that mandate minimum royalty payments or establish transparent and equitable royalty distribution models. However, the implementation of such regulations is complicated by the global nature of streaming platforms, which operate across numerous jurisdictions with varying legal frameworks. Reaching an international consensus on these issues has proven difficult, hindering efforts to create a uniform global standard for artist compensation. Another key area of government policy is the regulation of data privacy related to streaming services. These platforms collect vast amounts of data on user listening habits, which can be used for targeted advertising and other commercial purposes. Governments are increasingly focusing on regulating data privacy in the digital music industry, ensuring that user data is protected

and used responsibly. This involves establishing clear guidelines for data collection, storage, and use, as well as implementing mechanisms for users to access and control their data.

Beyond copyright, antitrust, and streaming regulations, government policies related to arts funding and cultural promotion significantly influence the music industry. Many governments provide funding for arts organizations, music education programs, and initiatives aimed at supporting emerging artists and fostering artistic development. These initiatives play a vital role in nurturing talent and promoting cultural diversity. Government support for music education, for example, ensures a pipeline of future musicians and contributes to the overall health of the music industry. Arts councils and other government bodies often provide grants, residencies, and other forms of assistance to artists, helping them overcome financial barriers and focus on their creative work. This support is particularly important for independent artists and those from marginalized communities, who often face significant challenges in accessing resources and opportunities. However, government funding for the arts is not always plentiful and faces competition for scarce resources. Decisions about how and where to allocate funding can have a significant impact on the range of musical styles and artists supported. The allocation of funding is often subject to political influences and may not always reflect the needs and priorities of the music community as a whole. Moreover, the effectiveness of government programs in supporting artists and promoting cultural diversity often depends on their design, implementation, and ongoing evaluation.

In conclusion, the role of government regulation and policy in shaping the music industry is multifaceted and farreaching. From copyright laws to antitrust regulations, streaming policies, and arts funding, government intervention significantly influences the industry's structure, competitiveness, and the opportunities available to artists. Balancing the need to protect artists' rights, promote competition, and foster a vibrant cultural landscape presents ongoing challenges for policymakers. Effective governance requires a nuanced understanding of the industry's complexities, a commitment to transparency and accountability, and a willingness to adapt to the everevolving technological and economic landscape. The future health of the music industry depends significantly on the wisdom and foresight of governments in creating a regulatory environment that is fair, equitable, and supportive of artistic expression. Navigating the intricate relationship between government and the music industry requires continuous dialogue, collaboration, and a commitment to ensuring that the industry's potential for creativity and economic growth is fully realized while protecting the rights and livelihoods of the artists at its core.

Economic Inequality and the Distribution of Wealth in the Industry

The preceding chapters have explored the regulatory and legal landscape of the music industry, revealing a complex interplay of copyright laws, antitrust regulations, and government policies impacting artists and corporations alike. However, the narrative is incomplete without a thorough examination of the stark economic realities shaping the industry. This section delves into the profound economic inequality that permeates the music business, analyzing the disproportionate distribution of wealth amongst its various stakeholders – the multinational conglomerates, the artists themselves, and the supporting cast of producers, songwriters, and session musicians.

The most glaring disparity lies in the chasm between the immense profits generated by major record labels and streaming platforms and the meager returns received by the artists who create the music. While industry giants rake in billions annually, a vast majority of musicians struggle to earn a living wage from their art. This isn't merely a matter of a few unlucky individuals; it's a systemic issue rooted in exploitative contracts, opaque royalty structures, and a power imbalance that consistently favors the corporations. Consider the common practice of "360 deals," which grant record labels a share not only of album sales and streaming royalties but also of merchandise, touring revenue, and even endorsements. Such contracts, often presented to aspiring artists as the only pathway to success, effectively bind musicians to their label for years, with minimal control over their financial destiny. The artist bears the risk, while the label reaps the rewards, regardless of the success or failure of the music. These deals frequently lead to situations where artists invest substantial amounts of their own money into recording and promoting their work, only to see a minimal return – if any at all – from the sales and streams, leaving them deeply in debt and financially crippled.

The opacity of royalty payments further compounds this problem. Many artists lack transparency in how their royalties are calculated and distributed, leaving them vulnerable to manipulation and exploitation. The complex accounting practices employed by labels and streaming platforms often obscure the true revenue generated by an artist's work, leaving musicians reliant on the good faith (often misplaced) of their representatives. Furthermore, the payment mechanisms of streaming services often favor quantity over quality, with per-stream royalties being minuscule, even for immensely popular tracks. This system compels artists to produce vast quantities of content, often sacrificing artistic integrity and creative experimentation to maintain a stream of income, creating a relentless cycle of production rather than thoughtful artistry.

The digital revolution, while transforming music consumption and distribution, has further exacerbated these inequalities. The ease with which music can be copied and shared online has led to widespread piracy, which significantly impacts artists' incomes. While streaming services have become dominant, the royalty rates paid to artists per stream are frequently criticized as insufficient and unfair. The massive user base of streaming platforms allows them to generate enormous profits, while artists receive a fraction of these earnings, largely due to complex licensing agreements and often skewed royalty splits. It is argued that while streaming has facilitated global music access, it has simultaneously created a system where the vast majority of revenue is concentrated in the hands of a few major players. The impact of this distribution model on independent artists is profound; with minuscule per-stream royalties, independent artists are almost entirely reliant on touring and other revenue streams to support their musical careers. This leaves them significantly vulnerable to market fluctuations and often forces them to perform multiple gigs per week or undertake extraneous work, significantly limiting their creative time and potentially impacting their overall wellbeing.

The concentration of power within the music industry is another significant factor contributing to economic inequality. A few multinational corporations control the majority of the market share, dominating almost every aspect of the music value chain, from record production and distribution to streaming platforms and music publishing. This monopolistic tendency limits competition, reduces opportunities for independent artists and labels, and empowers these companies to dictate terms that are consistently disadvantageous to those with less bargaining power. This concentration of power enables these corporations to negotiate highly favorable contracts, securing the lion's share of profits while minimizing their contribution to the artistic process. This situation leaves artists struggling not only for fair compensation but also for the space and opportunity to promote and distribute their music effectively.

This dominance further manifests in the realm of artist development and support. Emerging artists often rely on the support of established labels for funding, promotion, and distribution. However, the access to these vital resources is often unevenly distributed, with independent artists and those from marginalized communities facing considerable barriers. The emphasis on commercially driven decisions often overshadows artistic merit, leading to a skewed representation of musical styles and potentially stifling innovation and creative diversity.

Moreover, the economic inequalities within the music industry extend beyond the artists themselves, impacting a wide range of other stakeholders. Producers, songwriters, and session musicians frequently receive minimal compensation for their contributions, often facing unpredictable income streams and a constant struggle for financial stability. These professionals, crucial to the creative process, are often overlooked in the discussions surrounding industry revenues and profits, highlighting the broader reach of the economic disparities prevalent in the music business. Often, these essential contributors are forced to accept low payment rates or work on a project-to-project basis, lacking the stability and fair compensation they deserve for their expertise and talent. This highlights a deeper systemic issue – a devaluation of the human element within the music production process, where creativity is often sacrificed at the altar of profit maximization.

Addressing these economic inequalities requires a multipronged approach. Increased transparency in royalty payments is crucial, ensuring that artists receive accurate and timely information about the revenue generated by their work. Strengthening the legal protections afforded to artists, particularly in the context of exploitative contracts, is essential. Government regulation plays a pivotal role in leveling the playing field, ensuring fair competition and preventing monopolies. Furthermore, promoting and supporting independent artists and labels is essential to foster a more diverse and equitable music ecosystem. Finally, raising public awareness about the economic injustices prevalent within the music industry is critical to mobilizing change and supporting artists' efforts to secure fair compensation and recognition for their artistry. The future of music depends on a radical re-evaluation of the industry's economic model, one that prioritizes the well-being and financial security of artists and all stakeholders, rather than solely focusing on the profit maximization of a few powerful corporations. The current system is not sustainable and its inherent inequalities threaten to stifle innovation, reduce creative output, and ultimately diminish the richness and diversity of musical expression for future generations.

The Impact of Technological Advancements on Economic Structures

The advent of digital technologies has fundamentally reshaped the economic landscape of the music industry, triggering a seismic shift from the tangible realm of physical sales to the intangible world of digital distribution. This transformation, while initially promising democratization and expanded access to music, has yielded a complex and often paradoxical outcome, significantly altering the economic structures and power dynamics within the industry. The transition from vinyl records and cassette tapes to CDs, and subsequently to digital downloads and streaming platforms, has dramatically altered the revenue streams for artists and record labels alike. The ease and affordability of digital reproduction, initially hailed as a boon for artists seeking wider audiences, inadvertently opened the door to widespread piracy, severely impacting sales and royalties. The once lucrative physical album sales, a primary source of income for both artists and labels, dwindled significantly as digital downloads and streaming gained traction.

This shift didn't simply entail a change in format; it fundamentally altered the relationship between artists, consumers, and the intermediaries controlling distribution. The emergence of peer-to-peer file-sharing networks like Napster in the late 1990s exemplified the disruptive potential of digital technology. While Napster's ultimate demise due to legal challenges highlighted the industry's capacity to protect its interests, it also underscored the inherent difficulty in controlling the flow of digital music in the face of technological innovation. The subsequent rise of legal digital music platforms, such as iTunes and later streaming services like Spotify and Apple Music, presented an ostensibly legitimate alternative, but these platforms introduced their own set of economic challenges.

The introduction of streaming services fundamentally altered the traditional business model of the record industry. Whereas physical album sales offered a relatively straightforward revenue structure, streaming presents a far more complex and opaque system. Royalties are calculated based on a per-stream model, generating minuscule payouts per individual listen. While the sheer volume of streams on major platforms can translate into substantial overall revenue for certain artists, the majority receive only a fraction of the profits generated by their work. This model places an immense burden on artists to generate massive streams to achieve financial viability, often resulting in a cycle of constant content creation, potentially at the expense of artistic integrity and creative experimentation. The pressure to produce prolifically can lead to a homogenization of musical styles as artists cater to algorithm-driven trends to maximize their chances of accumulating substantial streams. The focus shifts from artistic expression towards maximizing platform visibility, influencing production choices and potentially limiting creative exploration.

Furthermore, the concentration of power within the streaming sector mirrors that of the traditional record industry. A small number of global corporations control the vast majority of the streaming market, wielding significant influence over music distribution, artist discovery, and ultimately, the financial well-being of musicians. This consolidation of power reinforces the pre-existing power imbalance within the industry, empowering a select few at the expense of a much larger pool of artists vying for attention and financial compensation. These major streaming platforms often engage in aggressive negotiation tactics, dictating contract terms favorable to their business models.

This effectively leaves independent artists, who frequently lack the leverage to negotiate effectively, with limited bargaining power, further exacerbating the economic inequalities within the music industry.

The economic implications extend beyond the artists themselves. Producers, songwriters, and session musicians, integral to the music creation process, also experience the consequences of these changes. Their compensation, frequently already meager, is further diminished within the per-stream royalty model. The lack of transparency in royalty distributions creates an atmosphere of uncertainty and vulnerability for these crucial contributors, making financial stability a constant and often unattainable goal. The ease and efficiency of digital collaboration, while beneficial in certain aspects, also contributes to this issue. Producers and songwriters may find themselves working on numerous projects concurrently, with each project potentially generating a minuscule income, resulting in a precarious financial situation.

The introduction of digital technology has also had a profound impact on copyright and intellectual property rights. The ease with which music can be copied and distributed online has exacerbated the challenges surrounding piracy. While technological measures have been implemented to combat piracy, the cat-and-mouse game between copyright holders and those seeking to circumvent these measures continues unabated. The struggle to effectively address piracy adds another layer of complexity to the financial realities of the music industry, leaving artists and rights holders to grapple with lost revenue and a constantly evolving technological landscape. The legal battles and ongoing efforts to implement effective antipiracy measures consume significant resources, diverting funds from other aspects of the industry, including artist support and development.

In addition to piracy, the shift to digital distribution has led to an increased emphasis on data-driven decision-making within the industry. The availability of extensive data on listening habits, genre preferences, and consumer behavior allows streaming platforms and labels to make more informed decisions regarding artist promotion and marketing. However, this data-driven approach can lead to a certain level of homogenization and predictability in musical production, as labels and artists focus on producing music that aligns with established trends and maximizes algorithmic reach. This can stifle innovation and artistic experimentation, as artists might feel pressured to prioritize commercial viability over artistic integrity. This data-driven approach, while facilitating efficiency in certain aspects, can ultimately constrain creativity, ultimately leading to a less diverse and engaging musical landscape.

The technological advancements in music production have also fundamentally shifted the economic power dynamics within the industry. The relative ease and affordability of digital audio workstations (DAWs) and other music production tools have lowered the barrier to entry for aspiring musicians and producers, seemingly democratizing the creative process. However, this accessibility does not automatically translate into economic equity. While independent artists now possess the means to produce and distribute their music without relying on large record labels, they still face significant challenges in attracting audiences, building a fan base, and generating sufficient revenue to sustain their careers. The sheer volume of content created in this more democratized landscape exacerbates the challenges of gaining visibility and standing out from the crowd,

leading to increased competition for limited resources and opportunities.

Moreover, the emphasis on digital marketing and social media presence requires artists to dedicate significant time and resources to promoting their work online. This often entails managing social media accounts, engaging with fans, and navigating complex digital marketing strategies, skills not necessarily associated with the core artistic process. These additional tasks place further burden on artists, demanding expertise beyond musical talent, demanding a multitasking approach that can consume time and resources better spent on the creative process itself.

The impact of technological advancements on the economic structures of the music industry is multifaceted and farreaching. While digital technology has expanded access to music and democratized the creative process to some extent, it has also created new challenges and exacerbated preexisting inequalities. The shift to digital distribution, the emergence of streaming services, and the pervasiveness of piracy have fundamentally altered the revenue streams for artists and labels alike. The concentration of power within the digital music ecosystem, coupled with opaque royalty structures and the pressure to maximize streams, has led to an environment where financial stability remains elusive for many musicians. Addressing these economic inequalities requires a concerted effort from all stakeholders, including artists, labels, streaming platforms, and policymakers, to create a more equitable and sustainable model for the future of the music industry. A systemic review and reform are crucial to ensuring that the digital revolution benefits all involved in the creation and enjoyment of music, rather than only a select few.

Future Economic Trends and Their Potential Impact

The preceding analysis of the music industry's current economic woes sets the stage for considering its future. Extrapolating from present trends, several key economic forces will likely shape the industry's landscape in the coming years. One significant trend is the continued dominance of streaming services. While their market share is already substantial, further consolidation and the emergence of new, perhaps more aggressive, players cannot be ruled out. This consolidation could lead to even greater control over music distribution and pricing power, potentially further squeezing artists' already thin profit margins. The current per-stream model, notorious for its low payouts, is unlikely to change drastically unless artists and industry advocates successfully lobby for regulatory changes or leverage collective bargaining power. However, the potential for innovative compensation models, such as incorporating listener engagement metrics or offering tiered subscription models with varying royalty distribution percentages, exists.

Another crucial factor is the rise of artificial intelligence (AI) and its applications in music creation and distribution. AIpowered music generation tools are becoming increasingly sophisticated, raising concerns about copyright and authorship. While AI could potentially democratize music production by enabling individuals without formal training to create music, it also threatens to inundate the market with AI-generated content, further intensifying competition and potentially devaluing human creativity. The economic implications of widespread AI-generated music are complex and largely unexplored. It could lead to a two-tiered system, where high-quality, human-created music commands higher prices and achieves greater recognition, while AI-generated music occupies a lower market segment, mirroring the existing stratification within the industry. The legal and ethical implications regarding ownership, copyright, and royalty payments for AI-generated music need to be addressed urgently before it becomes a widespread phenomenon.

The metaverse and Web3 technologies also hold significant potential for reshaping the music industry's economic structures. Virtual concerts, NFT-based music sales, and immersive fan experiences offer new avenues for revenue generation for artists and labels. However, the current lack of widespread adoption and the technical complexities associated with these technologies could limit their immediate impact. The metaverse, in particular, poses a challenge for artists who lack the resources and technological expertise needed to create engaging virtual performances. Furthermore, the fluctuating value of cryptocurrencies and the prevalence of scams and fraudulent activities within the NFT space pose risks for artists hoping to leverage these technologies for financial gain. The success of metaverse and Web3 initiatives largely depends on the maturation of the technologies themselves, their wider adoption by consumers, and the implementation of robust regulatory frameworks to protect both artists and fans from exploitation.

Moreover, the ongoing evolution of digital rights management (DRM) and anti-piracy technologies will undoubtedly influence the future economic landscape. While DRM has been partially successful in limiting unauthorized copying, the constant battle between copyright holders and those seeking to circumvent these measures will likely continue. The development of more robust and adaptable

DRM technologies is crucial for protecting artists'

intellectual property and generating revenue from their work. However, it is also essential to strike a balance between protecting intellectual property and ensuring accessibility to music for consumers. Overly restrictive DRM measures could alienate fans and stifle the growth of the digital music market.

Beyond technological advancements, macroeconomic factors will undoubtedly impact the music industry. Economic downturns can significantly affect music consumption, impacting sales and streaming numbers, leading to decreased revenue for artists and labels. Furthermore, inflation and changing consumer spending habits will continue to influence the demand for music, potentially impacting pricing strategies and consumer behavior. Changes in advertising revenue and sponsorship models will also alter the economic relationships between artists, labels, and brands. The potential for consolidation within the advertising sector might lead to a decrease in available funds for artist sponsorship, intensifying the existing competition for a shrinking pool of resources.

The role of government regulation and policy will also play a significant role. Policymakers globally must grapple with the challenges of balancing copyright protection, consumer rights, and the needs of artists and labels in the digital era. Fairer royalty structures for streaming platforms, improved mechanisms for collecting and distributing royalties, and stronger anti-piracy measures are crucial for ensuring a sustainable economic model. Regulatory frameworks that support innovation while protecting artists' rights are essential to navigating the complex economic challenges of the digital music era. The effectiveness of such regulations, however, will depend on their ability to adapt to the everevolving technological landscape and maintain a delicate balance between protecting artists' rights and fostering a competitive and dynamic music industry.

The political climate itself can significantly impact the music industry's economic well-being. Changes in tax laws, trade agreements, and government subsidies can directly affect artists' income and the financial viability of labels. Political instability or economic sanctions in various regions can disrupt music distribution networks, impacting international sales and collaboration opportunities. Political polarization can also influence consumer behavior and demand, impacting music consumption trends and the overall economic health of the industry. For instance, political boycotts of certain artists or labels could have a significant impact on their revenue streams. Likewise, government support for arts and culture initiatives could provide vital funding for artists and music education programs, contributing to the overall health of the sector.

Looking ahead, the future of the music industry's economy depends on a complex interplay of technological innovation, economic forces, government regulation, and geopolitical events. The challenges are significant, but so are the opportunities. Innovative business models, fairer royalty structures, effective anti-piracy measures, and greater transparency within the industry are all essential elements for creating a sustainable and equitable future for musicians and the industry as a whole. The industry's ability to adapt to these rapid changes, while advocating for artists' rights and promoting creative expression, will ultimately determine its long-term economic viability. Ignoring these challenges risks widening the existing chasm between the industry's haves and have-nots, potentially stifling creativity and leading to a less vibrant and diverse musical landscape. The future of music depends on a collective effort – from artists and labels to streaming services and policymakers – to create a fairer and more sustainable ecosystem for all involved.

The Rise of Streaming Services and Their Impact on Artists Income

The ascendance of streaming services represents a seismic shift in the music industry, one that has profoundly reshaped the landscape of music consumption and, critically, the financial realities for artists. While offering unprecedented access to a global audience, these platforms have also introduced a complex and often exploitative system of compensation that leaves many musicians struggling to make ends meet. The "per-stream" royalty model, the cornerstone of most major streaming services, is at the heart of this problem. The minuscule amounts paid per play, often fractions of a cent, simply don't translate into a sustainable income for the vast majority of artists, particularly those outside the established mainstream.

This model's inherent flaw lies in its failure to accurately reflect the value of a musical work. Unlike physical sales or traditional licensing deals, which offered a more predictable revenue stream, streaming payouts are heavily dependent on unpredictable listener habits and algorithmic whims. A song might achieve millions of streams yet still generate a paltry sum for the artist, while a viral hit might momentarily boost earnings only to plummet as quickly as it rose, leaving creators with inconsistent and unreliable income. This inherent volatility makes financial planning nearly impossible and forces many musicians to supplement their creative work with unrelated jobs, significantly impacting their ability to dedicate the time and resources needed to hone their craft.

The issue is further compounded by the opaque nature of royalty calculations and distribution. Many artists remain largely unaware of the exact mechanics behind how their streams are tallied and how much they are actually earning. This lack of transparency often facilitates the underpayment or even complete non-payment of royalties, leaving musicians vulnerable to exploitation. The sheer volume of transactions handled by streaming platforms, coupled with complex licensing agreements and international copyright laws, adds to the inherent difficulty in tracking and verifying payments, creating a perfect storm for widespread underpayment.

Furthermore, the dominance of a few major streaming giants exacerbates the problem. The market is increasingly concentrated in the hands of a handful of powerful corporations, creating a situation akin to a monopoly, where these companies wield substantial control over pricing and distribution. This consolidated power allows them to dictate the terms of service, including the notoriously low perstream rates, while artists have little leverage to negotiate for more equitable compensation. The bargaining power lies overwhelmingly with the platforms, leaving musicians with little choice but to accept the offered terms or risk being shut out of a crucial distribution channel. This imbalance of power is a significant contributor to the precarious financial situation of many artists today.

The rise of playlist culture further complicates matters. While playlists can offer significant exposure to new listeners, their algorithmic nature and the influence of curators often mean that artists lack control over their placement and visibility. A coveted spot on a popular playlist can generate a surge in streams and revenue, but the lack of consistent algorithm-driven placement leaves the majority of artists playing a constant game of chance, relying on unpredictable algorithms rather than their artistic merit. Moreover, the "pay-to-play" schemes, where artists or their labels are pressured to pay for playlist placement or promotion, represent a blatant abuse of power and further erode the fairness and integrity of the system. While not explicitly illegal, this practice casts a long shadow over the already questionable ethics of the streaming economy.

The impact extends beyond the individual artist. The precarious financial climate created by the streaming model is harming the broader music ecosystem. Independent artists, lacking the financial resources and support systems of major label acts, are particularly vulnerable. Their limited bargaining power often compels them to accept unfair contracts or forgo potential income altogether just to secure online distribution. Similarly, music producers, session musicians, and other vital contributors to the music-making process also experience the trickle-down effect of low streaming royalties, their earnings diminished by the overarching inadequacies of the current system. This systemic underpayment not only undermines the livelihoods of countless individuals involved in music creation but also threatens to stifle creative innovation and diversity. Investing in and developing musical talent becomes a gamble when the returns on that investment are so uncertain and low.

In addition to the royalty structure itself, the terms and conditions imposed by streaming services often include unfavorable clauses that further disadvantage artists. These contracts, often complex and lengthy, often grant the platforms extensive rights over an artist's music, including usage rights for advertising and other commercial purposes, without commensurate compensation. The lack of legal protection for artists in these contractual arrangements often leaves them with little recourse when their work is exploited. Many artists, especially those early in their careers, lack the resources or legal expertise to navigate the complexities of these contracts, leading to them unknowingly agreeing to terms that are significantly detrimental to their long-term interests.

The consequences of this model are tangible and farreaching. Many musicians are forced to abandon their artistic aspirations due to the impossibly difficult financial circumstances created by the current streaming system. The relentless pressure to maintain a constant online presence and produce a steady stream of content to meet the demands of algorithmic visibility, all while earning minimal income, has led to a culture of creative burnout and mental health struggles within the industry. This creates a feedback loop where the relentless pursuit of exposure through multiple platforms and digital marketing campaigns further depletes an artist's resources, leaving little time for actually creating music.

The solution requires a multi-pronged approach. First and foremost, a significant increase in per-stream rates is essential. Artists deserve fair compensation for their work, and the current rates simply don't reflect the value they create. This requires concerted lobbying efforts and advocacy by artist unions and industry organizations to pressure streaming services to adopt more equitable royalty structures. Moreover, increased transparency in royalty calculations and distribution is paramount. Artists need to have clear and readily accessible information about how their earnings are determined and how their money is being managed.

Regulatory reform is also crucial. Governments need to step in to establish clear guidelines and regulations to protect artists' rights and ensure fair compensation in the digital music market. This includes scrutinizing the power wielded by major streaming platforms to prevent monopolistic practices and promote fair competition. Strengthened copyright laws and effective anti-piracy measures are equally essential to prevent the unauthorized use of artists' work and protect their intellectual property rights.

However, technological solutions might also play a role in addressing the problem. Innovative models, such as incorporating listener engagement metrics into royalty calculations, could potentially offer a fairer system that reflects the actual value a listener places on a song. Directto-fan models, bypassing intermediaries altogether, and offering fans exclusive access and perks in return for subscriptions or one-off purchases can enable musicians to maintain a more equitable relationship with their audience. Furthermore, the exploration of alternative revenue streams, like merchandise sales, live performances, and brand partnerships, becomes even more important to maintain financial viability in the current climate.

Ultimately, addressing the financial precariousness of artists in the streaming era requires a collaborative effort. Artists, industry stakeholders, policymakers, and consumers must work together to demand a fairer, more sustainable, and ethical system that respects the value of creative work and ensures the future of music. The ongoing struggle to achieve this demonstrates the urgent need for reform and a thorough re-evaluation of the dominant paradigm of digital music consumption. The future of music hinges on the willingness of all parties involved to prioritize the rights and well-being of artists, placing creativity and fairness at the heart of the industry's economic model.

The Role of Social Media in Music Discovery and Promotion

The rise of social media has fundamentally altered the way music is discovered and promoted, presenting both unprecedented opportunities and significant challenges for artists and the industry. While it offers a direct line to fans, bypassing traditional gatekeepers like record labels and radio, the landscape is far from utopian. The democratizing potential of platforms like Instagram, TikTok, YouTube, and Twitter has been undeniable, empowering independent artists to reach global audiences without the need for substantial financial backing. However, this newfound access comes with its own set of complexities, exposing artists to a hypercompetitive environment characterized by relentless selfpromotion, algorithm-driven trends, and the constant pressure to maintain an engaging online presence.

One of the most significant impacts of social media is the shift in music discovery. Previously reliant on radio airplay, music television, and print media, consumers now increasingly discover new artists through targeted algorithms and social media recommendations. Platforms like TikTok, with its short-form video format, have become particularly effective at catapulting previously unknown artists into the spotlight. A viral video, featuring a catchy snippet of a song, can generate millions of views overnight, propelling the artist into the public consciousness and driving substantial streams on major streaming platforms. This viral potential represents a powerful tool for independent artists, allowing them to gain significant traction without the need for expensive marketing campaigns or radio play. However, the

reliance on viral trends is inherently fickle and unpredictable, leaving artists at the mercy of unpredictable algorithmic whims. A song that goes viral today might be forgotten tomorrow, leaving artists perpetually scrambling to maintain momentum.

This inherent volatility underscores the double-edged sword of social media promotion. While organic virality can offer a significant boost, it's often difficult to replicate and sustain. Many artists find themselves investing significant time and effort into crafting engaging content, meticulously curating their online personas, and interacting constantly with their followers, all while navigating the ever-changing landscape of social media algorithms. This necessitates a considerable investment of time and resources, which can be challenging for artists who are already struggling to balance their creative work with the demands of everyday life. Furthermore, the pressure to constantly produce new content and maintain a consistent online presence can lead to creative burnout and mental health challenges. The relentless demand for engagement can transform the creative process into a performative act, hindering artistic expression and authenticity.

The rise of social media influencers and paid promotions further complicates the landscape. Many artists rely on collaborations with influencers to promote their music, paying significant sums for sponsored posts and shout-outs. While this can generate significant reach, it also raises questions about authenticity and the value of organic engagement. The blurring of lines between genuine fan interaction and paid promotion can erode trust with the audience, potentially impacting long-term success. Moreover, the financial burden of these promotional strategies can be unsustainable for many independent artists, placing a significant financial strain on their already precarious budgets. The cost of professional marketing and the constant need to stay visible can ultimately prove to be more detrimental than beneficial.

The competitive nature of social media also impacts the perception of musical artistry. The platforms often favor artists who cultivate a strong online persona and can consistently produce engaging content, irrespective of their musical talent. This emphasis on visual appeal and online presence can shift the focus away from the music itself, leading to a homogenization of the artistic landscape. The pressure to fit into existing trends and algorithms can stifle originality and individuality, promoting a form of artistic conformity that overshadows true creativity. The pursuit of viral fame can overshadow the intrinsic value of artistic expression, transforming the musical journey into a calculated quest for online validation.

The ethical considerations surrounding social media promotion also warrant attention. The proliferation of fake followers, bots, and engagement-buying services undermines the integrity of the system. Many artists resort to these practices to inflate their follower counts and engagement metrics, creating a false sense of popularity and success. This not only harms the credibility of artists who engage in such behaviors but also distorts the overall competitive landscape, making it more difficult for genuine artists to gain recognition. This fabricated engagement creates a skewed perception of success, further pushing artists into a cycle of unsustainable and ultimately counterproductive practices.

The role of record labels in leveraging social media also requires scrutiny. While some labels provide valuable support and guidance to their artists in navigating the social media landscape, many others use it primarily as a tool to maximize profits, prioritizing superficial metrics over genuine artistic development. The pressure on artists to create content that maximizes engagement rather than reflects their creative vision creates a tense and often exploitative power dynamic. The imbalance of power between label and artist, often exacerbated by restrictive contracts, makes it difficult for musicians to assert their creative control and ensure their work is fairly represented.

Despite these challenges, social media remains a crucial tool for music discovery and promotion. Its democratizing potential has empowered independent artists, creating opportunities previously inaccessible. The key lies in harnessing its power responsibly and ethically, avoiding the pitfalls of excessive self-promotion, algorithm dependence, and unethical marketing practices. Ultimately, success on social media requires a nuanced understanding of the platform's unique dynamics and a commitment to genuine connection with audiences, prioritizing artistic integrity and long-term sustainability over fleeting viral moments. The future of music promotion on social media will require a more balanced and ethical approach, focusing on fostering genuine engagement and supporting artists' creative autonomy. The industry needs to shift its focus from shortterm gains to a more sustainable and artist-centric model, ensuring a healthy and diverse musical landscape for years to come. This necessitates a critical reassessment of the prevailing power dynamics and a collective effort to create a more equitable environment where artists can thrive both creatively and financially. Only through such a transformative shift can social media truly fulfill its democratizing potential and empower the next generation of musicians.

The Death of the Album and the Rise of the Single

The shift from album-centric consumption to the dominance of the single is a seismic change, reflecting broader transformations in how we consume media in the digital age. The album, once the cornerstone of the music industry, a carefully curated artistic statement spanning multiple tracks, a cohesive narrative, has been eclipsed by the immediacy and convenience of the single. This isn't merely a matter of format; it represents a fundamental alteration in listener behavior and industry economics.

One of the key drivers of this shift is the rise of streaming services. Platforms like Spotify, Apple Music, and others incentivize single consumption. Algorithms prioritize individual tracks based on listener preference and popularity, pushing songs into playlists and recommendations, effectively bypassing the album as a cohesive unit. Listeners, accustomed to instant gratification and on-demand access, are less likely to invest the time and attention required to listen to an entire album from start to finish. Instead, they curate their own personalized playlists, cherry-picking their favorite tracks from a vast library of individual songs. This fragmented listening experience undermines the artistic vision of albums designed as integrated works, and the album's narrative, thematic unity, or overall concept is frequently lost in translation.

The economics of streaming further exacerbate this trend. Streaming royalties are often paid per stream, rather than per album sale, rewarding artists who generate high numbers of individual song plays. This incentivizes the release of multiple singles rather than investing resources in crafting a complete album. The financial pressure to maximize streams has led to a strategy of releasing singles in quick succession, often as a prelude to, or even in lieu of, a full-length album. This "drip-feed" method of releasing music aims to maintain consistent engagement and chart performance, but arguably sacrifices artistic integrity in favor of short-term gains.

The rise of social media has also amplified the prominence of the single. Short-form video platforms like TikTok have proven exceptionally effective at promoting individual tracks. A catchy hook or a visually compelling video snippet can quickly go viral, catapulting an unknown artist to fame or giving established artists a significant boost. This form of rapid dissemination is ideally suited for singles, allowing a concentrated burst of popularity before listener interest inevitably wanes. Trying to achieve similar viral success with an entire album is considerably more difficult, requiring consistent engagement across multiple tracks.

The decline of physical media further contributes to the single's ascendancy. The once ubiquitous CD and vinyl, which facilitated the album as the dominant unit of purchase, have largely become niche markets. The digital realm offers instant access to individual tracks, eliminating the need for purchasing an entire album. This ease and efficiency are inherently attractive to consumers, further solidifying the single's place as the primary mode of music consumption.

The impact on artists is considerable. The pressure to produce chart-topping singles can constrain creative freedom. Artists may feel compelled to conform to existing trends and stylistic expectations to maximize their chances of viral success, stifling artistic experimentation and innovation. This homogenization of sound can lead to a lack of diversity and a decline in musical depth. Albums that once provided a canvas for creative exploration and multifaceted expression are now often reduced to a collection of radiofriendly singles, potentially sacrificing artistic coherence for commercial success.

The relationship between artists and record labels has also undergone a significant shift in this new landscape. Labels, once gatekeepers controlling the dissemination of music, now face a far more fragmented marketplace. Their role has increasingly shifted from album curation and promotion to managing individual tracks and orchestrating social media campaigns aimed at maximizing streams. This focus on short-term gains can lead to increased pressure on artists, who may find themselves struggling to balance artistic vision with the relentless demands of the streaming market.

The financial implications are stark. While streaming revenue can be substantial for some artists, the majority receive considerably lower royalties than their predecessors who sold albums in physical formats. This means that artists need to generate exponentially more streams to achieve the same level of income, placing immense pressure on the creation of catchy singles that can achieve viral success. This new economic reality often means that artists need to supplement their income through various means, such as touring, merchandise sales, and brand endorsements. It has made achieving sustained financial stability in the music industry far more challenging.

Furthermore, the diminished role of the album raises questions about the artistic value of long-form musical expression. The album format, for decades, fostered creative ambition and allowed artists to build narratives, express complex themes, and explore musical ideas in depth. The emphasis on individual singles risks simplifying and reducing the musical experience, focusing on easily consumable hooks and repetition rather than nuanced artistic expressions.

The shift towards singles is not without its benefits. The ease of access to music offers previously unheard-of opportunities for independent artists to reach global audiences without the need for major label backing. The democratization of music distribution through online platforms creates a fertile ground for innovation and allows diverse genres and styles to thrive. However, the inherent unpredictability of the streaming landscape and the focus on short-term success creates a precarious and highly competitive environment.

The industry, as a whole, needs to re-evaluate its priorities and find a more sustainable balance between artistic expression and commercial success. While the single will likely continue to be the dominant mode of music consumption, fostering an environment where both albums and singles can thrive is essential. This would involve exploring more equitable revenue models for artists, supporting long-form musical projects, and acknowledging the value of artistic exploration beyond the pursuit of viral hits. The future of music lies not solely in optimizing for individual track success, but in embracing a broader spectrum of artistic expression while ensuring the financial viability of the musicians who create it. Only then can we hope to ensure a rich and diverse musical landscape for generations to come. The current system often prioritizes profit over artistry, and unless adjustments are made, a crucial aspect of cultural expression may suffer. The narrative, the artistic journey, the meticulously crafted work of musicians risk being sacrificed at the altar of immediate, short-term gratification. The challenge lies in finding a balance that allows for both artistic vision and financial sustainability in a digital landscape that favors the fleeting popularity of the single over the enduring value of the album.

The Impact of Music Playlists and Algorithmic Curation

The rise of streaming services has not only shifted the consumption pattern from albums to singles; it has also introduced a powerful new gatekeeper: the algorithm. These sophisticated systems, designed to personalize the listening experience, curate playlists and recommend tracks based on complex calculations of user behavior, listening history, and perceived preferences. While algorithms offer a seemingly personalized and efficient way to discover new music, their influence on the shape of the music industry and the careers of artists is profound and often problematic.

One of the most immediate impacts is on discoverability. In the pre-streaming era, artists relied on radio airplay, critical reviews, and physical media sales to reach audiences. Now, an artist's success is heavily dependent on algorithmic favor. A song's placement in a popular playlist or its prominence in personalized recommendations can catapult an artist to fame, while conversely, an algorithm's oversight can effectively silence even talented musicians. This creates a system where a single algorithm's decision holds the power to make or break a career, often without transparency or recourse.

This dependence on algorithms introduces inherent biases that can perpetuate existing inequalities within the music industry. Algorithms are trained on vast datasets of existing listening habits. If these datasets predominantly reflect the popularity of certain genres or artists, the algorithms are likely to reinforce those trends, further marginalizing underrepresented genres or artists. For example, if the data predominantly features male artists within a certain genre, the algorithm may favor similar artists in the future, making it harder for female artists to break through, even if their music is of equal or higher quality. This creates a selfperpetuating cycle of skewed representation, mirroring and amplifying existing biases within the industry.

The lack of transparency in algorithmic curation further compounds this problem. The precise methods used by streaming services to create playlists and recommendations are often kept secret. This opacity makes it difficult to understand how these decisions are made, making it nearly impossible for artists to strategize or challenge potentially biased outcomes. While services often claim their algorithms are objective, the very nature of their creation involves subjective human choices in what data is included, how it's weighted, and what constitutes a "successful" outcome. This lack of transparency is not merely an inconvenience but actively hinders artists' ability to navigate the increasingly algorithmic landscape.

Furthermore, the emphasis on short-term gains encouraged by the streaming model exacerbates the bias inherent in algorithmic systems. Artists and labels are incentivized to create music that aligns with prevailing trends identified by algorithms, potentially at the expense of artistic integrity and originality. This can lead to a homogenization of sound, with artists feeling compelled to conform to predictable formulas to maximize their chances of algorithmic visibility. The quest for a viral hit, tailored to algorithm-driven trends, frequently takes precedence over long-term artistic development and the creation of lasting, meaningful work.

The curated playlist, a seemingly benign feature of streaming services, also significantly influences musical taste and consumption. These playlists, often created by human curators (though increasingly informed or even automatically generated by algorithms), act as powerful tastemakers, shaping listeners' preferences and introducing them to new artists. The power wielded by these playlists is immense. A placement on a popular playlist can generate a significant increase in streams, potentially launching an artist into the mainstream. However, the curation of these playlists, although often presented as objective, is invariably influenced by subjective choices, potentially excluding diverse sounds or lesser-known artists.

The financial implications of this algorithmic curation cannot be overstated. While some artists benefit enormously from algorithmic promotion, the vast majority struggle to compete in an increasingly crowded and unpredictable market. The focus on short-term gains driven by algorithms further incentivizes a "hit-driven" approach to music creation, meaning fewer resources are invested in albums that require longer engagement, while maximizing individual tracks designed for quick popularity. This approach is detrimental to artists who prioritize artistic vision over immediate financial returns, creating a system that favors quick-hits over deeper, more nuanced musical projects.

Moreover, the use of algorithms to generate playlists and recommendations raises complex questions about copyright and ownership. The datasets used to train these algorithms often include vast quantities of copyrighted material, raising questions about the rights of artists and copyright holders. While legal frameworks are struggling to catch up to the rapid advancements in technology, the exploitation of copyrighted material in the development of algorithmic systems has not been fully addressed.

The impact of algorithmic curation is far-reaching, extending beyond the artists themselves. It impacts the overall musical landscape, potentially leading to a homogenization of sound and a decline in artistic diversity. The concentration of

power in the hands of a few major streaming platforms and their algorithms creates a potentially monopolistic environment, where a small number of entities exert disproportionate control over the distribution and consumption of music. This lack of competition inhibits innovation and limits the exposure of diverse musical voices.

Moving forward, it is essential to address the biases and opaque nature of algorithmic curation. Increased transparency in the algorithms used by streaming services is crucial. This would allow artists to better understand the factors influencing their discoverability and provide avenues for redress if they feel unfairly marginalized. Furthermore, the development of more equitable revenue models for artists is paramount, reducing the pressure to conform to algorithmic preferences and promoting a more sustainable financial ecosystem for musicians.

The industry needs to promote a more diverse and inclusive approach to algorithmic curation, ensuring the algorithms are trained on more representative datasets and designed to promote artistic diversity rather than simply replicating existing biases. This requires collaboration between artists, labels, and streaming platforms to foster a system that values artistic expression alongside commercial success. The development of ethical guidelines and regulatory frameworks to address the potential harms of algorithmic bias is also necessary. It is important that policymakers and industry leaders work together to create a more just and equitable system for artists in the digital age. The challenge lies in finding a balance that ensures a vibrant and diverse musical landscape, one that prioritizes artistic integrity, diversity of expression, and the long-term sustainability of the industry itself. Only then can the true power of music, its ability to unite, inspire, and challenge, be unleashed in its full potential.

The Future of Music Consumption Predictions and Possibilities

The current landscape of music consumption, dominated by streaming services and algorithmic curation, presents a dynamic and uncertain future. While the convenience and accessibility of platforms like Spotify and Apple Music are undeniable, their influence extends far beyond mere convenience, impacting the very fabric of the music industry. Predicting the future is inherently speculative, but by analyzing current trends and emerging technologies, we can sketch some plausible scenarios for how music consumption might evolve.

One significant development to watch is the continued rise of personalized music experiences. Algorithms will undoubtedly become even more sophisticated, capable of not only predicting our preferences but also anticipating our moods and emotional needs. Imagine a future where your smart home system seamlessly integrates with your music streaming service, adjusting the music playing based on your activity and emotional state. This hyper-personalization, while appealing to some, raises concerns about the potential for musical homogeneity. Will the algorithms, in their quest for maximum engagement, stifle musical exploration and experimentation, leading to a landscape of overly familiar and predictable sounds? The potential for "filter bubbles" in music is a real concern, where algorithms reinforce existing tastes, limiting exposure to new genres and artists.

Furthermore, the metaverse and virtual reality present exciting possibilities for music consumption. Imagine attending a virtual concert featuring your favorite artist, interacting with fellow fans from around the world, and experiencing a level of immersion previously unimaginable. These immersive virtual environments offer opportunities for artists to connect with their audiences in innovative ways, generating new revenue streams and engaging fans on a deeper level. However, the technical barriers to entry, the need for specialized equipment, and potential access disparities could restrict the accessibility of these experiences. The metaverse, therefore, will likely exist as a supplementary medium, rather than a complete replacement, for traditional music consumption.

The development of artificial intelligence (AI) in music creation itself holds both promise and peril. AI tools can assist artists in composing, arranging, and producing music, accelerating the creative process and facilitating experimentation. However, the ethical questions surrounding AI-generated music, including issues of authorship, copyright, and artistic integrity, are significant and demand careful consideration. Will AI ultimately replace human musicians, or will it serve as a powerful tool to enhance their creative capabilities? The answer likely lies somewhere in between: a symbiotic relationship where AI augments human creativity, not replaces it entirely. Yet, this potential integration necessitates a frank discussion about proper attribution and fair compensation, which current copyright frameworks may not be adequately equipped to handle.

Another critical aspect of the future of music consumption is the ongoing evolution of audio technologies. High-resolution audio, spatial audio, and immersive sound experiences are gaining traction, offering listeners a richer and more nuanced listening experience. The shift towards high-fidelity audio might lead to a resurgence of physical media like vinyl records and high-quality digital downloads, offering a tangible and superior sonic experience compared to the often compressed audio of many streaming services. While convenience may drive the majority of music listening, a segment of the population clearly values superior sound quality and the unique experience of physical media, representing a potential market segment for higher-quality audio formats.

The future of music discovery also holds significant uncertainties. While algorithms currently dominate the landscape, other methods may gain prominence. Usergenerated content platforms, social media, and influencer marketing might become increasingly crucial in helping listeners discover new artists and music. The shift towards decentralization, empowered by technologies like blockchain and NFTs (non-fungible tokens), could democratize music distribution and provide artists with more direct control over their work and compensation. This shift could mitigate the power of centralized streaming platforms and give artists more agency over their careers. However, the complexities of blockchain technology and the volatile nature of NFT markets pose challenges that need careful consideration. It remains to be seen if these technologies will effectively empower artists or simply create new layers of complexity and potential exploitation.

Furthermore, the ongoing debates surrounding fair compensation for artists within the streaming model will continue to shape the future of music consumption. The current revenue models, often criticized for their low payouts to artists, may undergo significant revisions as artists, labels, and policymakers seek more equitable solutions. The emergence of new platforms and business models, like artistowned streaming services or subscription models that directly benefit artists, might disrupt the dominance of existing platforms. The demand for fairer compensation and greater transparency in revenue distribution is unlikely to diminish and could lead to significant changes in the industry's financial landscape.

The integration of music with other technologies will also continue to evolve. Music is increasingly used in virtual and augmented reality applications, video games, and interactive experiences. This integration expands the potential audience for music and creates new revenue opportunities for artists. The use of music in advertising, film, and television will continue to be crucial for artists' revenue streams, highlighting the continuing interconnectedness between music and other media. However, this integration requires a careful balance between effective use and exploitation, ensuring that the musical elements are not reduced to mere background noise.

Finally, the issue of copyright and intellectual property rights in the digital age will remain a central challenge. The ease of digital copying and distribution necessitates ongoing adaptations in legal frameworks to protect artists' rights. The complexities of copyright in a world of AI-generated music and user-generated content present novel legal and ethical challenges that require careful and thoughtful consideration. The balance between protecting artists' rights and fostering innovation and creativity remains a difficult but essential task for policymakers and the industry as a whole. A transparent and equitable system is necessary to ensure fair compensation and creative freedom for artists in the years to come. The future of music consumption is not merely about technological innovation; it's about the evolution of our relationship with music and the continued quest for a sustainable and equitable ecosystem for artists and listeners alike.

AIGenerated Music and its Impact on Artists Livelihoods

The rapid advancement of artificial intelligence (AI) has infiltrated nearly every facet of modern life, and the music industry is no exception. AI-powered tools now offer capabilities ranging from composing melodies and harmonies to generating entire musical arrangements, potentially revolutionizing the creative process. However, this technological leap has ignited a fierce debate, particularly concerning its impact on the livelihoods of human artists. The core question revolves around whether AI will serve as a collaborative tool, augmenting human creativity, or ultimately supplant human musicians altogether. The answer, as with most technological disruptions, is likely multifaceted and nuanced.

One immediate concern centers on the potential displacement of musicians. If AI can generate music that is indistinguishable from, or even surpasses, human-created compositions, the demand for human artists might dwindle. This could disproportionately impact musicians who rely on composing and arranging as their primary income source. Imagine a future where film scores, video game soundtracks, and even commercial jingles are predominantly generated by AI, rendering human composers largely redundant. Such a scenario would have devastating consequences for countless musicians struggling to make a living in an already fiercely competitive industry.

Beyond the immediate threat of job displacement, the issue of copyright and ownership presents significant ethical and legal challenges. If an AI generates a musical piece, who owns the copyright? Is it the developer of the AI software, the user who prompted the AI to create the music, or does the AI itself hold some form of intellectual property rights? Current copyright laws are ill-equipped to handle these complexities, creating a legal gray area that could lead to widespread exploitation and uncertainty for artists. The lack of clear legal precedent leaves artists vulnerable to having their creative work appropriated and monetized without proper compensation or attribution.

Furthermore, the issue of artistic integrity is paramount. AIgenerated music, while potentially innovative and technically impressive, often lacks the emotional depth, personal expression, and nuanced storytelling that characterize truly great human-created music. Music often serves as a vessel for conveying personal experiences, reflecting cultural contexts, and sharing universal human emotions. Can an algorithm, however sophisticated, truly replicate the complexities of human emotion and experience in a way that resonates with listeners on an authentic level? The risk is that the proliferation of AI-generated music could lead to a homogenization of musical styles, a lack of originality, and a devaluation of the human element that makes music so powerful.

The impact extends beyond individual artists. The music industry itself relies on a complex ecosystem of creators, performers, producers, engineers, and label executives. The widespread adoption of AI-generated music could disrupt this intricate network, potentially causing job losses across the board. Record labels, facing a potential surplus of easily generated AI-created music, might shift their focus away from nurturing and promoting human artists, further exacerbating the existing challenges faced by struggling musicians. This could stifle artistic innovation and lead to a homogenized musical landscape dominated by algorithms and profit maximization.

However, it's crucial to acknowledge that AI also offers significant potential benefits for musicians. AI tools can automate tedious tasks, freeing up artists to focus on the more creative aspects of music making. Imagine a composer using AI to assist with orchestration, allowing them to experiment with more complex arrangements without the time-consuming process of manual notation. AI can also serve as a tool for generating new ideas and exploring uncharted sonic territories. It can help musicians overcome creative blocks and experiment with different styles and genres, expanding their creative palette and pushing the boundaries of musical innovation.

The key lies in finding a balance between leveraging the technological advancements of AI and protecting the livelihoods and creative integrity of human artists. This requires a collaborative approach involving artists, technologists, policymakers, and industry leaders. One important step is to develop clearer legal frameworks that address issues of copyright, ownership, and attribution in the context of AI-generated music. This includes exploring new models for compensation that fairly reward both human artists and AI developers for their contributions. Additionally, the music industry needs to adopt ethical guidelines for the use of AI in music creation, ensuring transparency and avoiding exploitation.

Another crucial aspect is to invest in education and training programs that equip musicians with the skills needed to navigate this evolving technological landscape. Musicians need to adapt to the new tools and techniques emerging in the field, learning how to effectively integrate AI into their creative workflows. This might involve mastering new software, learning to collaborate with AI, and developing a deeper understanding of the ethical considerations surrounding AI-generated music.

Educational initiatives are critical to ensuring that musicians are not left behind in this rapid technological advancement.

Moreover, the focus should shift towards fostering a symbiotic relationship between AI and human artists. Instead of viewing AI as a threat, musicians can embrace it as a powerful tool to augment their creative capabilities. By combining the ingenuity and emotional depth of human artistry with the efficiency and analytical capabilities of AI, we can unlock entirely new levels of musical innovation. This requires a shift in mindset, moving away from a purely competitive framework to a collaborative one, where humans and AI work together to push the boundaries of musical expression.

The ethical considerations surrounding AI-generated music extend beyond the immediate economic impact on artists. They also raise fundamental questions about the nature of creativity, originality, and artistic expression. If AI can create music that is both technically proficient and emotionally resonant, does that diminish the value of human artistic expression? Or does it simply expand the definition of what constitutes "art"? These are complex philosophical questions that require careful consideration, as they touch upon the very core of what makes human creativity unique and meaningful.

In conclusion, the emergence of AI-generated music presents both significant challenges and exciting opportunities for the music industry. The potential for displacement of human artists is undeniable, and the ethical and legal questions surrounding copyright, ownership, and artistic integrity demand immediate attention. However, the potential for AI to augment human creativity and unlock new sonic frontiers should not be dismissed. By fostering collaboration, establishing clear ethical guidelines, investing in education, and adapting legal frameworks, we can navigate this technological shift in a way that benefits both human artists and the future of music itself. The future of music is not a zero-sum game; it is a dynamic interplay between human creativity and technological innovation, and it is crucial to ensure that the human element remains central to the musical experience. Ignoring the ethical implications could lead to a homogenized, emotionally sterile musical landscape, while embracing the responsible integration of AI offers the potential for a vibrant and innovative future for music creation and appreciation.

Copyright and Ownership Issues Surrounding AICreated Music

The advent of AI music composition tools has thrown the established legal frameworks governing copyright and ownership into disarray. Current copyright law, largely designed for human creators, struggles to grapple with the unique circumstances of AI-generated music. The fundamental question—who owns the copyright to a song composed by an algorithm?—remains largely unanswered, leaving artists, developers, and users in a precarious legal limbo. This uncertainty fosters a breeding ground for exploitation, with the potential for widespread infringement and the erosion of artists' rights.

One of the key challenges lies in defining the role of each party involved in the creation of AI music. Is the copyright held by the developer of the AI software, who created the algorithm capable of generating music? This argument centers on the idea that the software itself is the creative tool, analogous to a paintbrush or a piano, and therefore the developer holds the same ownership rights as the creator of a traditional art tool. However, this analogy is flawed; the AI isn't just a tool; it is capable of generating original compositions based on input parameters. Furthermore, the degree of human involvement in shaping the final output varies widely, adding further complexity to the legal equation.

Consider the scenario where a musician utilizes AI software to generate a musical piece. They may input specific parameters, such as a desired tempo, key, or instrumentation, and the AI then generates a musical composition based on these guidelines. However, the human user still exercises a degree of creative control over the final product, deciding which elements to retain, modify, or discard. In this case, determining the relative contribution of the human and the machine is crucial in assigning copyright. A simple tweaking of parameters may not warrant co-ownership, whereas a significant degree of human intervention and editing might justify a joint copyright. However, establishing a quantitative measure of "significant" contribution remains a significant hurdle.

Another contentious issue arises from the use of pre-existing musical material in training AI models. Many AI music generators are trained on vast datasets of copyrighted music. This raises concerns about copyright infringement, particularly if the AI generates a piece that closely resembles a pre-existing work. Establishing a clear line between inspiration and direct copying in the context of AI is incredibly challenging. Can we reasonably expect an AI, trained on thousands of copyrighted works, to never generate something reminiscent of those works, even if it doesn't directly replicate them? The legal response to this is far from settled, and precedent is still being established through a patchwork of court cases.

The potential for derivative works also adds to the complexity. If a musician uses AI-generated music as a starting point for their own compositions, adding their own creative elements and arrangements, who owns the copyright to the resulting work? Is it the original AI developer, the user who prompted the AI, or the musician who incorporated the AI-generated music into their own composition? This problem is exacerbated by the potential for multiple layers of AI involvement. Imagine a scenario where one AI generates a melody and another AI generates a harmony for that melody. The ownership implications alone become exponentially complex.

The legal landscape surrounding AI-generated music is further complicated by international differences in copyright law. What constitutes legal ownership in one country might be viewed quite differently in another. The global reach of the music industry necessitates a harmonized approach to these issues, but achieving such harmonization is a monumental task, given the diverse and sometimes conflicting legal frameworks in place around the world. Without a unified global standard, artists face the frustrating possibility of their rights being protected in some territories but vulnerable in others.

Beyond the purely legal aspects, the ethical implications are equally profound. If AI becomes the primary source of music creation, what happens to the livelihoods of human musicians? Will the widespread availability of readilygenerated music devalue the work of human composers and performers? The potential for mass unemployment in the music industry is a significant concern. And even if AI generates music that doesn't directly replace human artists, it may still significantly alter their work and the industry's structure. Will musicians become primarily curators of AIgenerated music, or will they become obsolete entirely? These are critical questions that require careful consideration and proactive policy measures.

Furthermore, the issue of artistic integrity and originality is paramount. While AI can generate technically proficient music, some argue it lacks the emotional depth and expressive nuance that characterizes truly great human compositions. Music is often a deeply personal expression of human experience, and some contend that algorithms, however sophisticated, cannot fully replicate the richness and complexity of human emotions. This raises fundamental questions about the nature of art itself and the potential for AI to diminish the value and impact of human creative endeavors. Is AI-generated music truly "art," or is it a mere imitation, lacking the essence of human creativity? This philosophical debate is only beginning to take shape, with no clear consensus in sight.

Moreover, the question of attribution adds another layer of ethical complexity. How should we attribute authorship to AI-generated music? Should the AI software itself be credited as a co-creator? Such a crediting would blur the line between human artistry and algorithmic output, raising complex questions about intellectual property rights and creative agency. The existing copyright systems are not equipped to deal with non-human creators, and adapting these frameworks to incorporate AI as a collaborator or coauthor will require significant legal reform and innovative thinking.

To address these multifaceted issues, a multi-pronged approach is necessary. Firstly, there is an urgent need for legal reforms to clarify copyright ownership and attribution for

AI-generated music. This includes international cooperation to establish a consistent legal framework across different jurisdictions. Secondly, the music industry needs to develop ethical guidelines for the use of AI in music creation, ensuring transparency and fairness to all stakeholders. This would involve developing mechanisms for compensating human artists whose work is used to train AI models and for fairly compensating the individuals involved in using and adapting AI-generated music.

Thirdly, investment in education and training programs for musicians is crucial. Musicians need to adapt to the changing technological landscape, learning how to effectively integrate AI into their creative processes. This might involve mastering new software, learning collaborative techniques, and understanding the ethical and legal implications of AIgenerated music. The development of such programs is essential to enable artists to thrive in this evolving creative ecosystem.

Finally, fostering collaboration between artists, technologists, policymakers, and industry leaders is paramount. A collaborative approach, focused on navigating the ethical and legal complexities of AI music creation, is crucial in fostering an environment where AI serves to augment rather than supplant human creativity. The goal should not be to eliminate human musicians but to empower them with the necessary tools and knowledge to flourish in the age of AI music technology. This will ensure a vibrant and diverse musical landscape where both human ingenuity and technological innovation contribute to the creation of inspiring and impactful music. The challenge, therefore, is to navigate the complex interplay of legal frameworks, ethical considerations, and technological advancements to shape a future where human creativity and AI innovation coexist harmoniously in the world of music.

AI as a Tool for Music Creation Benefits and Drawbacks

The burgeoning field of AI-powered music creation presents a double-edged sword for the music industry. On one hand, it offers unprecedented opportunities for artists to expand their creative horizons, enhance productivity, and reach wider audiences. On the other, it poses significant challenges to established norms of authorship, copyright, and the very definition of artistic merit. The potential for exploitation and the displacement of human musicians are real and pressing concerns that demand careful consideration.

One of the most immediate benefits of AI music tools is increased accessibility. Previously, the technical proficiency required to create professional-quality music was a significant barrier to entry for many aspiring musicians. AI tools, however, democratize the creative process, allowing individuals with limited musical training to compose and produce sophisticated tracks. This opens up new avenues for artistic expression and allows for a greater diversity of voices in the music landscape. Imagine a songwriter with a brilliant melodic idea but lacking the technical skills to fully realize it. AI tools can fill this gap, acting as a collaborative partner to help translate their vision into a finished product.

This democratizing effect is particularly potent in genres that rely on complex instrumentation or intricate production techniques, previously only attainable by experienced professionals with access to expensive equipment and studio time. The barrier to entry isn't eliminated entirely – a strong musical idea and understanding of music theory are still crucial – but the technological hurdle is significantly lowered.

Furthermore, AI tools can dramatically enhance the productivity of established artists. A musician might use AI to generate a variety of musical ideas, exploring different melodic and harmonic possibilities much faster than could be achieved through traditional methods. This speeds up the songwriting process, allowing artists to experiment more freely and generate a larger volume of work. A composer might utilize AI to generate backing tracks, freeing up their time to focus on the more nuanced aspects of their composition, such as melody, lyrics, and overall arrangement. Consider the case of a film composer facing tight deadlines. AI could be used to create a wide array of initial soundtracks, allowing for efficient exploration of themes and variations, before human refinement and orchestration. This increased efficiency isn't about replacing human creativity but about augmenting it, allowing artists to focus on the aspects of their craft that require uniquely human skills.

However, the benefits are heavily countered by substantial drawbacks. The most significant concern revolves around copyright and ownership. As previously discussed, the current legal framework struggles to cope with the complexities of AI-generated music. The question of authorship – who owns the rights to a song created by an AI – remains a highly contested area, leading to uncertainty and the potential for exploitation. This ambiguity can be particularly damaging to independent artists who might unwittingly infringe on existing copyrights when using AI tools, exposing them to costly legal battles and the loss of their creative work. Furthermore, the use of vast datasets of copyrighted material in training AI models raises serious ethical questions. While the developers may argue that the AI is merely "learning" from these existing works, the generated music may bear striking resemblances to copyrighted material, leading to accusations of plagiarism or copyright infringement. The lack of clear legal precedents makes navigating this treacherous landscape particularly challenging for both artists and AI developers alike.

Another significant concern is the potential for the devaluation of human artistic talent. The ease with which AI can generate musical pieces raises concerns about the future of human musicians. Will the widespread availability of AIgenerated music lead to a decline in demand for human composers and performers? Will audiences value the work of human artists less highly, especially if AI can generate music that is equally technically proficient, if not more so in certain aspects? The potential for mass unemployment within the music industry is a very real threat, requiring proactive measures to mitigate its impact. This might involve government initiatives to support and reskill musicians, helping them to adapt to the changing landscape and integrate AI tools into their work. It could also involve the development of new business models that fairly compensate musicians for their creative contributions, even when collaborating with AI systems. Furthermore, it is crucial that the public develops a more sophisticated understanding of the process of AI music generation and its role in supporting – rather than supplanting – human creativity.

Beyond the economic implications, the ethical implications of AI-generated music are profound. The question of artistic integrity and originality is paramount. While AI can generate technically proficient music, many argue that it lacks the emotional depth and nuanced expression characteristic of great human compositions. Music often serves as a powerful conduit for human emotions, reflecting our experiences, anxieties, and joys in a uniquely personal way. Some believe that AI, despite its sophistication, cannot truly replicate the depth and complexity of human emotional expression. This raises fundamental questions about the nature of art itself

and the potential for AI to diminish the value and impact of human creative expression. Is AI-generated music truly "art," or is it merely a sophisticated imitation, lacking the essence of human experience and intention?

The issue of attribution adds another layer of complexity.

How should we attribute authorship to AI-generated music? Is the AI software itself a co-creator? The existing frameworks of copyright law are not equipped to address the issue of non-human creators, requiring significant legal and philosophical reform to adapt to the reality of AI as a collaborative partner in artistic creation. The problem of transparency in AI systems also raises concerns. Many AI music generators are "black boxes," making it difficult to understand the processes by which the music is created. This lack of transparency hinders artists' ability to exercise control over the creative process and understand the potential legal implications of their use of the technology.

The development of AI music technology also raises questions about the future of artistic collaboration. Will human musicians increasingly become collaborators with AI systems, or will they be replaced altogether? This shift will not only impact the livelihoods of musicians but also the evolution of artistic styles and expressions. The potential for homogeneity is a concern, as reliance on a limited set of AI algorithms and training data could lead to music that lacks originality and diversity. The challenge lies in harnessing the potential of AI to augment human creativity without sacrificing the uniquely human elements that make music such a powerful and expressive art form.

Addressing these multifaceted challenges requires a comprehensive approach involving legal reforms, ethical guidelines, educational initiatives, and fostering collaboration between stakeholders. International cooperation is crucial to establish a consistent legal framework for AI-generated music, addressing issues of copyright, ownership, and attribution. The development of ethical guidelines for the use of AI in music creation will ensure fairness and transparency, protecting the rights of human artists and preventing exploitation. Investments in educational programs will help musicians adapt to the changing technological landscape, enabling them to effectively integrate AI tools into their creative processes and navigate the complex legal and ethical considerations. Finally, open dialogue and collaboration between artists, technologists, policymakers, and industry leaders are crucial to shape a future where AI augments rather than supplants human creativity in the music industry. Only through a concerted and collaborative effort can we ensure a future where both human ingenuity and technological innovation contribute to a vibrant and diverse musical landscape.

The Impact of AI on Music Education and Training

The integration of artificial intelligence (AI) into music education and training is poised to revolutionize how musicians learn, practice, and perform. While the prospect of AI tutors and automated feedback systems might seem futuristic, the technology is already making inroads into various aspects of musical pedagogy. However, this technological advancement is not without its ethical and practical challenges, requiring a careful consideration of its implementation and long-term impact.

One of the most significant benefits of AI in music education is its potential to personalize the learning experience. Traditional music education often follows a one-size-fits-all approach, where students are taught the same material at the same pace, regardless of their individual needs and learning styles. AI, however, can tailor instruction to suit each student's strengths and weaknesses, providing personalized feedback and targeted exercises. Imagine an AI-powered app that analyzes a student's playing, identifying areas needing improvement and offering customized exercises to address those specific issues. This could involve identifying incorrect fingerings, rhythmic inaccuracies, or intonation problems, providing immediate and targeted feedback to enhance the learning process. Such personalized learning could significantly improve efficiency and effectiveness, accelerating student progress and increasing engagement.

Furthermore, AI can provide immediate and objective feedback, a feature often lacking in traditional music education. While human instructors offer valuable insights and guidance, they may be limited in their ability to provide instantaneous feedback on technical aspects of performance. AI, on the other hand, can analyze a student's playing in realtime, offering precise measurements of timing, intonation, and dynamics. This real-time feedback can be invaluable in helping students develop good habits and correct errors early on, preventing the development of ingrained bad techniques. Consider the example of a young violinist struggling with vibrato. An AI system could analyze the student's vibrato, providing detailed feedback on its speed, consistency, and amplitude, allowing for immediate adjustments and refinement. This constant, objective feedback can be particularly beneficial for self-taught musicians or those in remote areas with limited access to experienced instructors.

The accessibility of musical instruction is another area where AI holds significant promise. AI-powered platforms can provide access to high-quality music education to individuals in underserved communities or those with limited resources. Online courses and interactive tutorials can bridge geographical barriers, allowing students from all over the world to learn from leading instructors. Imagine a student in a rural community with limited access to music teachers being able to access personalized lessons from a worldrenowned musician through an AI-powered platform. This democratizing effect of AI could significantly increase the diversity and inclusivity of music education, allowing more people to pursue their musical passions regardless of their location or socioeconomic background.

Moreover, AI can expand the range of musical tools and resources available to students. AI-powered music composition tools, for instance, can allow students to experiment with different musical styles and techniques, fostering creativity and innovation. Students can use these tools to compose their own music, receive feedback on their compositions, and explore the vast world of musical possibilities. This hands-on approach can be a valuable supplement to traditional instruction, allowing students to develop a deeper understanding of music theory and composition through practical application. Furthermore, AI can generate accompaniment tracks, providing students with the opportunity to practice their performance skills with a virtual ensemble. This is particularly useful for instrumentalists who might not have access to a live accompanist or a full ensemble.

However, the implementation of AI in music education also presents significant challenges. One major concern is the potential for over-reliance on technology, leading to a decline in the importance of human interaction and mentorship in music education. While AI can provide valuable feedback and personalize the learning experience, it cannot replace the nuanced guidance and support that a human instructor can offer. The social and emotional aspects of learning music, such as collaboration, performance anxiety, and creative expression, are best addressed through human interaction. Therefore, a balanced approach is crucial, integrating AI tools to enhance learning rather than replacing the human element entirely.

Another challenge lies in ensuring the accuracy and fairness of AI-generated feedback. The algorithms used by AI systems are trained on vast datasets of musical data, and any biases present in these datasets could be reflected in the feedback provided to students. This could lead to unfair or inaccurate assessments, particularly for students from diverse musical backgrounds or those who adopt unconventional approaches to music-making. It's crucial to develop robust and unbiased AI systems that accurately assess musical performance without penalizing individuality or creativity. Regular audits and ongoing refinement of AI systems are necessary to mitigate this risk.

Furthermore, the cost and accessibility of AI-powered music education tools could exacerbate existing inequalities in access to music education. While AI holds the potential to democratize access to music education, the cost of developing and implementing these technologies may make them inaccessible to many schools and individuals. It's vital to ensure that the benefits of AI in music education are equitably distributed, avoiding a situation where only affluent institutions and students can benefit from this technology. This may require government investment in open-source AI tools and initiatives to provide affordable access to these technologies for underserved communities.

The ethical implications of using AI in music education must also be carefully considered. Questions surrounding data privacy, intellectual property rights, and the potential for AI to replace human instructors need to be addressed.

Clear guidelines and regulations are necessary to ensure the responsible use of AI in music education, protecting the rights and interests of students and educators alike. Transparent algorithms and open access to the data used to train AI systems are crucial to ensure accountability and prevent biases from undermining the educational process.

Finally, the role of human educators in the age of AI needs to be redefined. Rather than being replaced, human educators should become facilitators and mentors, guiding students through the learning process and providing context, encouragement, and emotional support. The human element of music education remains irreplaceable, with its emphasis on creativity, collaboration, and emotional growth. AI should be used to augment the capabilities of human educators, enhancing their effectiveness and allowing them to focus on higher-level skills such as fostering creativity, critical thinking, and collaborative learning.

In conclusion, the integration of AI into music education and training holds immense potential to personalize learning, provide immediate feedback, democratize access, and expand musical resources. However, its implementation requires a cautious and responsible approach, addressing the challenges of over-reliance on technology, ensuring fairness and accuracy in AI-generated feedback, mitigating the risks of exacerbating existing inequalities, and considering the ethical implications of its use. A collaborative effort among educators, technologists, policymakers, and industry leaders is crucial to ensure that AI serves as a powerful tool to enhance music education rather than undermine its essential human elements. The future of music education lies not in a replacement of human interaction but in a carefully considered integration of human expertise and technological innovation, fostering a more inclusive, engaging, and effective learning environment for all.

The Future of AI in the Music Industry Ethical Considerations

The rapid advancement of artificial intelligence (AI) is poised to reshape the music industry in profound ways, extending far beyond its current applications in music education. While AI-powered tools already assist in tasks like music production, mastering, and even songwriting, the future promises even more transformative capabilities. However, this technological leap forward brings with it a complex web of ethical considerations that demand careful scrutiny. Failing to address these concerns risks exacerbating existing inequalities, undermining artistic integrity, and creating a system that prioritizes profit over creativity and fairness.

One of the most significant ethical dilemmas revolves around the use of AI in music creation. While AI can generate musical pieces, often indistinguishable from human compositions, the question of authorship and copyright remains unresolved. Who owns the copyright to a song generated by an AI? Is it the programmer who created the algorithm, the user who inputted the parameters, or does the AI itself possess some form of intellectual property rights? These are complex legal and philosophical questions that are far from settled. The lack of clarity could lead to exploitation of artists, with companies potentially utilizing AI to generate music without proper compensation to human creators, further undermining already precarious incomes in the industry. Imagine a scenario where a major record label uses an AI to produce a chart-topping hit, reaping immense profits while avoiding the expense of hiring and paying human songwriters and musicians. This raises serious concerns about the displacement of human artists and the potential for AI to become a tool for suppressing creative talent, particularly for those already struggling to gain recognition and financial stability.

Furthermore, the use of AI in music production raises concerns about the homogenization of music. AI algorithms are trained on vast datasets of existing music, which means they are likely to reproduce existing musical styles and trends. This could lead to a reduction in musical diversity and innovation, as AI-generated music might lack the unique characteristics and originality that come from human creativity and experience. While AI can assist in refining and enhancing existing musical ideas, its potential to generate entirely new and innovative sounds is still limited, raising the question of whether the future of music will be dictated by algorithms, limiting artistic exploration and the emergence of fresh, diverse sounds. The risk of stylistic stagnation is a significant concern; the vibrant tapestry of musical genres and subgenres could become increasingly homogenous, reducing the richness and diversity that defines the human musical experience.

The impact of AI on music distribution and consumption also raises ethical concerns. AI-powered algorithms are already being used by streaming platforms to curate playlists and recommend music to users. However, these algorithms can perpetuate biases, reinforcing existing power structures and limiting exposure to lesser-known artists. The "filter bubble" effect can confine users to a narrow range of music, reducing their exposure to diverse musical styles and cultures. This creates a feedback loop that favors popular artists and genres, potentially silencing the voices of marginalized artists and communities. The lack of transparency in these algorithms also poses a problem. Without understanding how these systems function, it's difficult to assess their fairness and address potential biases.

This lack of accountability can exacerbate the existing power imbalances within the music industry, further marginalizing independent artists and those from underrepresented groups.

Another crucial issue lies in the potential for AI to be used to create deepfakes of musicians' voices and performances. This technology could be used to create unauthorized recordings, infringe on copyright, and even damage the reputations of artists. Imagine a situation where a musician's voice is used to create a song endorsing a political figure or product without their consent—the potential for harm, both professional and personal, is immense. The challenges in detecting and preventing these deepfakes are significant, and existing legal frameworks are struggling to keep pace with this rapidly evolving technology. This necessitates urgent development of robust detection methods and regulatory frameworks to protect artists from exploitation and reputational damage.

The issue of accessibility and equity also deserves attention. The high cost of developing and implementing AI-powered music technologies could exacerbate existing inequalities in the music industry. Smaller, independent artists might lack the resources to invest in these technologies, putting them at a disadvantage to larger labels and corporations that can afford to leverage AI's power for music creation, distribution, and promotion. This unequal access to technology risks further consolidating power in the hands of a few large players, leaving independent artists struggling to compete in an increasingly technology-driven market. A crucial step toward mitigating this inequality is ensuring fair and equitable access to AI tools and resources for all musicians, regardless of their size or budget. This may necessitate government intervention, supporting the development of open-source AI tools and creating funding programs to help independent artists adopt and utilize these technologies.

In conclusion, the future of AI in the music industry presents immense opportunities for innovation and efficiency, but these advancements must be carefully managed to avoid exacerbating existing ethical and equity issues. Addressing the challenges related to copyright, authorship, musical diversity, algorithmic bias, deepfakes, and accessibility is crucial to ensuring a fair and equitable future for the music industry. A collaborative approach involving artists, technologists, policymakers, and industry leaders is essential to develop guidelines and regulations that promote responsible innovation, protect artists' rights, and safeguard the integrity and diversity of music for future generations. The goal should not be to replace human creativity but to augment it, fostering a symbiotic relationship between technology and artistic expression that benefits both artists and music lovers alike. The music industry must actively engage in shaping the ethical framework surrounding AI, ensuring that this powerful technology serves as a force for good, promoting fairness, innovation, and artistic freedom. Failure to do so risks creating a future where the music industry is dominated by a few powerful entities, leaving independent artists and their unique voices marginalized and unheard.

The Rise of Independent Labels and Their Impact on the Industry

The rise of independent music labels represents a seismic shift in the power dynamics of the music industry, a direct challenge to the long-held stranglehold of major labels. For decades, these behemoths dictated the terms of engagement, controlling nearly every aspect of an artist's career, from songwriting and recording to distribution and marketing. Artists, often young and inexperienced, were routinely forced into exploitative contracts, sacrificing significant portions of their earnings and creative freedom for the promise of mainstream success. The major labels, in turn, focused on maximizing profits, prioritizing commercially viable artists and genres over artistic merit or originality. This system, while profitable for the labels, often left artists feeling undervalued, exploited, and creatively stifled.

The emergence of independent labels, however, offers a viable alternative, a pathway to artistic freedom and financial fairness that was largely absent from the traditional model. Armed with the tools of the digital revolution—affordable recording equipment, accessible distribution platforms, and the vast reach of the internet—independent labels have carved a significant niche for themselves, providing a breeding ground for innovation and fostering a more diverse and vibrant musical landscape. This shift isn't merely about a change in ownership; it signifies a fundamental change in the relationship between artists and their representatives. Independent labels, by their very nature, are often artistcentric, prioritizing the creative vision and artistic integrity of the musicians they represent.

One of the most significant advantages offered by independent labels is greater creative control for artists. In the major label system, A&R executives often exert considerable influence over an artist's musical direction, pushing for commercially palatable sounds that may compromise the artist's artistic vision. Independent labels, however, are more likely to embrace experimentation and artistic risk-taking, allowing artists to explore their creative boundaries without the pressure to conform to mainstream trends. This newfound freedom allows artists to develop a unique sonic identity, forging a stronger connection with their audience and building a more loyal fan base.

Furthermore, independent labels often offer artists fairer and more transparent deals. Major label contracts are notorious for their complexity and opacity, often containing clauses that heavily favor the label and leave artists vulnerable to exploitation. Independent labels, on the other hand, tend to adopt more equitable business practices, offering artists a larger share of the profits and greater transparency in financial matters. This increased fairness fosters a more collaborative and trusting relationship between artist and label, leading to a more sustainable and mutually beneficial partnership.

The rise of digital distribution platforms has played a crucial role in the success of independent labels. Services like Spotify, Apple Music, and Bandcamp provide independent artists with unprecedented access to global audiences, bypassing the gatekeeping role previously held by major labels. This direct-to-consumer approach allows artists to retain a larger share of their earnings and build a direct relationship with their fans, creating a more intimate and engaged fan base. This direct connection, fostered through social media and email marketing, enables artists to build loyalty and cultivate a community around their work, factors often lacking in the major label model.

However, the journey for independent labels is not without its challenges. While digital distribution platforms have democratized access to audiences, they also present new challenges in terms of competition and revenue generation. The sheer volume of music available on these platforms makes it difficult for independent artists to stand out from the crowd, requiring strategic marketing and promotion to reach a wider audience. The complexities of navigating the digital music landscape, including royalty payments, streaming analytics, and marketing strategies, can also be daunting for independent labels and artists who may lack the resources and expertise of their major label counterparts.

Moreover, independent labels often face financial constraints that limit their resources and marketing reach. Unlike major labels, which have vast marketing budgets and established distribution networks, independent labels often rely on bootstrapping and creative resourcefulness to promote their artists. This can limit their ability to reach wider audiences and compete with the marketing power of major labels. This disparity in resources highlights the ongoing need for support and investment in independent labels, enabling them to compete effectively in an increasingly competitive landscape.

Despite these challenges, the increasing influence of independent labels signifies a significant shift toward a more equitable and artist-centric music industry. The growing number of successful independent artists demonstrates the viability of this alternative model, providing a pathway to artistic freedom, financial fairness, and sustainable careers for musicians. The future of the music industry is likely to be one of increased diversity and pluralism, with a dynamic interplay between major labels and independent labels, each offering unique advantages and catering to different needs and artistic visions.

The role of technology continues to evolve, impacting both independent and major labels. While digital platforms provide unparalleled reach, they also introduce complexities in terms of revenue models and algorithmic biases. Independent labels have shown a remarkable ability to adapt and innovate, leveraging social media, targeted marketing, and direct engagement with fans to overcome these challenges. Their agility and resourcefulness have enabled them to compete effectively in the digital marketplace, carving out a space for themselves in a landscape dominated by major labels.

Moreover, the increasing demand for authenticity and artistic originality is driving consumers toward independent artists and labels. Audiences are increasingly discerning, recognizing and appreciating the unique artistic voices fostered by independent labels. This preference for originality and authenticity is fueling the growth of independent music, underscoring the value of creative freedom and artistic integrity in the music industry. The shift towards a more artist-centric approach is not only beneficial for the artists but also enriches the overall musical landscape, fostering innovation and diversity in musical styles and expression.

Looking ahead, the future of independent music labels appears bright. Continued technological advancements and increasing consumer demand for authentic and diverse music will likely fuel further growth in the independent sector. The ability of independent labels to adapt and innovate, coupled with the increasing awareness of the shortcomings of the traditional major label system, suggests that independent labels will continue to play an increasingly vital role in shaping the future of the music industry. This is not merely about economic empowerment; it is about artistic freedom, fostering a more diverse and vibrant music scene that reflects the rich tapestry of human creativity.

The narrative of the independent label is one of resilience, innovation, and a steadfast commitment to artistic integrity. They represent a counter-narrative to the often exploitative practices of major labels, providing a supportive ecosystem where artists can thrive and flourish. The continued success of independent labels serves as a powerful testament to the power of community, collaboration, and a dedication to creating authentic and meaningful music. Their contribution to the musical landscape extends far beyond economic empowerment; it is about preserving the spirit of independent creation, ensuring a future where diverse artistic voices can be heard, celebrated, and valued. Their continued growth is not just a trend; it is a reflection of a fundamental shift in the music industry, one driven by a deep-seated desire for authenticity, artistic freedom, and a more equitable distribution of creative output. The future of music, in many ways, rests in the hands of these independent labels and the artists they champion.

Distribution Strategies and Marketing Tactics of Independent Labels

The success of independent music labels hinges not only on their artist-centric approach and fairer contracts but also on their ability to effectively navigate the complexities of music distribution and marketing. Unlike major labels with their vast budgets and established networks, independent labels often employ creative and resourceful strategies to reach audiences and build sustainable businesses. This requires a deep understanding of the evolving digital landscape and a willingness to adapt and innovate.

One of the most significant changes in music distribution is the rise of digital platforms. While offering unprecedented reach, these platforms present a complex web of challenges. The sheer volume of music uploaded daily means that simply having a presence on Spotify or Apple Music isn't enough. Independent labels must employ strategic marketing to ensure their artists' music is heard above the noise. This requires a sophisticated understanding of platform algorithms, playlist curation, and targeted advertising. Many independent labels invest heavily in digital marketing, utilizing social media campaigns, targeted advertising on platforms like Facebook and Instagram, and email marketing to cultivate direct relationships with fans. This direct connection fosters loyalty and provides valuable feedback, allowing the label to refine its strategies and better understand its audience.

However, simply uploading music to streaming services isn't enough. Many successful independent labels are employing a multi-pronged distribution strategy. This involves utilizing multiple platforms, each catering to a different segment of the audience. For example, Bandcamp, with its focus on direct sales and fan engagement, allows for a higher revenue share for the artist and label compared to streaming services. This approach allows independent labels to cultivate a strong core fan base, generating revenue through direct sales while also building brand recognition on larger streaming platforms. Further diversifying their distribution, many independent labels also engage in physical releases – vinyl records, CDs, and cassettes. These physical formats cater to a specific niche market of music enthusiasts who appreciate the tangible nature of owning music. The limited edition and collector's appeal of these releases can generate significant revenue and enhance brand loyalty.

Beyond digital and physical distribution, many independent labels explore other avenues. Licensing their artists' music for film, television, and video games generates significant revenue and exposes their music to a wider audience. Sync licensing, in particular, has become increasingly important for independent labels, generating considerable income streams and expanding their reach beyond their core fanbase. Securing sync deals requires proactive networking, building relationships with music supervisors, and carefully tailoring their pitch to fit the specific requirements of each project.

The marketing tactics employed by independent labels are equally diverse and innovative. Social media marketing plays a pivotal role, with many labels employing a multiplatform strategy encompassing Facebook, Instagram, Twitter, TikTok, and other emerging platforms. This requires understanding the nuances of each platform and tailoring content to resonate with the specific audience on each. Many independent labels invest in high-quality visuals and engaging video content, knowing that visually appealing content is crucial in the attention-grabbing world of social media. They also actively engage with their online community, responding to comments, fostering discussions, and building a sense of community around their artists.

Public relations and press outreach remain critical aspects of marketing. Independent labels often collaborate with publicists or work directly with journalists and bloggers to secure media coverage. This might involve sending press kits, organizing interviews, and pitching stories to relevant media outlets. Securing features in blogs, magazines, and online publications can significantly increase the visibility of their artists and draw in new fans. Building relationships with music journalists and influencers is crucial, creating a network of supporters who can champion their artists' work.

A crucial element of the independent label's marketing approach is grassroots marketing. This often involves organizing live performances, creating merchandise, and engaging directly with fans at local events. Connecting with audiences on a personal level, fostering a sense of community, and building personal relationships between artist and fan is a key differentiator for independent labels. Organizing local shows, appearances at festivals, and actively participating in the community creates a strong connection with the fanbase. This intimate engagement fosters loyalty and builds a foundation for long-term success.

Another significant strategy is collaborative marketing. Independent labels often partner with other labels, artists, or businesses to cross-promote their work and reach new audiences. This might involve co-headlining tours, creating joint merchandise, or participating in collaborative marketing campaigns. Such partnerships can be extremely cost-effective, creating synergistic benefits for all parties involved.

Finally, many independent labels actively engage in email marketing. This direct method of communication allows them to build a targeted list of fans and directly share news, promotions, and upcoming events. Collecting email addresses through website sign-ups, social media, and live events builds a highly valuable contact list for direct marketing efforts. Effective email campaigns create a sense of personal engagement, reminding fans about new releases, upcoming gigs, and other initiatives.

Navigating the complexities of music distribution and marketing demands creativity, resourcefulness, and a deep understanding of the evolving digital landscape. Independent labels demonstrate a remarkable ability to adapt and innovate, often outpacing major labels in their agility and direct connection to fans. While challenges remain, the strategies employed by successful independent labels highlight the power of strategic thinking, targeted marketing, and a genuine commitment to building community and personal relationships with their artists and fans. Their success underscores the vital role of independent labels in fostering a diverse and vibrant music scene. The future of the music industry will likely continue to see a dynamic interplay between independent and major labels, each contributing unique strengths and perspectives to the everevolving world of music. The resilience and innovation of independent labels, however, ensures their continued presence as a significant force in shaping the future of music.

Success Stories of Independent Labels and Their Artists

The preceding discussion highlighted the strategic acumen required for independent labels to thrive in the competitive music landscape. Now, let's delve into the tangible successes of specific independent labels and the artists they've championed, showcasing the effectiveness of their innovative strategies. These examples demonstrate that bypassing the major label system isn't just a viable path, it can be a profoundly rewarding one, fostering artistic integrity and financial independence.

One compelling case study is that of Sub Pop Records, a label synonymous with the grunge movement of the 1990s. Initially bootstrapped with a small loan and a fervent DIY ethos, Sub Pop launched the careers of iconic bands like Nirvana, Soundgarden, and Pearl Jam. Their success wasn't simply a matter of luck; it was a carefully cultivated strategy rooted in fostering a strong sense of community and identifying raw talent before the major labels caught on. Sub Pop understood the power of underground networks and built relationships with key music journalists and college radio stations, ensuring their artists received vital exposure at a critical stage of their development. This grassroots approach, coupled with a keen ear for musical trends, enabled Sub Pop to not only discover groundbreaking artists but also to build a loyal fanbase that propelled their artists to international stardom. The label's commitment to artistic freedom also played a pivotal role, allowing artists to retain creative control and develop their unique styles without the constraints of major label interference. The financial success of Nirvana, in particular, showcased the immense potential of independent labels to compete with, and even surpass, the giants of the industry. The lesson learned from Sub Pop is clear: a strong sense of community, astute artist selection, and a commitment to artistic integrity can yield extraordinary results.

Another successful independent label, Matador Records, has similarly demonstrated the power of a carefully curated roster and a sophisticated understanding of music marketing. Matador, known for its eclectic mix of alternative and indie rock artists, has launched the careers of numerous critically acclaimed bands, including Pavement, Belle & Sebastian, and Interpol. Their success stems from their willingness to take risks on unconventional artists, often embracing those whose musical styles defied easy categorization. This commitment to artistic diversity has not only built a strong and recognizable brand identity but also attracted a fiercely loyal fanbase that appreciates the label's unique taste and commitment to quality. Matador's marketing strategies are equally noteworthy, often relying on clever word-of-mouth campaigns and collaborations with independent media outlets. They understood that building a devoted fanbase through targeted marketing and fostering a strong brand identity is crucial for longevity and success in the independent realm. They weren't simply chasing charttopping hits; they were cultivating a dedicated community of music lovers. Their success underscores the importance of maintaining artistic integrity and cultivating a strong brand identity in the ever-shifting music landscape.

Moving beyond the more established labels, let's consider the impact of smaller, newer independent labels. The rise of Bandcamp has provided a crucial platform for these smaller entities, allowing them to connect directly with their fans and retain a significantly larger share of the revenue generated from music sales. The success stories here often involve labels that focus on a specific genre or subgenre, building a niche community around a shared musical passion. This hyper-focus allows these labels to cultivate intimate relationships with both their artists and their fans. These labels often utilize social media and email marketing to connect directly with their audience, building a personal connection that fosters loyalty and supports repeat sales. They leverage the unique features of Bandcamp to host exclusive releases and interact directly with customers. This fosters a sense of community that's incredibly difficult for major labels to replicate, and it translates directly to financial success for the artists and the labels alike. The direct-to-fan model, facilitated by platforms like Bandcamp, proves that success in the independent music industry doesn't require mainstream saturation; it requires deep engagement with a highly-engaged audience.

The impact extends beyond financial success. Independent labels often provide artists with significantly more creative control than their major label counterparts. This autonomy allows for the creation of more authentic and personal music, resulting in a richer and more diverse music landscape. The stories of artists who have flourished under the guidance of these labels often emphasize the importance of this creative freedom. They describe an environment of collaboration and trust, where artistic vision takes precedence over commercial considerations. This allows for the nurturing of unique musical voices that might otherwise be lost or diluted in the homogenizing pressures of the mainstream music industry. Artists often cite the ability to retain ownership of their work and maintain a direct connection with their fans as crucial factors in their overall satisfaction and success.

Furthermore, the success of independent labels often directly contributes to a more vibrant and diverse musical ecosystem. By taking risks on artists who might be overlooked by major labels, these smaller labels contribute to a richer sonic tapestry, representing a broad range of styles and genres. This fosters a more creative and innovative music industry, preventing the stagnation that can occur when the industry is dominated by a few powerful entities. The willingness to take chances on unconventional artists and explore new sounds demonstrates a key difference between independent and major labels, highlighting the vital role these smaller operations play in maintaining the dynamic vibrancy of the music industry.

The examples provided only scratch the surface of the myriad success stories emerging from the independent music sector. The common thread throughout these narratives is a commitment to artistic integrity, innovative marketing strategies, and a genuine connection with artists and fans. These elements, combined with a willingness to adapt to the evolving digital landscape, are essential components of the success formula employed by independent labels. This isn't simply a matter of avoiding the pitfalls of major labels; it's a statement about building a sustainable and fulfilling career in the music industry based on artistic vision, fan connection, and entrepreneurial spirit. The future of the music industry undoubtedly lies in a dynamic interplay between major and independent labels, but the resilience and innovation showcased by independent labels and their artists promise a future where diverse voices can flourish, unburdened by the often-limiting constraints of mainstream pressures. The power of independent music isn't just a trend; it's a testament to the enduring value of creativity, authenticity, and direct engagement in an industry frequently consumed by commercial pressures. The ongoing success of these labels proves that a different path, one characterized by collaboration and artistic freedom, can indeed lead to sustained success and a more vibrant musical landscape.

Challenges Faced by Independent Labels in a Dominated Market

The preceding examples showcased the triumphs of independent labels, painting a picture of resourceful entrepreneurship and artistic freedom. However, this success story exists in stark contrast to the uphill battle many independent labels face daily. The music industry, despite its outward appearance of vibrancy and inclusivity, remains fundamentally structured to favor the major players. Independent labels constantly navigate a complex web of challenges that significantly limit their reach and potential for growth.

One of the most significant hurdles is access to capital. Major labels operate with vast financial resources, allowing them to invest heavily in artist development, marketing campaigns, and sophisticated distribution networks. Independent labels, often run by small teams with limited budgets, struggle to compete on this level. Securing funding, whether through loans, investors, or grants, is a constant struggle, often diverting energy and resources away from the core mission of artist development and creative output. The disparity in financial resources translates directly into limitations in marketing and promotion. Major labels can afford high-profile advertising campaigns, extensive radio play, and prominent placements in streaming services. Independent labels must rely on more creative, and often less effective, strategies, such as grassroots marketing, social media campaigns, and collaborations with smaller blogs and publications. This disparity in marketing power directly impacts an artist's ability to reach a wider audience, hindering their potential for commercial success.

Distribution is another significant obstacle. Major labels have established relationships with global distribution networks, ensuring their artists' music reaches listeners worldwide through a variety of channels—physical retailers, digital platforms, and streaming services. Independent labels often lack these established partnerships, forcing them to navigate a complex and often opaque distribution landscape. This can involve negotiating with multiple distributors, dealing with complex licensing agreements, and facing significant delays in getting music to market. The logistical complexities and financial burdens associated with distribution can significantly drain resources, leaving less available for artist development and other essential label functions. Furthermore, the sheer volume of music released daily means that getting noticed amidst the noise is a constant challenge for independent artists and their labels. The lack of resources and established relationships can significantly hamper an independent label's ability to effectively compete in the saturated marketplace.

Furthermore, the negotiation of favorable contracts presents a formidable challenge. Major labels often leverage their considerable bargaining power to secure highly advantageous deals, leaving artists with a smaller share of the profits. Independent labels, while striving for fairer contracts, often lack the legal expertise and negotiating strength to ensure that their artists receive a just compensation for their work. The lack of resources and bargaining power can often lead to exploitative contracts that disadvantage independent artists and limit their financial success. This often necessitates a deep understanding of contract law and business acumen, which might not be readily available to a team focused primarily on creative expression.

The dominance of major labels also extends to their influence over key industry stakeholders. Major labels wield substantial power over radio airplay, playlist curation, and media coverage, creating a system where artists signed to major labels are often given preferential treatment. This creates a bias that favors already established artists and entities, making it more difficult for independent artists to gain traction and receive meaningful exposure. The inherent power imbalance heavily favors large conglomerates, which are able to leverage their position to control the narrative and gatekeep opportunities. This creates a cyclical effect that reinforces the dominance of major labels and makes it even more challenging for independent labels to break through.

The ever-evolving technological landscape adds another layer of complexity. While technology has democratized music production and distribution, it also presents new challenges for independent labels. Understanding and adapting to changing platforms, formats, and technologies requires continuous investment in skills, infrastructure, and resources—all of which are costly and time-consuming. Staying ahead of the curve requires constant learning and adaptation, something that can be a significant strain for independent labels with limited budgets and staff. The costs associated with mastering, distributing and promoting music across a multitude of platforms can be prohibitive for those without significant financial resources.

Beyond the purely commercial challenges, independent labels face a crucial dilemma concerning artistic integrity. Major labels often exert significant control over an artist's creative output, prioritizing commercial viability over artistic expression. This can lead to creative compromises that dilute an artist's unique voice and vision. Independent labels, while frequently prioritizing artistic freedom, face the countervailing pressure to create commercially successful products to ensure the label's sustainability. This delicate balance requires skillful navigation and strategic decisionmaking, demanding a sophisticated understanding of both the artistic and commercial dimensions of the music industry.

Moreover, the lack of industry mentoring and support networks further compounds the challenges faced by independent labels. Major labels offer established systems of support, including access to experienced professionals in areas such as marketing, legal affairs, and finance. Independent labels often lack this support structure, forcing them to navigate the complexities of the music industry with limited guidance. This lack of mentorship can be particularly challenging for smaller, newer labels, leaving them vulnerable to making costly mistakes. Networking and community support are vital for navigating the industry, yet building these crucial networks requires both time and resources, which might be stretched thin for independent labels struggling to establish a firm foothold.

Finally, the constant pressure of competition creates a highstakes environment in which survival itself requires unwavering resilience. Navigating the competitive landscape necessitates a multifaceted approach encompassing shrewd marketing, deft negotiation, and an indefatigable work ethic. The need to generate constant new revenue streams, stay current with industry trends, and maintain a high level of creative output imposes immense demands on an alreadystretched team, demanding a level of commitment and versatility that's rarely seen in more established business sectors. The constant pressure to stay afloat, often without the safety nets afforded to large corporations, fosters a highstress environment demanding remarkable tenacity and passion.

In conclusion, while the success stories of independent labels are inspiring, they do not fully represent the totality of the challenges faced in a market dominated by major players. The financial disparities, distribution complexities, contract negotiations, industry influence, technological demands, artistic integrity concerns, mentorship gaps, and competitive pressures create an inherently challenging landscape. These challenges highlight the need for increased support systems, fairer industry practices, and a greater appreciation for the vital role independent labels play in fostering artistic diversity and innovation. The future of the music industry hinges upon a more balanced ecosystem, one that recognizes and supports the contributions of both major and independent labels, allowing for a truly vibrant and inclusive musical landscape to thrive.

The Future of Independent Labels and their Role in the Music Ecosystem

The preceding analysis highlighted the significant hurdles faced by independent labels in a music industry dominated by major players. However, the narrative is far from complete. The resilience and innovative spirit displayed by independent labels suggest a future brimming with potential, provided certain critical shifts occur within the industry's landscape. The survival and even flourishing of independent labels are not simply a matter of romantic idealism; their existence is crucial for the health and diversity of the music ecosystem. Their continued presence guarantees a space for artists seeking creative freedom and equitable partnerships, a space often squeezed out by the profit-driven mechanisms of major labels.

One of the most promising developments is the increasing accessibility of technology. While the initial investment in sophisticated recording equipment and mastering software might still present a barrier to entry, the cost has plummeted significantly in recent years. Digital distribution platforms, such as Bandcamp and DistroKid, have dramatically reduced the cost and complexity of getting music to listeners, bypassing the traditional gatekeepers controlled by major labels. This democratization of production and distribution empowers artists to maintain greater control over their creative work and financial compensation, potentially mitigating some of the exploitative practices prevalent in traditional label deals.

Furthermore, the rise of streaming services, while presenting its own set of challenges, has also created new opportunities for independent labels. While major labels often dominate the algorithms and playlists of these platforms, independent labels are finding ways to leverage social media marketing, targeted advertising, and direct engagement with fans to cultivate a loyal audience base. This direct-to-fan approach circumvents the need to rely on traditional media outlets, which are often influenced by major label interests. Successful independent labels are demonstrating the effectiveness of fostering authentic connections with listeners, building community around their artists, and cultivating long-term relationships that generate sustainable revenue.

This increased accessibility is not without its challenges. The sheer volume of music released daily means that cutting through the noise requires a savvy and multifaceted approach. Independent labels must not only produce highquality music but also actively engage in strategic marketing, social media outreach, and community building. This requires a level of resourcefulness, adaptability, and entrepreneurial spirit that is often overlooked in discussions of the industry's challenges. The key to success lies in the ability to build a strong brand identity, cultivate a loyal fan base, and create a sustainable business model that can withstand the constant pressures of a highly competitive environment.

Another crucial factor influencing the future of independent labels is the growing awareness among artists of the limitations of major label deals. Many artists, disillusioned by the restrictive contracts and limited creative control offered by major labels, are increasingly seeking out independent labels that offer greater artistic freedom and fairer financial terms. This shift in artist attitudes reflects a growing preference for collaboration over exploitation and autonomy over conformity. This trend is creating a strong demand for the services offered by independent labels, driving growth and encouraging innovation within the sector. As more artists recognize the value proposition of independent labels—creative freedom, equitable partnerships, and direct connection with fans—the sector's growth will only accelerate.

The legal landscape is also evolving to support independent labels. Increased scrutiny of exploitative contracts, coupled with a greater understanding of intellectual property rights, is fostering a climate of greater transparency and fairness within the industry. Organizations dedicated to supporting independent artists and labels are actively working to provide legal assistance and education, equipping independent labels with the knowledge and resources necessary to navigate complex contracts and protect their artists' rights. This trend towards greater legal support and awareness contributes to a more balanced playing field, giving independent labels a stronger bargaining position when negotiating with distributors, streaming services, and other industry stakeholders.

However, challenges remain. Access to capital continues to be a significant hurdle. While crowdfunding platforms and angel investors are becoming increasingly prevalent, securing sufficient funding to support artist development, marketing, and distribution remains a constant struggle. Independent labels often lack the financial resources of major labels, limiting their ability to compete on a global scale. Addressing this funding gap requires creative solutions, such as collaborative funding models, government grants for arts organizations, and the development of more sophisticated investor networks that are attuned to the needs of the independent music sector.

The continued growth of independent labels also hinges on the development of a robust support infrastructure. This includes mentoring programs, educational initiatives, and networking opportunities that connect independent labels with experienced professionals in areas such as legal affairs, marketing, finance, and technology. The creation of collaborative platforms that facilitate knowledge sharing and resource exchange can significantly reduce the costs and complexities of navigating the music industry, empowering independent labels to focus on their core mission: supporting artists and fostering creative expression.

Looking ahead, the future of independent music labels is intimately tied to the evolution of the music industry as a whole. The industry needs to move beyond its current, heavily centralized structure towards a more balanced ecosystem. This balanced system should foster collaboration between independent and major labels while providing opportunities for smaller players to thrive. A move towards more transparency, fairer contracts, and a greater understanding of the value of artistic diversity is vital. The continued success of independent labels is not merely a niche concern, but a fundamental requirement for a vibrant, diverse, and truly representative music industry. Their ability to champion artistic expression, foster fair partnerships, and nurture creativity represents a crucial counterbalance to the often-commercialized forces that shape the mainstream music scene. Ultimately, the future of music rests upon a landscape that allows both independent and major labels to flourish, creating an ecosystem where artistic merit and commercial success can coexist. The path forward necessitates a concerted effort from artists, labels, industry professionals, and policymakers alike, working collaboratively to create a more equitable, sustainable, and creatively rich musical landscape for generations to come.

Diversity and Inclusion in the Music Industry Addressing Systemic Inequalities

The preceding discussion focused on the challenges and triumphs of independent labels, highlighting their crucial role in maintaining a diverse and vibrant music ecosystem. However, even within this comparatively more equitable sphere, significant systemic inequalities persist, undermining the potential for genuine inclusivity. This section delves into the pervasive issues of diversity and inclusion within the broader music industry, examining how systemic biases and discriminatory practices actively hinder the representation and opportunities available to artists from marginalized communities.

The lack of diversity in the music industry is not merely a matter of aesthetics; it's a reflection of deep-seated structural inequalities that operate at every level, from the creation and distribution of music to the decision-making processes that shape the industry's overall direction. Consider the composition of major record labels' executive boards, A&R teams, and marketing departments. A consistent pattern emerges: a stark overrepresentation of white men, a demographic that does not reflect the diverse tapestry of musical talent and audiences globally. This lack of representation significantly impacts the types of music that are promoted, the artists who are signed, and the stories that are told through music.

The underrepresentation of women in leadership positions within the music industry is particularly glaring. While women make up a significant portion of the musicconsuming audience, their presence in executive roles and decision-making positions remains notably low. This disparity leads to a skewed perspective on what constitutes successful music, often prioritizing genres and styles that resonate with the dominant demographic rather than reflecting the broader spectrum of musical expression. The consequences are far-reaching, limiting opportunities for women artists to achieve mainstream success and perpetuating harmful stereotypes about their musical capabilities. The pervasive "glass ceiling" effects women at all levels, limiting their advancement and access to crucial resources.

The challenges faced by artists of color are similarly profound. Racial bias in the music industry manifests in numerous ways, from subtle microaggressions to overt discrimination. Artists of color often face difficulties securing fair record deals, gaining access to radio play, and achieving recognition from mainstream media outlets. Their unique musical styles and cultural perspectives are frequently overlooked or appropriated, their contributions minimized or marginalized. This systematic marginalization results in a homogenized musical landscape, failing to reflect the rich diversity of musical traditions that exist across different cultures and communities.

The impact of these systemic inequalities extends beyond simply limiting opportunities for individual artists. It shapes the overall cultural narrative, perpetuating stereotypes, and reinforcing harmful power dynamics. The dominance of a particular aesthetic and sonic preference within the mainstream music landscape often leads to the silencing of other voices and perspectives, hindering innovation and creativity. The industry's tendency to favor established norms over originality prevents the discovery and promotion of artists who offer unique and groundbreaking approaches to music-making.

Moreover, the financial implications of these systemic inequalities are significant. Artists from marginalized communities frequently receive lower pay, less promotional support, and fewer opportunities for career advancement compared to their counterparts from the dominant demographic. This disparity creates a system where financial success is disproportionately concentrated in the hands of a select few, perpetuating the existing power imbalance and creating a cycle of disadvantage for artists who lack the resources and support to overcome these systemic barriers.

Beyond the lack of representation in leadership and decisionmaking roles, systemic inequality operates through the very structures that govern the music industry. The gatekeeping mechanisms of traditional record labels, radio stations, and music festivals have historically favored certain genres and artists, while excluding others. These gatekeeping mechanisms are often unconsciously biased, reflecting the pre-existing prejudices and limited perspectives of those in positions of power. This bias is reinforced through the process of A&R (Artists and Repertoire), where decisions about which artists to sign and which music to promote are frequently made based on subjective assessments that inadvertently perpetuate existing power structures.

Furthermore, the issue of equitable payment is a crucial aspect of the fight for diversity and inclusion. The exploitation of artists, particularly those from marginalized communities, has been a longstanding problem in the music industry. Unfair contracts, restrictive clauses, and a lack of transparency in royalty payments are common practices that disproportionately affect artists who lack the resources and bargaining power to negotiate favorable terms. These practices perpetuate a system where artists are forced to accept unfavorable deals, sacrificing their creative autonomy and financial well-being.

Addressing these pervasive inequalities requires a multipronged approach. One crucial step is to foster greater diversity and representation within the leadership and decision-making structures of the music industry. This means actively recruiting and promoting individuals from marginalized communities to leadership positions, creating pathways for advancement, and implementing policies that ensure equitable representation. This commitment must be reflected at every level – from the executive suites of major record labels to the programming departments of radio stations and music festivals.

Furthermore, the industry needs to adopt more equitable contracting practices. Transparency and fairness should be paramount in all interactions between artists and record labels. Contracts should be clear, concise, and easily understandable, eliminating ambiguities that could be exploited to the detriment of artists. Independent organizations and legal support networks can play a crucial role in providing education and resources to artists, empowering them to negotiate more favorable terms.

Initiatives promoting mentorship and educational programs can help bridge the gap and provide support for artists from marginalized communities. These programs could focus on providing access to industry professionals, developing essential skills in areas like marketing, finance, and legal affairs, and creating networks of support among artists. By fostering a culture of collaboration and mutual support, these initiatives can create more equitable opportunities for all.

Finally, the industry needs to critically examine and address the underlying biases that permeate its processes and decision-making structures. This requires a commitment to self-reflection and a willingness to confront uncomfortable truths about the ways in which systemic biases shape the industry landscape. Initiatives promoting diversity and inclusion must be more than symbolic gestures; they must be grounded in concrete actions and meaningful change. Only through a concerted effort to dismantle these systemic inequalities can the music industry truly become a more inclusive and representative space for artists from all backgrounds and communities. The future of music hinges on its ability to embrace its diverse tapestry of voices and experiences, reflecting the rich and multifaceted cultural landscape from which it springs. Failing to do so not only limits the creative potential of the industry but also reinforces harmful social structures and deprives audiences of the wealth of talent that remains hidden due to systemic biases.

Gender Inequality and the Experiences of Women in Music

The pervasive lack of diversity discussed earlier extends acutely to gender, creating a landscape where women face systemic barriers to success and equitable treatment within the music industry. While women constitute a significant portion of music consumers, their presence in leadership roles and decision-making positions remains strikingly low. This imbalance isn't merely a matter of representation; it shapes the very fabric of the industry, influencing the types of music produced, promoted, and ultimately, consumed.

The "glass ceiling" effect is profoundly evident in the executive ranks of major record labels. A quick glance at the leadership teams reveals a stark reality: a disproportionate number of men occupy CEO, CFO, and A&R positions. This lack of female leadership translates to a dearth of female perspectives informing strategic decisions, influencing artist development, and shaping the overall direction of the industry. Without women at the table, the industry risks neglecting the unique needs and challenges faced by female artists, leading to systemic bias in contract negotiations, marketing strategies, and promotional opportunities. The consequences are far-reaching, stifling female talent and hindering the creation of a truly inclusive and representative music scene.

The underrepresentation extends beyond executive suites, permeating the creative and technical aspects of music production. Female producers, engineers, and songwriters often encounter subtle yet impactful forms of discrimination. Their contributions might be overlooked or undervalued, their expertise questioned or dismissed, and their voices marginalized in creative collaborations. This subtle yet insidious bias creates an environment where women find it challenging to establish themselves as industry leaders, limiting their growth, and preventing them from reaching their full potential.

Moreover, the challenges faced by female artists differ significantly from those of their male counterparts. The pressure to conform to specific beauty standards and societal expectations often overshadows their musical talent. Female artists may encounter gendered critiques, with their artistic merit frequently judged based on their appearance rather than their musical skills. This double standard contributes to a cycle of self-doubt and underperformance, hindering their ability to thrive in a hyper-competitive industry.

The issue of compensation further underscores the pervasive inequality. Studies have repeatedly shown that female artists, particularly those starting their careers, often earn less than their male counterparts for comparable work. This pay gap widens in genres dominated by male artists, where female musicians face added challenges in negotiating favorable contracts and securing fair royalties. The lack of transparency and standardization in royalty payments further exacerbates the problem, allowing for exploitation and silencing the voices of those who lack the resources or power to negotiate better terms.

The industry's promotional machinery often reinforces existing gender biases. Radio airplay, music video rotations, and media coverage disproportionately favor male artists, limiting the reach and exposure of female musicians. This bias in media representation perpetuates harmful stereotypes and limits the public's awareness of female talent, contributing to a self-fulfilling prophecy where women struggle to gain mainstream recognition.

The experiences of women in specific genres further highlight the complexity of gender inequality. For instance, in traditionally male-dominated genres like hip-hop and rock, female artists often encounter intense scrutiny and prejudice, their artistry often questioned or dismissed due to preconceived notions about their place within the genre. Even genres traditionally associated with women, such as pop, are not immune to gender bias, with female artists frequently facing pressure to conform to specific aesthetic standards or to prioritize commercial appeal over artistic integrity.

The legal landscape also poses significant challenges to female artists. Contracts are frequently complex and opaque, designed to favor the label's interests. Female artists, often lacking the financial resources and legal expertise to navigate these complicated agreements, may unknowingly sign unfavorable terms, limiting their earning potential and creative control. The absence of robust legal support systems and access to experienced legal counsel further exacerbates the problem, leaving female artists vulnerable to exploitation and unfair practices.

Beyond the individual experiences of women in the music industry, the broader societal implications of gender inequality are significant. The lack of female representation reinforces harmful stereotypes about women's roles in music, undermining their legitimacy and credibility. This has cascading effects, limiting opportunities for future generations of female musicians and perpetuating a cycle of underrepresentation.

Addressing gender inequality within the music industry requires a multifaceted strategy. One essential step is to increase female representation in leadership positions within record labels, publishing companies, booking agencies, and other key organizations. This requires proactive measures such as targeted recruitment initiatives, mentorship programs, and leadership development opportunities designed specifically for women.

Furthermore, the industry needs to adopt more transparent and equitable compensation practices. This includes establishing clear and standardized royalty structures, ensuring fair payment for all artists regardless of gender, and promoting transparency in contract negotiations. Greater access to legal support and educational resources can empower female artists to better understand and negotiate their contracts.

Improving media representation is also crucial. Radio stations, music publications, and other media outlets should actively promote female artists and challenge existing biases in their coverage. This includes highlighting female artists' achievements, challenging gender stereotypes, and providing balanced representation across different genres and styles.

Ultimately, overcoming gender inequality in the music industry demands a fundamental shift in mindset and culture. This requires a commitment from industry leaders, artists, and consumers to actively challenge discriminatory practices, foster inclusivity, and create a more equitable and just space for female musicians to thrive. This is not simply a matter of fairness; it's a matter of recognizing and celebrating the incredible talent and contribution of women to the rich tapestry of music. Only through concerted effort can we dismantle the systemic barriers that prevent women from realizing their full potential within the music industry and ensure that future generations have the opportunity to thrive on their merits alone.

Racial Disparities and the Underrepresentation of Artists of Color

The systemic inequalities discussed thus far, while deeply concerning in their own right, represent only a portion of the larger picture of injustice within the music industry. The pervasive lack of diversity extends, with even greater intensity, to race. Artists of color, particularly Black and Latinx artists, face a complex web of systemic barriers that significantly hinder their ability to achieve equitable success compared to their white counterparts. This isn't merely a matter of unequal representation; it's a reflection of deepseated racism that permeates every level of the industry, from songwriting and production to distribution and marketing.

The disproportionate representation of white artists in mainstream success is starkly evident. One only needs to examine the Billboard charts, award show nominations, and radio airplay to observe the overwhelming dominance of white artists, particularly in genres perceived as commercially viable. This isn't coincidental; it's the result of a system that consistently prioritizes, promotes, and profits from the music of white artists while simultaneously marginalizing the talent and contributions of artists of color.

A significant aspect of this marginalization involves the historical and ongoing exploitation of Black musical styles. Genres like blues, jazz, rock and roll, hip-hop, and R&B – all born from the creative genius of Black artists – have consistently been appropriated and commodified by the music industry, with white artists often reaping the lion's share of financial rewards and mainstream recognition. The stories of Black musicians whose innovations and creativity formed the foundation of these genres, yet who were denied proper compensation and credit, are numerous and tragically familiar. This history of appropriation fuels a cycle of systemic inequality that continues to disadvantage Black artists today.

The power dynamics within the industry itself exacerbate these issues. A significant lack of diversity within the executive suites of major record labels, publishing houses, and talent agencies perpetuates biased decision-making processes. The dearth of Black and Brown executives and A&R representatives means that the perspectives, experiences, and musical styles of artists of color are often overlooked or undervalued. Decisions regarding which artists to sign, which songs to promote, and how to market music are made overwhelmingly by individuals who may not fully understand or appreciate the cultural nuances and artistic merit of music created by artists of color. This lack of representation translates to fewer opportunities for artists of color to be discovered, developed, and given the platform they deserve.

Furthermore, artists of color often face significantly more obstacles in securing funding and investment. Access to capital is crucial for artists to record music, produce videos, and tour, yet many artists of color lack the networks and resources to secure adequate financial backing. Venture capitalists, investors, and angel investors frequently show a bias towards artists who align with their own demographics and cultural understanding, inadvertently perpetuating cycles of underinvestment in artists of color.

The marketing and promotional strategies employed by the music industry also contribute significantly to racial disparities. The imagery, messaging, and target demographics used in marketing campaigns often reinforce existing stereotypes and limit the visibility of artists of color. Radio airplay, music video rotations, and media coverage still disproportionately favor white artists, perpetuating the cycle of underrepresentation and limiting the reach and exposure of artists of color. This bias in media representation subtly, yet powerfully, shapes listener perceptions and influences the popularity and success of artists across racial lines.

Beyond these structural issues, individual artists of color frequently encounter microaggressions and overt racism within the industry. These can range from subtle biases in feedback and creative direction to outright discrimination and exclusion. Many artists of color report experiences of having their musical talent questioned or dismissed, their contributions minimized, and their ideas ignored or stolen. This creates a hostile and unwelcoming environment that discourages creativity, undermines confidence, and ultimately limits artistic expression.

The legal landscape also presents significant challenges for artists of color. Complex and often unfair contracts, coupled with a lack of access to quality legal representation, leave many artists vulnerable to exploitation. The bargaining power between established record labels and emerging artists, particularly artists of color who may lack the resources and connections to negotiate effectively, is dramatically uneven. This disparity in power contributes to contracts that often favor the label's interests, leaving artists with limited financial gain and creative control.

The consequences of these systemic inequalities are profound. The underrepresentation of artists of color not only limits their individual opportunities but also diminishes the diversity and richness of the music landscape. By perpetuating a system that favors certain demographics, the industry loses out on the vast spectrum of creativity, innovation, and cultural expression that artists of color could bring.

Addressing racial disparities in the music industry demands a multifaceted and sustained effort. Increased diversity in leadership positions within record labels, publishing houses, and talent agencies is crucial. This requires intentional recruitment practices, mentorship programs, and a commitment to fostering inclusive workplaces where artists of color feel valued and supported.

Moreover, greater transparency and accountability in contract negotiations are essential. The industry needs to move away from opaque and exploitative practices that disadvantage artists of color and move toward fair and equitable compensation models.

Beyond organizational changes, fostering greater access to funding and investment opportunities for artists of color is critical. Initiatives to support Black-owned record labels, publishing companies, and management firms could help level the playing field and provide a pathway to success for artists who may face barriers in gaining access to traditional channels of funding.

The media also has a vital role to play. Radio stations, music publications, and other media outlets need to actively challenge existing biases in their coverage, ensuring equitable representation of artists of color across genres and styles. High-profile media outlets must be actively committed to amplifying the voices and stories of artists of color, not simply as a symbolic gesture but as a genuine effort to create a more inclusive and equitable landscape.

Furthermore, education and awareness campaigns targeting industry professionals, artists, and consumers can play a significant role in promoting cultural sensitivity and combating prejudice. Open dialogue and critical selfreflection are crucial for addressing the deep-seated biases that permeate the industry. A commitment to fostering a culture of empathy and understanding will create an atmosphere where artists of color feel supported, respected, and empowered.

Ultimately, overcoming racial disparities in the music industry requires a fundamental shift in mindset and culture. It's not enough to simply address individual instances of discrimination; the industry needs to actively dismantle the systemic barriers that perpetuate racial inequality. This requires a collective commitment from industry leaders, artists, and consumers alike to create a more just and equitable music industry where artists of color can thrive and achieve their full potential. This is not just a matter of social justice; it's a matter of recognizing and celebrating the crucial contributions of artists of color to the rich tapestry of global music. The future of music hinges on the industry's capacity for genuine and meaningful change, moving beyond superficial gestures towards transformative action. Only then can the industry genuinely reflect the vibrant diversity of its listeners and truly realize its potential for global artistic expression.

LGBTQ Representation and Issues of Discrimination

The fight for equality within the music industry, as we've seen, extends far beyond racial disparities. A significant and often overlooked aspect of this struggle centers on the experiences of LGBTQ+ artists and professionals. While the industry often projects an image of flamboyant selfexpression, a closer examination reveals a stark reality: pervasive discrimination and systemic barriers that significantly hinder the success and well-being of LGBTQ+ individuals.

The challenges faced by LGBTQ+ artists often begin long before they step into a recording studio. Many LGBTQ+ youth, particularly those from marginalized communities, lack access to the same resources and opportunities that their heterosexual counterparts enjoy. This includes access to music education, mentorship, and networking opportunities crucial for launching a music career. The lack of visible LGBTQ+ role models can further compound this issue, leading to a sense of isolation and discouragement that prevents many talented individuals from pursuing their musical dreams.

Even when LGBTQ+ artists manage to gain a foothold in the industry, they often face subtle and overt forms of discrimination that can significantly impact their career trajectories. Microaggressions, such as being misgendered, facing homophobic jokes, or being excluded from conversations about personal lives, create a hostile and unwelcoming environment. These seemingly minor instances of discrimination, when compounded over time, can have a significant cumulative effect on an artist's mental health and professional success. The pressure to conform to heteronormative standards, often implicitly enforced through marketing and publicity strategies, can also lead LGBTQ+ artists to suppress aspects of their identities, limiting their artistic expression and authenticity.

The issue of visibility is critically important. Many LGBTQ+ artists find themselves navigating a complex decision: whether to openly embrace their identity or to remain closeted for fear of jeopardizing their careers. The fear of backlash from conservative audiences, radio programmers, or industry executives can lead artists to conceal their sexual orientation or gender identity, resulting in a lack of authentic representation in mainstream music. This creates a vicious cycle; without sufficient visible LGBTQ+ artists, the industry reinforces the idea that LGBTQ+ identities are not commercially viable or palatable to a broader audience.

The marketing and promotion of LGBTQ+ artists often reflect this underlying bias. Marketing campaigns frequently avoid overt representations of LGBTQ+ identities, fearing that it will alienate portions of their target audience. This can translate into a lack of visibility and recognition for LGBTQ+ artists, as their music and images are less likely to be featured in prominent media outlets or on major streaming platforms. The algorithms that govern these platforms, often designed without considering the needs and interests of LGBTQ+ communities, further contribute to this marginalization.

Beyond the challenges faced by artists, LGBTQ+ professionals working behind the scenes in the music industry also encounter significant hurdles. A lack of diversity within record labels, publishing houses, and talent agencies perpetuates a climate of exclusion and inequality. The scarcity of LGBTQ+ executives and decision-makers leads to a lack of understanding and empathy towards the needs and concerns of LGBTQ+ artists and employees. This can translate into biased decision-making processes, affecting opportunities for signing, promotion, and creative input.

The legal landscape also presents unique challenges for LGBTQ+ artists and professionals. Issues like fair compensation, equitable contract negotiations, and access to legal representation are all significantly impacted by the existing power imbalances. Many LGBTQ+ artists, especially those from marginalized communities, lack the resources and networks to navigate complex legal matters, leaving them vulnerable to exploitation and unfair treatment.

Moreover, the music industry's historical association with certain harmful stereotypes and tropes regarding LGBTQ+ individuals further exacerbates the problem. The industry's reliance on problematic caricatures of queer identity frequently reinforces harmful stereotypes, limiting opportunities and creating a climate of fear and uncertainty. This can manifest in discriminatory casting choices for music videos, problematic lyrics, or even simply in a general lack of sensitivity and understanding towards LGBTQ+ experiences.

The consequences of these systemic inequalities are farreaching. The lack of LGBTQ+ representation in the music industry not only limits the opportunities for individual artists and professionals, but also impoverishes the artistic landscape as a whole. By excluding a vibrant and diverse community of artists, the industry loses out on a rich tapestry of unique perspectives, creative expressions, and cultural contributions. The stories of LGBTQ+ artists, their struggles, and their triumphs offer essential insights into the human experience, yet these stories are too often left untold or relegated to the margins.

Addressing these issues requires a multifaceted approach. Firstly, greater representation in leadership positions within the music industry is crucial. Intentional recruitment practices, mentorship programs, and a commitment to fostering inclusive workplaces are essential steps toward creating an environment where LGBTQ+ artists and professionals feel safe, valued, and empowered. This includes actively seeking out and promoting the work of LGBTQ+ artists, not just as a token gesture, but as a genuine effort to showcase the full range of talent and creativity within the community.

Secondly, transparent and equitable contract negotiations are vital. Artists need access to qualified legal representation and resources that allow them to fully understand and negotiate favorable contracts. This requires a shift in power dynamics, fostering a more collaborative and respectful relationship between artists and industry professionals. Independent labels and alternative distribution models can also provide avenues for LGBTQ+ artists to circumvent the exploitative practices of major labels.

Thirdly, the media plays a crucial role in challenging harmful stereotypes and promoting greater inclusivity. Radio stations, music publications, and streaming platforms need to actively work towards equitable representation of LGBTQ+ artists, ensuring that their music and stories are given the same visibility and attention as those of their heterosexual counterparts. This includes actively supporting LGBTQ+ artists and challenging the ingrained biases in their own selection processes.

Finally, fostering a culture of allyship and understanding is essential. Open dialogue, education, and awareness campaigns can contribute significantly to promoting greater sensitivity and inclusivity within the industry. Industry professionals, artists, and consumers alike have a responsibility to challenge homophobic and transphobic attitudes and behaviors, creating an environment where LGBTQ+ individuals feel safe to express themselves authentically.

The future of music depends on the industry's willingness to confront its history of exclusion and discrimination, embracing its diversity as a source of strength and innovation. Only by actively dismantling systemic barriers and creating an inclusive environment can the music industry truly reflect the diverse voices and experiences of its global community, showcasing the full spectrum of human experience through music. The journey towards equality is a continuous process, demanding ongoing commitment, vigilance, and a fundamental shift in the industry's cultural landscape. It's a fight for not only social justice, but also for the preservation and enrichment of music itself.

Advocacy Groups and Initiatives Promoting Social Justice in Music

The fight for a more equitable and just music industry isn't solely fought on the front lines of individual artists' struggles. A crucial, and often overlooked, element of this ongoing battle is the tireless work of advocacy groups and initiatives dedicated to promoting social justice and equity within the industry's complex ecosystem. These organizations operate on various fronts, tackling systemic issues from unequal pay and representation to combating harmful stereotypes and fostering inclusive practices. Their impact, though often understated, is profoundly shaping the landscape of the music world, pushing for a more representative and equitable future.

One prominent example is the Recording Academy's efforts, while often criticized for inconsistencies and a lack of transparency in their awards process, to address diversity and inclusion. Their initiatives, while sometimes falling short of their stated goals, represent a significant attempt by a major industry player to acknowledge and address these crucial issues. Their programs aimed at supporting emerging artists from underrepresented groups, for instance, provide crucial funding, mentorship, and networking opportunities that can significantly impact the trajectory of early careers. However, true impact hinges on meaningful accountability and demonstrable results – a consistent challenge for such large organizations. The need for transparency in their selection processes, as well as a more rigorous evaluation of the longterm impact of their programs, remains a critical area of concern and potential improvement.

Beyond the Recording Academy, numerous non-profit organizations are actively working to amplify marginalized voices and challenge systemic inequalities. Organizations like the Black Music Coalition, for instance, actively advocate for Black artists and professionals within the industry, pushing for greater representation in leadership roles and demanding accountability regarding fair compensation and creative control. Their work includes lobbying efforts, public awareness campaigns, and direct support for Black artists facing exploitation or discrimination. They also play a vital role in fostering community among Black musicians and professionals, providing a network of support and shared experiences in an industry that can often feel isolating and unwelcoming. Their success often lies in their grassroots approach, building powerful coalitions and raising awareness within the wider community, thus pressuring the industry to change from both the inside and the outside.

Similarly, organizations focused on LGBTQ+ rights within the music industry are actively working to combat discrimination and promote inclusivity. These groups provide crucial legal and advocacy support for artists and professionals facing harassment or unfair treatment, and also champion greater visibility and representation for LGBTQ+ artists in mainstream media. They often work closely with other social justice organizations, recognizing the intersectional nature of discrimination and the importance of coalition building. Challenges often include securing funding, navigating complex legal processes, and challenging deeply entrenched biases within a system reluctant to change. However, their persistent efforts to push for inclusive language in contracts, to challenge harmful stereotypes, and to ensure equitable access to opportunities represent crucial steps in transforming the industry.

The fight for fair compensation for artists is another key area of focus for many advocacy groups. The historical power imbalance between artists and record labels has resulted in exploitative contracts and a lack of transparency in royalty payments. Numerous groups are working to challenge these imbalances, advocating for fairer compensation models and greater transparency in how artists are compensated for their work. This involves not only legal challenges to existing contract structures but also campaigns aimed at raising public awareness of the widespread nature of artist exploitation. Some are developing alternative distribution models that allow artists greater control over their own music and earnings, bypassing the traditional gatekeepers of the music industry. This movement represents a significant challenge to the established power structures, demanding a fundamental shift in the industry's business model.

Moreover, the focus extends beyond direct financial compensation to include other forms of equity. Many groups are working to ensure greater representation of women and artists from marginalized communities within all aspects of the music industry – from songwriting and production to marketing and executive leadership. These initiatives involve mentoring programs, workshops, and networking opportunities designed to empower underrepresented groups and provide them with the tools and connections necessary to succeed in a historically biased environment. The success of these initiatives is often measured in the number of women and underrepresented groups gaining leadership positions, the rise in representation on record labels, and the increasing visibility of artists from various backgrounds in mainstream media.

A significant challenge faced by many of these advocacy groups is securing sufficient funding to sustain their operations and expand their impact. While some receive grants from foundations or government agencies, others rely heavily on individual donations and fundraising events. This often leads to limited resources and a constant struggle to maintain effective operations and reach a wider audience. The financial dependence on external sources can also limit their ability to be truly independent and to challenge powerful vested interests within the music industry. This highlights the ongoing need for more robust financial support for social justice initiatives in the music industry.

Finally, there is a growing recognition of the interconnectedness of social justice issues within the music industry. Many advocacy groups are working collaboratively to address multiple forms of discrimination and inequality simultaneously. This collaborative approach recognizes that systemic injustices often overlap and intersect, and that a holistic approach is necessary to achieve lasting change. By working together, these groups are creating a stronger and more effective force for change, leveraging their collective resources and expertise to address the industry's most pressing challenges. The future of equitable representation in music will likely depend not only on the continued advocacy of these groups, but also on the degree of collaboration and engagement from all stakeholders involved in the music industry. The road ahead remains a long and arduous one, but the collective efforts of these dedicated advocates are making a tangible and increasingly necessary impact on the world of music.

The Power of Music Criticism and its Impact on Artists Careers

The influence of music critics extends far beyond simple reviews; it shapes the very trajectory of an artist's career, acting as a powerful gatekeeper to both critical acclaim and commercial success. Their words, published in influential publications or broadcast on respected radio shows, can launch a previously unknown artist into the stratosphere or, conversely, condemn a seasoned performer to relative obscurity. This power stems from the perceived authority and expertise of critics, often cultivated over years of experience and a demonstrated understanding of musical history and theory. Readers and listeners alike often look to these figures as trusted guides in the vast and often overwhelming landscape of contemporary music.

This trust, however, is not without its complexities. The very notion of objective criticism is inherently debatable. A critic's personal tastes, their musical background, and even their subconscious biases inevitably seep into their judgments. What one critic hails as a masterpiece, another might dismiss as derivative or uninspired. This subjectivity, while a source of lively debate among music aficionados, also highlights the potential for critical misjudgments and the inherent limitations of any single perspective. The impact of a negative review, particularly from a high-profile critic, can be devastating for an artist, potentially stifling their career before it truly begins.

The power dynamics between critics and artists are further complicated by the commercial interests at play.

Major record labels and publicists often cultivate relationships with influential critics, sometimes subtly influencing their opinions through privileged access to artists, early releases, and exclusive interviews. While this doesn't always equate to outright bribery, the potential for unconscious bias and the subtle manipulation of narrative is undeniable. This symbiotic relationship, while sometimes beneficial for both parties, raises ethical concerns about transparency and the potential for conflicts of interest. The line between legitimate journalistic practice and promotional activity can become frustratingly blurred.

Furthermore, the accessibility and reach of music criticism have been dramatically altered by the rise of the internet and social media. While traditional print and broadcast media retain significant influence, online platforms have democratized the critical landscape. Anyone with an internet connection can now express their opinions, offering reviews and commentary on music platforms like YouTube, Spotify, and blogs. This accessibility has both positive and negative consequences. On the one hand, it empowers a far wider range of voices, allowing independent artists and lesserknown musical genres to garner attention. On the other hand, the absence of editorial oversight and the proliferation of unsubstantiated claims raise concerns about the validity and reliability of online criticism. The flood of opinions, often lacking nuance or critical rigor, can make it difficult for artists to discern genuine critical feedback from the noise.

The changing nature of music consumption also impacts the influence of music critics. Streaming services, for instance, offer personalized recommendations based on individual listening habits, often circumventing traditional gatekeepers. While critics still hold sway over a significant segment of the audience, their influence is arguably less decisive than it once was. The dominance of streaming playlists and algorithmic curation has created a new landscape where viral success can often eclipse critical acclaim. A song can become a global phenomenon based solely on its popularity on TikTok or other social media platforms, regardless of what established critics think. This shifts the power balance, diminishing the gatekeeping role of critics, and placing greater emphasis on viral trends and audience engagement.

Moreover, the increasing diversity of musical genres and subgenres adds another layer of complexity. A critic specializing in classical music may lack the expertise to provide a meaningful critique of experimental hip-hop, and vice versa. This specialization, while necessary for in-depth critical analysis, limits the scope of individual critics and can inadvertently marginalize certain genres or artists. The dominance of certain musical styles in major media outlets can create an echo chamber effect, amplifying certain voices and silencing others. This bias in representation has contributed to the marginalization of many musical genres and artists who struggle to gain critical traction in the mainstream media. This highlights the ongoing need for greater diversity and inclusivity within the world of music criticism.

The intersection of commercial success and critical acclaim remains a complex and fascinating topic. Many artists achieve widespread commercial success without receiving significant critical praise, while others achieve critical acclaim without achieving comparable commercial success. This disparity highlights the tension between artistic merit and audience preference, emphasizing the disconnect that can exist between critical judgment and popular reception. The commercial drivers of the music industry frequently prioritize immediate sales and chart performance over artistic integrity, leading to a focus on trends and catchy melodies that can sometimes overshadow critical considerations of musicality and originality.

The role of music criticism in shaping public perception and influencing commercial success is undeniable. It's a powerful force that can make or break an artist's career. Yet, this power is often wielded subtly, through careful word choices, perceived authority, and carefully curated narratives. The complexities of this power dynamic, further complicated by commercial interests, the rise of social media, and the changing consumption patterns of music, necessitates a critical examination of the ethical responsibilities of music critics and the role they play in the ever-evolving landscape of the music industry. The future of music criticism likely lies in a balanced approach, recognizing the limitations of subjective opinions while still providing insightful and thought-provoking commentary that enriches the experience of listening to music. The pursuit of diversity, inclusion, and transparency within the critical community will be critical in ensuring a more equitable and representative representation of the vast and ever-expanding world of music.

The debate about the objectivity of music criticism is an ongoing one, and rightly so. The very act of evaluating art is inherently subjective, a reflection of the critic's individual experiences, background, and understanding of the musical landscape. While some critics strive for an objective stance, completely devoid of personal bias, it's a nearly impossible task. Their analyses, no matter how rigorously reasoned, are still interpretations colored by their personal lens. The challenge, therefore, lies not in achieving unattainable objectivity, but in acknowledging and addressing this inherent subjectivity, providing context for their assessments, and promoting transparency in their critical approaches. A critical review should not simply pronounce judgment, but offer a nuanced explanation for that judgment, enabling readers to engage with the critique in a more informed and comprehensive manner.

Furthermore, the impact of a critical review, positive or negative, can vary significantly depending on the context and the standing of the critic. A glowing review in a prestigious publication carries much more weight than a similar review from a less established source. This unequal distribution of influence highlights the inherent power imbalance within the critical landscape, reinforcing the need for greater diversity and representation in the critical establishment. The voices of marginalized communities, often excluded from mainstream publications, must be amplified to provide a richer and more comprehensive picture of the global musical tapestry. By broadening the range of voices, we can counter the biases inherent in established critical structures and ensure a more equitable critical landscape.

The interaction between critics, artists, and the industry is not always straightforward. Some artists seek critical validation, actively courting positive reviews to boost their credibility and commercial prospects. Others, particularly those with established fan bases, may be less concerned with mainstream critical reception, focusing instead on their own artistic vision and direct engagement with their audiences. This difference in approach underscores the diversity of motivations within the music industry and the varied ways in which artists navigate the landscape of critical discourse. The symbiotic relationship between artists and critics is fluid and dynamic, shaped by factors as diverse as personal ambition, artistic vision, and the ever-shifting currents of public opinion.

The digital revolution has also profoundly affected the dissemination and consumption of music criticism. While traditional media outlets still hold significant influence, the rise of online platforms and social media has created a more fragmented and decentralized landscape. This has democratized access to criticism, allowing a wider range of voices to contribute to the discourse, but it has also created new challenges in evaluating the credibility and reliability of online reviews. The ease with which anyone can publish their opinions online can lead to a flood of poorly informed, biased, or even malicious criticisms, making it challenging for artists to discern genuine feedback from noise. The challenge, therefore, lies in developing strategies for navigating this chaotic digital landscape, identifying reliable critical sources, and creating more robust mechanisms for evaluating the quality and integrity of online reviews.

In conclusion, the power of music criticism, though evolving and contested, remains a significant force in shaping the careers of musicians. Understanding its intricacies, acknowledging its inherent biases, and navigating its shifting landscape is crucial for both artists and those seeking to understand the dynamics of the music industry. The future of music criticism lies in embracing diversity, enhancing transparency, and fostering a more inclusive and critically engaging discourse around music. Only then can we move towards a more equitable system where all voices are heard and judged fairly, fostering a richer, more representative, and truly global musical experience.

The Responsibility of Music Journalists in Promoting Ethical Practices

The previous sections explored the considerable influence wielded by music critics and the inherent complexities of their role. However, the ethical responsibilities extend beyond the realm of critical analysis to encompass the broader landscape of music journalism. Music journalists, in their capacity as reporters, investigators, and commentators, possess a unique opportunity—and an undeniable responsibility—to promote ethical practices within the industry. This involves more than simply reporting on industry news; it requires actively holding powerful figures accountable, advocating for artists' rights, and fostering a culture of transparency and fairness.

One crucial aspect of this responsibility lies in investigative journalism. The music industry, with its lucrative deals and intricate power dynamics, is susceptible to various forms of corruption and exploitation. Journalists equipped with investigative skills can uncover and expose these practices, shedding light on exploitative contracts, unfair royalty payments, and the silencing of artists who speak out against systemic abuses. This requires a commitment to rigorous fact-checking, meticulous research, and a willingness to challenge established narratives. Examples abound of artists who have been unfairly treated, their rights violated, and their voices suppressed by powerful industry players. Thorough investigations, supported by evidence and corroborated testimonies, can help bring these injustices to light, fostering public awareness and prompting necessary reform. The depth of this investigative work is paramount; superficial reporting might scratch the surface, but only a painstaking examination can expose the entrenched systems of exploitation.

Furthermore, music journalists have a responsibility to advocate for artists' rights. This includes highlighting issues such as fair compensation, creative control, and equitable representation within the industry. Artists, particularly those starting out, often lack the resources or legal expertise to navigate the complexities of contract negotiations or to challenge powerful industry figures. Journalists can play a crucial role by providing a platform for artists' voices, educating them about their rights, and amplifying their concerns to a wider audience. This could involve in-depth reports on industry standards, analyses of model contracts, and profiles of artists who have successfully fought for fair treatment. The power of storytelling is invaluable here; by humanizing the experiences of artists who have faced exploitation, journalists can engage readers emotionally and foster a sense of empathy and support for their cause. This goes beyond simply reporting on individual cases; it entails building a broader narrative of systematic challenges faced by many artists.

The role of music journalists in promoting transparency is equally crucial. The music industry thrives on carefully constructed images and carefully managed narratives. However, a commitment to transparency requires challenging these narratives, digging beneath the surface, and revealing the complexities of power dynamics and financial transactions. This necessitates critical engagement with press releases and promotional materials, questioning the claims made by industry figures, and seeking out alternative perspectives. A truly transparent industry fosters informed decision-making, empowering both artists and consumers. This also implies critically analyzing the use of promotional material, noting where facts might be stretched or where a biased approach to representation is being employed. The journalist's role extends to exposing these machinations and offering a counter-narrative grounded in facts and verifiable information. This commitment to truth is fundamental to building trust with readers and holding the industry accountable.

Another key ethical responsibility involves ensuring fairness and balance in reporting. The temptation to prioritize sensationalism or to align with particular industry players must be resisted. Journalists must strive to present all sides of a story, providing a platform for diverse viewpoints and ensuring that all voices are heard, especially those that might be marginalized or silenced. This requires a commitment to thorough research, an awareness of potential biases, and a willingness to challenge one's own perspectives. The inherent subjectivity of music criticism, explored earlier, must be acknowledged and addressed in the broader journalistic endeavor. Objectivity might be an elusive ideal, but striving for fairness and impartiality remains a crucial ethical obligation. This entails consciously combating personal biases and actively seeking diverse perspectives from individuals whose viewpoints might differ.

The digital age has added further complexity to the ethical landscape of music journalism. The proliferation of online platforms has democratized the dissemination of information, allowing a wider range of voices to be heard. However, it has also created challenges in terms of verifying information, combating misinformation, and ensuring that ethical standards are upheld across all platforms. Music journalists must be particularly vigilant in navigating this digital landscape, employing effective fact-checking techniques, and critically evaluating the sources of information. The rapid spread of unsubstantiated claims and biased reporting online underscores the increased responsibility for journalists to adhere to stringent ethical standards and provide readers with accurate and reliable information. Moreover, responsible reporting needs to consider the impact of algorithms, which can amplify certain narratives and marginalize others, reinforcing the need for conscious effort to ensure fair representation across all platforms.

Furthermore, the ethical responsibility of music journalists extends to addressing issues of diversity and inclusion within the industry. The music industry, like many others, has a history of systemic biases that have marginalized certain artists and genres. Journalists can play a crucial role in challenging these biases by providing coverage of underrepresented artists and genres, advocating for greater diversity in programming, and highlighting the systemic issues that perpetuate inequalities. This involves actively seeking out stories from marginalized communities, ensuring fair representation in the reporting of music news and providing a platform for voices that are often unheard. The role extends to promoting discussions on issues of race, gender, sexual orientation, and disability within the music industry, holding industry players accountable for their lack of inclusivity, and advocating for more equitable practices.

Finally, music journalists also have a responsibility to foster a culture of critical engagement with music itself. This means moving beyond simple reviews and offering insightful commentary that encourages deeper listening, sparks critical dialogue, and enriches the listener's experience. This type of critical engagement goes beyond assessing the technical aspects of music to address the cultural, social, and political contexts in which it is produced and consumed. It acknowledges the subjective nature of musical taste while encouraging a nuanced and informed understanding of music's power to shape our worldviews. By providing in-depth analysis, thoughtfully exploring various critical perspectives, and connecting music to broader cultural conversations, journalists can foster a more engaged and appreciative audience. This includes encouraging a culture of constructive dialogue, where opinions are expressed respectfully and where readers are encouraged to engage in critical thinking.

In conclusion, the responsibility of music journalists in promoting ethical practices within the music industry is multifaceted and demanding. It requires a commitment to investigative journalism, a dedication to advocating for artists' rights, a relentless pursuit of transparency, a dedication to fairness and balance in reporting, and a mindful navigation of the complexities of the digital age. Through their work, music journalists can hold powerful figures accountable, amplify the voices of marginalized artists, and foster a culture of ethical engagement with music itself. The pursuit of these ideals is essential not only for the health and integrity of the music industry but also for the benefit of artists, listeners, and society at large. The ethical frameworks discussed above are not just aspirational goals but essential components of a thriving and equitable music world. Failure to uphold these standards will only perpetuate the imbalances and exploitative practices that have plagued the industry for too long. The future of music journalism lies in its commitment to these principles, ensuring a more just and representative landscape for all.

Bias and Subjectivity in Music Reviews and Their Implications

The seemingly innocuous act of writing a music review carries with it a weight far exceeding the length of the piece itself. While ostensibly a subjective appraisal of artistic merit, the review holds the power to shape public perception, influence sales, and even determine an artist's career trajectory. This power, however, is often wielded without sufficient awareness of the inherent biases and subjective filters through which the critic's judgment is formed. The consequences can be profound, particularly for emerging artists whose careers are still fragile and dependent on critical acclaim. A scathing review, even if poorly reasoned or fueled by personal prejudice, can significantly damage an artist's prospects, while a glowing review, irrespective of its accuracy, can propel them to unexpected heights.

The subjectivity inherent in evaluating music is undeniable. Musical taste is, after all, deeply personal and shaped by a complex interplay of cultural background, personal experiences, and individual preferences. What one listener finds profoundly moving, another may find utterly banal. This fundamental subjectivity isn't inherently problematic; music criticism thrives on diverse interpretations and perspectives. However, the problem arises when subjectivity masks itself as objectivity, when personal preferences are presented as universally applicable truths, or when unconscious biases skew the critical assessment.

One common source of bias stems from the critic's own musical background and affiliations. A critic heavily invested in a particular genre, for instance, may unconsciously favor artists within that genre, while dismissing those outside it. This can manifest as overly generous assessments of artists who align with their preferred aesthetic or harsh judgments of those who don't. A critic raised on classic rock, for instance, might be less receptive to the nuances of experimental electronic music, inadvertently dismissing innovative works simply because they challenge their pre-conceived notions of what constitutes "good" music. This isn't to suggest that critics should abandon their personal preferences, but rather that they should be acutely aware of how these preferences shape their critical assessments and strive to articulate their biases transparently.

Further complicating matters is the inherent power imbalance between the critic and the artist. The critic, often operating from a position of authority and influence, wields significant power over the artist's career. This power dynamic can lead to a critical landscape where deference to established artists and institutions trumps objective assessment. Emerging artists, lacking the established name recognition or critical backing of their more seasoned counterparts, often find themselves at a disadvantage. Their work may be subjected to more stringent scrutiny or dismissed more readily, simply because they lack the established credibility that comes with years of positive critical reception. This creates an uneven playing field, where established artists benefit from a presumption of quality while emerging artists must constantly prove themselves against pre-existing biases.

Genre biases also significantly impact the landscape of music criticism. Certain genres are routinely privileged over others. For instance, classical, jazz, and folk music historically received more serious critical attention than genres associated with marginalized communities like hip hop or electronic dance music. This historical bias continues to influence contemporary criticism, even when critics attempt to present themselves as objective. The implicit assumption that certain genres are more "sophisticated" or "artistically valid" than others perpetuates these inequalities, hindering the recognition and appreciation of diverse musical expressions. This bias often manifests not just in direct judgments, but in the sheer volume of coverage devoted to different genres. If a particular genre receives limited coverage, its artists are less likely to gain exposure, perpetuating a vicious cycle of critical neglect.

The commercial pressures faced by music publications also introduce a significant element of bias. Many critics work for outlets with financial ties to record labels or other industry stakeholders. This creates a potential conflict of interest, where critics might be subtly influenced to write favorably about artists associated with their employers or to avoid harshly critiquing powerful figures in the industry. Such pressures can distort critical judgment, prioritizing commercial interests over artistic merit and creating an environment where frank and honest assessment is compromised. This is further complicated by the blurring lines between advertising and editorial content in the digital age, where sponsorships and partnerships can inadvertently compromise the independence of critical assessments.

Beyond explicit commercial pressures, the broader context of the music industry itself contributes to biased critical practices. The industry's inherent structure, focused on profit maximization and market share, incentivizes a focus on commercially successful music, regardless of its artistic merits. Consequently, critics may be inclined to favor commercially successful artists, reinforcing existing power dynamics and hindering the recognition of innovative or challenging works that might not align with prevailing market trends. This means that critics often reflect, rather than challenge, the existing power structures within the music industry.

The implications of biased and subjective music criticism extend far beyond the realm of aesthetic judgment. For artists, a biased critical landscape can significantly hinder career progression, limiting access to opportunities, and perpetuating inequalities. The cumulative effect of negative or unfair reviews can damage an artist's reputation, impacting their ability to secure gigs, attract funding, or secure record deals. Conversely, unduly favorable reviews can lead to inflated expectations and potentially damage an artist's career through mismatched hype and artistic reality.

For listeners, biased criticism limits exposure to diverse musical expressions and perpetuates a homogenized musical landscape. When certain genres or artists are systematically marginalized through biased reviews, listeners are deprived of opportunities to discover new and enriching musical experiences. This ultimately impoverishes the musical landscape as a whole, hindering creativity and fostering a lack of appreciation for the vast diversity of musical forms.

Addressing the issue of bias and subjectivity in music criticism requires a multifaceted approach. Critics must engage in critical self-reflection, acknowledging their own biases and actively seeking to counteract them. This involves developing a conscious awareness of their personal preferences and attempting to understand how these preferences shape their critical assessments. Transparency is key; openly acknowledging potential biases allows readers to engage with reviews in a more informed and critical manner.

Music publications must also take a more proactive role in fostering ethical and unbiased criticism. This involves implementing measures to mitigate conflicts of interest, ensuring greater diversity among their critics, and encouraging more rigorous and transparent review processes. The creation of guidelines for ethical criticism, coupled with regular internal discussions about bias and subjectivity, could also help promote fairer and more responsible review practices.

Ultimately, striving for objective criticism in a subjective field like music might be an unattainable ideal. However, the goal should be to strive for fairness, acknowledging biases and engaging with diverse perspectives to create a more just and representative critical landscape. This includes actively seeking out and amplifying the voices of marginalized artists and genres, ensuring that all artists have a fair opportunity to be heard and appreciated. The pursuit of a more ethical and equitable approach to music criticism is not merely an academic exercise; it is crucial for the health and vitality of the music world, ensuring a richer, more diverse, and ultimately more meaningful musical landscape for artists and listeners alike.

The Changing Landscape of Music Journalism in the Digital Age

The rise of the internet and the subsequent explosion of digital media have irrevocably altered the landscape of music journalism. Where once a handful of influential print publications held sway, shaping public perception and dictating the trajectory of musical careers, today's landscape is a sprawling, fragmented ecosystem populated by blogs, podcasts, social media platforms, and a multitude of online publications, each vying for attention in a crowded digital marketplace. This shift has presented both immense opportunities and unprecedented challenges for music critics and journalists.

One of the most significant changes is the democratization of music criticism. The high barriers to entry that characterized print journalism – the need for formal journalistic training, connections within the industry, and the approval of gatekeepers – have largely dissolved in the digital realm. Anyone with an internet connection and a willingness to share their opinions can now establish themselves as a music critic, contributing to the ever-growing chorus of voices online. This has led to a dramatic increase in the volume of music criticism available, offering a wider range of perspectives and voices than ever before. However, it has also created a situation where the quality of criticism is uneven, with insightful and well-researched analyses existing alongside poorly written, opinionated, and sometimes even malicious critiques.

This proliferation of online platforms has also led to a decline in the power and influence of traditional music publications. Once the gatekeepers of musical taste, these publications now face stiff competition from independent bloggers, social media influencers, and dedicated music fan communities. This competition has forced many established publications to adapt, adopting digital strategies to maintain relevance and engage younger audiences. Some have successfully transitioned to a robust online presence, leveraging their established reputation to build large online followings. Others, however, have struggled to adapt, facing financial difficulties and ultimately being forced to shut down.

The digital age has also profoundly impacted the economic realities of music journalism. The shift from print to digital media has severely impacted advertising revenue, the lifeblood of many traditional publications. The rise of ad blockers and the difficulty of monetizing online content have further exacerbated these economic pressures, making it increasingly difficult for publications to maintain a sustainable business model and fairly compensate their writers. This has resulted in a decline in the number of fulltime music journalism jobs, leading to a rise in freelance work, which often comes with less job security and lower pay. The prevalence of unpaid or low-paid internships further reinforces this precarity, leading to a less diverse and representative pool of music journalists.

Furthermore, the digital environment fosters a culture of immediacy and brevity. In the fast-paced world of online media, long-form journalism is often sidelined in favor of quick reviews, short news updates, and bite-sized content designed to grab attention in a crowded newsfeed. This shift towards shorter, more easily digestible content can lead to superficial coverage, neglecting the nuanced and in-depth analyses that once characterized print music journalism. While concise and engaging writing is important, the pressure to constantly churn out short pieces can sacrifice analytical depth and critical rigor. Furthermore, this fastpaced environment often encourages emotional and sensationalist reactions, contributing to a climate of "hot takes" that prioritize rapid engagement over careful consideration.

The rise of social media presents a unique set of challenges and opportunities. Social media platforms, such as Twitter and Instagram, offer music journalists the ability to reach vast audiences and engage directly with readers. These platforms can provide instant feedback, facilitating discussions and debates about musical releases, fostering community amongst music lovers, and allowing journalists to cultivate a personal brand and audience. However, the algorithms that govern these platforms can also present challenges, potentially limiting exposure for certain voices and prioritizing content that prioritizes virality over substance. Additionally, the volatile and sometimes toxic nature of online discourse can create hostile work environments for music journalists, leading to censorship and self-censorship of valid perspectives.

The algorithmic nature of online platforms also influences the consumption of music journalism. Search engine optimization (SEO) and personalized algorithms shape what content individuals see, often prioritizing established publications and voices. This can make it challenging for emerging or underrepresented voices to gain traction and visibility, perpetuating existing inequalities within the field. The recommendation algorithms of streaming platforms further exacerbate this bias, as they often prioritize popular music over niche or experimental works, shaping musical consumption patterns and reinforcing a homogenous musical landscape. This has significant implications for the exposure and promotion of lesser-known artists and diverse musical genres, perpetuating existing power structures and limiting the discovery of new and innovative musical expressions.

Despite the challenges, the digital age also presents significant opportunities for music journalism. The lowered barriers to entry enable diverse voices and perspectives to be heard, leading to a richer and more representative landscape of critical commentary. Independent bloggers and online publications have the potential to challenge the established norms and promote artists and genres that might be overlooked by mainstream media outlets. Moreover, online platforms offer the opportunity to engage readers in new and innovative ways, through interactive features, live streams, and discussions. The creation of digital archives and online databases of music writing also provides access to a wealth of historical material, allowing for the study and appreciation of music journalism across various eras and contexts.

The future of music journalism hinges on adaptability and innovation. Journalists must embrace new technologies and platforms to reach wider audiences, while also maintaining high journalistic standards and ethical practices. This includes developing effective strategies to mitigate bias and ensure a just and representative representation of artists and genres. Moreover, it requires navigating the complexities of the digital media landscape, finding ways to generate income in a rapidly changing economic environment, and addressing the challenges of engaging readers in an environment saturated with content. Investing in journalistic training and skills development to empower a diverse pool of music journalists is essential to fostering a critical landscape that is truly representative of the vibrant tapestry of musical expression across the world. The journey ahead is complex, but the potential for a more vibrant, diverse, and impactful music journalism remains substantial.

The Future of Music Criticism and its Role in Shaping Musical Taste

The democratization of music criticism, fueled by the internet, presents a double-edged sword. While it has undeniably broadened the range of voices and perspectives, it has also diluted the authority and influence traditionally held by established critics. The sheer volume of online opinions, ranging from insightful analyses to uninformed ramblings, creates a challenge for discerning readers seeking credible guidance. Navigating this sea of information requires a critical eye and an understanding of the biases and motivations behind different sources. The rise of algorithmic curation on platforms like Spotify and YouTube further complicates matters. These algorithms, designed to maximize engagement, often prioritize popular trends over

artistic merit, potentially limiting exposure for underrepresented genres and artists, creating an echo chamber effect that reinforces existing preferences rather than challenging them. This algorithmic bias raises questions about the future of music discovery and the role of critics in guiding listeners toward less mainstream but equally valuable musical experiences. A concerted effort is needed to develop algorithms that promote diversity and expose listeners to a wider range of musical styles, fostering a more inclusive and representative musical landscape.

This situation demands a reassessment of the role of the music critic. No longer the sole arbiter of taste, the critic must evolve into a curator, a guide, and a contextualizer. Their expertise lies not just in evaluating the musical qualities of an album or performance, but in situating it within a broader cultural and historical context. They must connect the dots, revealing the influences and inspirations behind the music, and explaining its significance within the evolving narrative of musical expression. The critic's voice becomes particularly valuable in dissecting the complex marketing and promotional strategies employed by the music industry, helping listeners navigate the often-blurred lines between genuine artistic merit and manufactured hype.

This analytical function is essential in a world overwhelmed by information, providing a framework for understanding and appreciating the nuance of musical creation.

The future of music criticism also hinges on the development of new models for evaluating and rewarding quality work. The precarious financial landscape of online journalism, characterized by low pay, irregular work, and the prevalence of unpaid internships, discourages talented individuals from entering the field and limits the diversity of voices represented. Finding sustainable models for supporting music criticism is critical, whether through innovative subscription models, public funding initiatives, or alternative forms of patronage. Platforms and publications must recognize the intrinsic value of quality criticism and commit to fairly compensating those who dedicate their time and expertise to this essential function. This investment in human capital is vital to nurturing a critical ecosystem capable of enriching musical culture.

Moreover, the relationship between critics and artists needs re-evaluation. The adversarial relationship that sometimes characterized the past, with critics viewed as potential detractors, needs to give way to a more collaborative and nuanced dialogue. Critics can play a valuable role in promoting artists and helping them connect with a broader audience. Open communication and mutual respect can lead to a more fruitful exchange of ideas and contribute to a deeper understanding of the creative process. The focus should shift from mere judgment to engagement, fostering constructive criticism that encourages artistic growth rather than fostering animosity.

The digital landscape offers opportunities for greater interaction between critics, artists, and audiences. Interactive online platforms can facilitate discussions, debates, and collaborative projects, building bridges and fostering a deeper engagement with music. Live streams, podcasts, and online forums create avenues for direct engagement, breaking down the barriers between creators and consumers. This fosters a sense of community and shared appreciation for music, moving beyond the traditional hierarchical structure of criticism. The future of insightful critique may lie in the development of collaborative spaces where critics, artists, and audiences can engage in ongoing dialogue, fostering a deeper appreciation for the intricacies and complexities of music.

However, this democratized landscape necessitates a renewed focus on ethical considerations. The ease with which anyone can publish their views online requires a greater emphasis on accuracy, fairness, and accountability. Promoting media literacy amongst audiences is crucial in helping them distinguish between credible sources and biased or unreliable information. Transparency and clear disclosure of potential conflicts of interest are essential in maintaining the integrity of music criticism. The unchecked proliferation of online reviews and opinions risks undermining trust and eroding the value of thoughtful, wellresearched critiques. Developing robust mechanisms for detecting and combating disinformation, malicious attacks, and the manipulation of reviews is essential to safeguarding the integrity of the field.

The role of music criticism in shaping musical taste is not static; it evolves alongside technological advancements and cultural shifts. While the digital landscape presents significant challenges, it also offers exciting opportunities for innovation and engagement. To thrive in this dynamic environment, music critics must adapt their methods and embrace new technologies, while maintaining the fundamental principles of responsible journalism and critical thought. This necessitates a concerted effort from critics, platforms, artists, and audiences to foster a sustainable and ethical ecosystem that supports high-quality criticism, encourages diverse voices, and promotes a deeper appreciation of music in all its forms. The future of music criticism lies in its ability to navigate the complexities of the digital age while preserving its core mission: to enrich and deepen our understanding and appreciation of the power of music.

The ongoing evolution of artificial intelligence also presents both challenges and opportunities for music criticism. AIpowered tools can aid in tasks such as transcription, translation, and even the identification of musical patterns and influences. However, concerns about potential biases in algorithms and the ethical implications of AI-generated content need careful consideration. The critical role of human judgment and interpretation remains paramount, ensuring that AI is used as a tool to enhance, not replace, human expertise. The delicate balance between leveraging technological advancements and maintaining the integrity and human touch of music criticism will be a defining aspect of the field's future.

Furthermore, the increasingly globalized nature of music production and consumption requires critics to develop a more nuanced understanding of diverse musical traditions and cultural contexts. Promoting cross-cultural dialogue and challenging ethnocentric biases in musical taste are crucial in fostering a truly inclusive musical landscape. This requires a commitment to diversifying the field of music criticism, ensuring that voices from various backgrounds and perspectives are represented, enriching the critical conversation and offering a more comprehensive understanding of the global tapestry of musical creation.

The future of music criticism will also depend on its ability to engage with new generations of listeners. Critics must find innovative ways to connect with younger audiences who may consume music and media differently than previous generations. This requires a willingness to experiment with new formats, styles, and platforms, ensuring that criticism is accessible, engaging, and relevant to a wider range of listeners. The continued evolution of music criticism is inextricably linked to the evolution of music consumption itself, and the field must remain adaptable to thrive.

In conclusion, the future of music criticism is not a matter of decline but of adaptation and evolution. The challenges are undeniable – the fragmented media landscape, the precarious economic realities, and the challenges of maintaining integrity in a digitally saturated world. However, the opportunities are equally substantial: the potential for broader inclusivity, deeper engagement, and the creation of a more vibrant and collaborative critical ecosystem. The future of music criticism depends on the collective efforts of critics, artists, platforms, and audiences to nurture a sustainable, ethical, and engaging approach to appreciating the enduring power of music. The journey ahead is challenging, but the potential for enriching musical culture remains vast and exciting.

Financial Management and Budgeting for Musicians

The glittering world of music often obscures the harsh realities of its financial landscape. For many musicians, the dream of a sustainable career clashes with the unpredictable nature of income and the often-overlooked need for meticulous financial planning. While passion fuels the creative process, a solid understanding of financial management is the bedrock upon which a lasting musical career is built. This isn't about becoming a financial whiz; it's about implementing practical strategies that empower musicians to take control of their finances and make informed decisions that support their artistic endeavors.

The first step towards financial stability is accurate income tracking. This goes beyond simply noting gig payments. It involves meticulously recording every single source of revenue, from album sales and streaming royalties to merchandise proceeds, teaching fees, and grants. Detailed records are crucial not only for tax purposes but also for gaining a clear picture of the financial health of your musical enterprise. Consider using spreadsheets, accounting software, or dedicated apps designed for freelancers and independent contractors. These tools allow you to categorize income, track trends, and identify peak earning periods and potential areas for growth. For instance, if you consistently earn more from private teaching than live performances, that signals a potential need to re-evaluate your performance strategy or explore expanding your teaching business.

Expense management is equally crucial, and often overlooked. Many musicians mistakenly focus solely on income, neglecting the consistent drain of expenses. This oversight can lead to a perilous financial situation, especially during periods of lower income. Comprehensive expense tracking encompasses every cost associated with your music career, from studio time and instrument maintenance to marketing and travel expenses. This detailed record-keeping is vital for tax purposes, but also provides invaluable insights into your spending habits. Categorizing expenses—instrument repairs, studio fees, marketing materials, travel—allows you to identify areas where you might be overspending. For example, if marketing is consistently absorbing a significant portion of your budget with little return, it might be time to re-evaluate your marketing strategy, potentially focusing on more cost-effective methods like social media engagement or collaborations.

Budgeting is the next crucial step, and it's far more than just subtracting expenses from income. Creating a realistic budget requires a forward-looking approach, anticipating income fluctuations and factoring in both regular and irregular expenses. Consider incorporating a buffer for unexpected costs – instrument repairs, sudden medical bills – to avoid financial shocks. A well-structured budget helps visualize your financial situation, providing a roadmap for allocating funds effectively. The budgeting process necessitates a balance between your short-term and longterm financial goals. Short-term goals might include saving for new equipment or covering upcoming tour expenses. Long-term goals might encompass investing in your musical future, like purchasing a larger studio space or paying off debts.

Financial planning extends beyond budgeting. It entails making strategic decisions about saving, investing, and managing debt. Establishing an emergency fund is paramount; it serves as a safety net during periods of low income or unexpected expenses. The general recommendation is to have three to six months' worth of living expenses saved. This might seem daunting for a musician with fluctuating income, but even small, consistent savings contribute to building this crucial financial security. Investment options, such as retirement accounts and other low-risk investments, are essential for long-term financial security. While the allure of immediate gratification is strong, investing in your long-term financial stability is a vital component of sustaining a musical career.

Managing debt is another critical aspect of financial health. Music often requires significant upfront investments— instruments, equipment, recording studio time. Understanding different types of debt and developing strategies for managing them is crucial. High-interest debt should be prioritized for repayment, while longer-term, lower-interest debts can be addressed strategically. Financial literacy programs, online resources, and advice from financial advisors can offer invaluable guidance on responsible debt management. Never underestimate the power of seeking professional advice. A financial advisor specializing in the arts can provide customized guidance based on your unique circumstances and financial goals.

Beyond personal financial management, understanding the legal and financial aspects of the music industry is crucial. This includes navigating royalty payments, performance contracts, and publishing agreements. Many musicians unfortunately find themselves exploited due to a lack of understanding in these areas. It's essential to seek legal counsel when signing contracts, understanding the nuances of royalty structures, and safeguarding your intellectual property. Investing in a good entertainment lawyer might be one of the most prudent financial decisions a musician makes. Their expertise protects you from potentially exploitative contracts and ensures your rights are protected.

Negotiating fair rates for performances and collaborations is another vital aspect of financial success. It's crucial to understand your worth and confidently negotiate fees that reflect your experience and market value. Researching industry standards and consulting with peers can provide a valuable framework for determining appropriate compensation. Don't undervalue your work; establishing a fair and sustainable pricing strategy is crucial for your financial well-being.

Tax planning is often an afterthought, but it's a crucial component of responsible financial management. Understanding the tax implications of your income and expenses is vital for staying compliant and maximizing your tax benefits. Familiarize yourself with self-employment taxes and deductions specific to musicians. Consider consulting with a tax professional who specializes in the arts to ensure you're taking advantage of all applicable deductions and minimizing your tax burden. This proactive approach saves money and prevents future financial headaches.

Finally, fostering a strong professional network is crucial not only for creative collaborations but also for financial support. Connect with other musicians, industry professionals, and financial advisors who can offer guidance and support. Attending industry events and workshops can provide valuable networking opportunities, helping you build relationships that extend beyond the purely artistic realm. A robust network can become an invaluable source of information, referrals, and support.

Building a sustainable music career requires a multifaceted approach. While the creative passion is the driving force, financial stability is the foundation upon which that passion can flourish. By implementing the strategies outlined here – meticulous income and expense tracking, realistic budgeting, strategic financial planning, legal awareness, and professional networking – musicians can take control of their financial destiny and build a career that sustains both their artistic vision and their financial well-being. The path to musical success is paved not just with talent, but with financial savvy and responsible planning.

Networking and Building Relationships in the Music Industry

The previous section focused on the crucial role of financial literacy in building a sustainable music career. However, even the most meticulous financial planning will fall short without a robust network of supportive and influential individuals within the music industry. Success in the music business, much like in any other field, is rarely a solo endeavor. It's built on collaborations, mentorship, and a strategic cultivation of relationships. This isn't about simply collecting business cards; it's about fostering genuine connections that can lead to opportunities, collaborations, and crucial support throughout your career.

Networking within the music industry is a marathon, not a sprint. It requires consistent effort, genuine engagement, and a long-term perspective. Forget the image of the jaded industry veteran aloofly exchanging business cards. Effective networking is about building meaningful connections based on mutual respect and shared goals. It's about offering value, being genuinely interested in others, and consistently demonstrating your professionalism and talent.

One of the most effective networking strategies is attending industry events. These events range from large-scale conferences and festivals like South by Southwest (SXSW) or Coachella to smaller, more intimate showcases and workshops. The key is to approach these events with a clear strategy. Don't simply wander around hoping to stumble upon the next big opportunity. Instead, research the event beforehand, identify key individuals you'd like to connect with, and prepare a concise and engaging introduction.

Remember, it's about quality over quantity. A few meaningful conversations are far more valuable than a flurry of superficial exchanges.

Online networking is equally important. Platforms like LinkedIn, Instagram, and Twitter provide avenues for connecting with industry professionals, showcasing your work, and engaging in relevant conversations. However, it's crucial to use these platforms strategically. Don't spam potential contacts with generic messages; instead, personalize your outreach, highlighting your mutual interests or shared connections. Engage meaningfully with their content, demonstrating your genuine interest in their work and the industry as a whole.

Collaborating with other musicians is another crucial aspect of networking. This could involve co-writing songs, performing together, or even simply offering each other support and advice. These collaborative efforts not only enhance your creative output but also expand your network, introducing you to new audiences and potential collaborators. Moreover, these collaborations often lead to mutual referrals, further expanding your network organically.

Mentorship is a powerful tool for building a sustainable music career. Seek out individuals who have achieved a level of success you aspire to and who seem genuinely invested in helping others. Don't be afraid to reach out and express your admiration for their work and your desire to learn from their experience. Many successful musicians are happy to offer guidance and support to aspiring artists, recognizing the value of paying it forward. Remember, approaching a potential mentor should not be about seeking immediate favors but about building a genuine relationship based on mutual respect.

Building relationships with industry professionals such as managers, agents, publicists, and lawyers is paramount. These individuals possess valuable industry knowledge, connections, and expertise that can significantly advance your career. However, developing these relationships requires patience, persistence, and a clear demonstration of your talent and professionalism. Don't expect immediate results; instead, focus on building trust and establishing a long-term relationship based on mutual respect and shared goals.

Leverage your existing network. While it's important to expand your network, don't neglect the value of your current connections. Friends, family, teachers, and past collaborators can all play a role in supporting your career. They might not be industry insiders, but they can still offer invaluable support, encouragement, and referrals. Never underestimate the power of your existing relationships. Maintain these connections and nurture them; they can often be your most reliable source of support during challenging times.

Networking isn't merely about self-promotion; it's about reciprocal value exchange. What do you offer to those you hope to connect with? Do you possess a skill, resource, or perspective that can benefit others? Thinking this way shifts your approach from a transactional, "what can I get out of this?" mentality to a more mutually beneficial partnership. Consider how you might support the individuals in your network, offer assistance, or provide value in return for their connections or insights.

Networking requires active participation. Passive networking —simply attending events and hoping to be noticed—rarely yields significant results. Instead, be proactive; initiate conversations, introduce yourself, ask thoughtful questions, and genuinely engage with others. Show that you're not just looking for something from them, but that you're interested in learning, collaborating, and building genuine connections.

Finally, always remember the importance of follow-up. After attending an event or connecting online, make sure to follow up with relevant individuals, thanking them for their time and reiterating your interest in their work. A simple thankyou note, email, or social media message can reinforce your connection and keep you top of mind. This simple act of follow-up differentiates you from those who merely attend events but fail to cultivate lasting relationships. It demonstrates your professionalism and commitment to building meaningful connections.

Navigating the music industry requires a multifaceted approach that encompasses creative talent, financial acumen, and, critically, a strategic and well-cultivated network. By embracing these networking strategies and consistently investing in genuine connections, musicians can significantly increase their chances of building a sustainable and successful career. Remember, success in the music industry is rarely a solo effort; it's about the powerful synergy of talent, financial planning, and a robust, supportive network. The connections you build will not only lead to opportunities and collaborations but also provide invaluable emotional and professional support throughout your journey. Cultivating these relationships is a long-term investment that yields significant dividends.

Marketing and Promotion Strategies for Musicians

Building a sustainable music career necessitates more than just talent and networking; it demands a shrewd understanding and implementation of effective marketing and promotional strategies. While possessing exceptional musical ability is foundational, it remains largely ineffective without a robust plan to reach your target audience and build a loyal fanbase. This section delves into the multifaceted world of music marketing, providing practical advice and actionable strategies for musicians of all levels.

Social media has revolutionized the music industry, transforming the way artists connect with their fans and promote their work. It's no longer enough to simply have a presence; you must actively engage and cultivate a genuine community around your music. Platforms like Instagram, TikTok, Facebook, and Twitter offer distinct opportunities for reaching specific demographics and building brand loyalty. Each platform demands a unique approach, tailored to its specific user base and algorithm. For instance,

Instagram thrives on visually appealing content, making high-quality photos and videos crucial. TikTok, on the other hand, prioritizes short-form, engaging video content that encourages participation and viral spread. Facebook, with its broader demographic, allows for a more varied approach, combining image-heavy posts with longer-form updates and interactive elements. Twitter, known for its concise messaging, is ideal for rapid announcements, interacting with fans in real-time, and engaging in industry discussions.

Beyond simply posting content, successful social media marketing requires a strategic approach. Developing a content calendar can help maintain consistency and ensure your posts align with your overall marketing goals. This calendar should outline the type of content you'll post, the platform it will be posted on, and the intended message. Remember to track your results, using analytics to determine which strategies are most effective and making adjustments accordingly. A/B testing different types of content—videos versus images, different caption styles, various call-toactions—allows you to fine-tune your approach and optimize your reach. Don't underestimate the power of engaging with your followers; responding to comments, participating in conversations, and running contests can significantly enhance your engagement rates and build stronger relationships with your fanbase.

Paid social media advertising can accelerate your reach and target specific demographics. Platforms like Facebook and Instagram offer robust advertising tools that allow you to define your target audience based on factors such as age, location, interests, and listening habits. This targeted approach ensures your advertising budget is used efficiently, maximizing your return on investment. However, paid advertising should not replace organic content creation; it should complement it, amplifying your message and expanding your reach to new audiences. Experiment with different ad formats to determine what resonates best with your target audience. Track your results carefully to identify which ads are performing best and adjust your campaigns accordingly.

Public relations (PR) plays a vital role in building your brand and reaching a wider audience. PR isn't just about sending press releases; it's about cultivating relationships with journalists, bloggers, and influencers who can help amplify your message. This might involve pitching stories to relevant publications, attending industry events, or building relationships with key media contacts. A strong media kit, containing a press release, high-quality photos, and your biography, is essential for pitching stories. Your press release should focus on a compelling angle—a new album release, an upcoming tour, or a significant accomplishment—and be written in a clear and concise manner. Ensure all materials are professional and reflect your brand image. Remember, relationships are key in PR; building rapport with journalists and influencers will make it more likely they'll feature you in their publications or on their platforms.

Beyond traditional media outlets, consider working with music bloggers and influencers who specialize in your genre. These individuals often have highly engaged audiences and can provide valuable exposure to new listeners. Collaborating with them can take various forms—reviewing your music, featuring you on their blog or podcast, or participating in joint social media campaigns. Seek out influencers who align with your brand image and have an audience that overlaps with your target demographic. Always be transparent about any sponsored collaborations and ensure the influencer's content aligns with your overall brand message.

Live performance promotion is crucial for building a loyal fanbase and generating income. Your live shows are not just opportunities to perform; they are marketing opportunities. Before each show, promote it heavily through your social media channels, email list, and any other relevant platforms. Utilize engaging visuals, countdown timers, and behind-thescenes content to build anticipation. Consider offering presale tickets to your email subscribers, creating a sense of exclusivity and rewarding your most loyal fans.

Work with local venues and promoters to maximize your reach. Venues often have their own marketing channels and promotional efforts, which can amplify your reach to a wider audience. Build relationships with promoters, attending their shows and networking to create opportunities for future collaborations. Consider cross-promotion with other artists, particularly those with similar styles and audiences. Joint shows can introduce each other's fanbases to new music and broaden your reach.

Ticket sales are only one aspect of live performance promotion. Merchandise sales during and after shows can generate additional revenue and provide tangible reminders of your performances. Offer a range of products, from tshirts and posters to more unique items that reflect your brand identity. Consider collaborating with local artists or designers to create exclusive merchandise that adds value and appeal. High-quality merchandise not only generates revenue but reinforces your brand identity and provides fans with a tangible connection to your music.

Email marketing is a powerful tool for nurturing relationships with your fans and promoting your music and shows. Building an email list allows you to directly communicate with your most loyal fans, sharing updates, exclusive content, and promotions. Offer incentives to join your mailing list, such as access to early ticket sales or exclusive downloads. Develop a strategic email marketing plan that includes different types of campaigns, such as newsletters, promotional announcements, and event invitations. Ensure your emails are well-designed, engaging, and reflect your brand identity. Regularly analyze your email open and click-through rates to refine your messaging and improve your overall strategy.

Website presence is essential for providing a central hub for your fans to access your music, news, and tour dates. Your website should be easy to navigate, visually appealing, and mobile-friendly. Include your biography, discography, upcoming tour dates, and contact information. Consider adding a blog where you can share your thoughts, experiences, and insights into your musical journey. Ensure your website reflects your brand image and provides a positive user experience.

Effective marketing and promotion for musicians requires a blend of creativity, strategy, and consistent effort. Social media, PR, live performance promotion, email marketing, and a professional website work together to create a multifaceted approach that maximizes your reach and builds a sustainable fanbase. Remember, consistent effort and a focus on building genuine relationships are key to success. By implementing these strategies diligently and consistently adapting your approach based on the results, you significantly increase your chances of establishing a sustainable and thriving career in the music industry.

Legal and Business Aspects of a Music Career

Navigating the complex legal and business landscape of the music industry is crucial for any aspiring or established musician. The glittering facade of fame often obscures the intricate web of contracts, copyright laws, and business practices that can make or break a career. This section aims to shed light on these often-overlooked aspects, providing practical advice and cautionary tales gleaned from years of observing the industry's underbelly.

One of the most critical areas is contract negotiation. Record deals, publishing agreements, and even smaller contracts with promoters or venues can contain clauses that significantly impact an artist's financial success and creative control. Many artists, particularly those starting out, are pressured into signing contracts they don't fully understand, leading to exploitation and financial hardship. This is where having a knowledgeable legal representative is invaluable. A lawyer specializing in entertainment law can review contracts, identify potentially problematic clauses, and negotiate better terms on your behalf. Don't underestimate the power of having someone in your corner who understands the industry's intricacies and is willing to fight for your rights. This isn't just about maximizing financial returns; it's about protecting your artistic vision and longterm career trajectory.

Understanding copyright law is equally important. Copyright protects your musical compositions, lyrics, and recordings, granting you exclusive rights to reproduce, distribute, and perform your work. Registering your copyrights with the appropriate organizations is essential, providing legal evidence of your ownership and offering crucial protection against infringement. Failure to register your work can severely limit your ability to defend your rights against unauthorized use, leading to potential losses in income and reputation. The digital age has presented new challenges to copyright protection, with rampant online piracy and unauthorized streaming significantly impacting artists' revenue streams. It's critical to actively monitor the use of your work online and take appropriate legal action when infringement occurs. Ignoring online copyright violations only emboldens those who profit from unauthorized use of your creative efforts.

Beyond copyright, artists need to consider other aspects of intellectual property, such as trademarks and brand names. Developing a strong brand identity is essential in the crowded music market, and protecting that identity through trademark registration can prevent others from using similar names or logos, potentially causing confusion among consumers. This becomes especially relevant when merchandising and expanding your brand beyond just music. A well-defined brand can enhance your marketability and generate additional revenue streams.

The business side of music extends far beyond contracts and copyright. Effective financial management is critical, including budgeting, expense tracking, and tax planning. Many artists struggle with financial mismanagement, leading to debt and financial instability, often in the face of significant initial success. Engaging a financial advisor specializing in the entertainment industry can provide crucial guidance on financial planning, tax optimization, and investment strategies. They can help you navigate the complexities of royalty payments, touring income, and other revenue streams, ensuring your money is managed effectively and strategically. Remember, having a healthy financial foundation allows for long-term career sustainability and reduces the pressure to compromise artistic integrity for short-term financial gains.

Building a strong team is essential for long-term success. This extends beyond just a lawyer and a financial advisor; consider a publicist, manager, and potentially an agent. A skilled manager can handle various aspects of your career, including booking gigs, negotiating contracts, and managing your finances. A publicist focuses on securing media coverage and building your public profile. An agent represents you to securing major performances and deals, while a good lawyer protects your interests in legal and contractual matters. Choosing the right team members is crucial—look for individuals who share your vision and are committed to your long-term success. Avoid individuals who prioritize short-term gains over your creative integrity.

Understanding the intricacies of royalty payments is critical for ensuring proper compensation for your work. Royalties can come from various sources, including record sales, streaming services, and public performances. It's crucial to understand how these royalties are calculated and distributed, and to ensure you receive the payments you are entitled to. Keep thorough records of all your musical works, performances and sales. Regularly review your royalty statements to ensure accuracy and identify any discrepancies. Don't be afraid to challenge inaccuracies or seek advice from legal professionals if you suspect you are not receiving the appropriate compensation.

The music industry is often portrayed as a glamorous world of fame and fortune. The reality, however, is often far different, characterized by intense competition, cutthroat business practices, and legal complexities. By understanding and navigating these legal and business aspects with diligence and the right support system, musicians can significantly increase their chances of building a sustainable career that allows them to not only achieve their creative goals but also maintain financial stability and artistic integrity. Remember, your career is a valuable asset; protect it through informed decision-making and professional guidance. Never hesitate to seek out expertise when navigating the complexities of contracts and legal matters, and remember that understanding the business side of the music industry is just as important as developing musical talent. By prioritizing both, you are building a foundation for a career that is not only sustainable but also fulfilling.

The digital revolution has profoundly altered the landscape of music distribution and consumption. The rise of streaming services has created both opportunities and challenges for artists. While these platforms offer unprecedented access to global audiences, they also introduce complex royalty structures and lower per-stream payouts compared to traditional sales models. Artists must develop strategies to maximize their revenue within this new ecosystem, including understanding the intricacies of streaming royalties, actively promoting their music on different platforms, and exploring alternative revenue streams, such as merchandise sales, live performances, and fan subscriptions.

Negotiating with digital distributors and streaming platforms requires a keen understanding of their various contracts and royalty structures. Each platform has its own system for calculating and distributing royalties, and the terms can vary significantly. It's crucial to carefully review these agreements before signing any contracts, ensuring that you understand the payment terms, reporting methods, and any restrictions on your music's usage. Working with a legal representative can ensure you get a fair deal and protect your interests. Moreover, continuously monitoring your performance data on each platform allows you to adjust your strategies and maximize your reach and earning potential.

Beyond the digital realm, the live performance aspect remains crucial to the financial sustainability of many artists. This includes not only performing at concerts and festivals, but also securing corporate gigs, private events, and even teaching or giving workshops. Diversification of performance opportunities is key to building a consistent income stream. Effectively managing expenses associated with touring, including travel, accommodation, equipment, and personnel, is also vital to ensuring profitability. Careful budgeting and meticulous record-keeping are essential to tracking income and expenses, ensuring you're making informed decisions regarding your performance schedule and financial planning.

Finally, exploring alternative revenue streams beyond traditional music sales and performances becomes essential for long-term success in the current market. These could include merchandise sales (t-shirts, albums, posters, etc.), producing and selling online courses, offering music lessons, or launching a Patreon or other fan-subscription based platform. Engaging directly with your fan base and nurturing these relationships offers additional revenue streams and fosters a loyal community. Building a direct connection with your audience through these alternative methods not only improves financial stability but also enriches the artist-fan relationship and cultivates long-term loyalty, creating a more sustainable and fulfilling career. In short, the successful musician of today needs to be not just a talented artist, but also a shrewd business person, adept at managing legal complexities, negotiating favorable contracts, and diversifying their income streams.

Maintaining Mental and Physical Wellbeing in a Demanding Industry

The relentless pursuit of musical success often comes at a steep personal cost. The music industry, with its unpredictable nature, intense competition, and constant pressure to perform, can take a significant toll on an artist's mental and physical well-being. Burnout, anxiety, and depression are not uncommon, and many artists find themselves struggling to cope with the demands of their profession. This section is dedicated to exploring practical strategies for maintaining a healthy balance, ensuring a sustainable and fulfilling career in the long run.

Ignoring self-care is a recipe for disaster. The pressure to constantly create, perform, and promote oneself can lead to a vicious cycle of exhaustion, impacting creativity, performance quality, and ultimately, career longevity. Many artists fall prey to this cycle, pushing themselves to the brink of collapse before realizing the importance of prioritizing their well-being. This is not a sign of weakness; it is a realistic acknowledgement of the demanding nature of the industry.

One of the most crucial aspects of self-care is establishing healthy boundaries. Learning to say "no" to commitments that drain your energy or compromise your mental health is essential. Overcommitting is a common trap; aspiring artists, eager to prove themselves, often accept every opportunity that comes their way, leading to overwhelm and burnout. It's crucial to evaluate each opportunity carefully, considering its potential impact on your overall well-being. Prioritize projects and collaborations that align with your artistic vision and contribute positively to your mental state.

Remember that your creative energy is a finite resource, and protecting it is paramount.

Stress management is a critical skill for anyone navigating the challenges of the music industry. Chronic stress can manifest in various ways, from physical ailments like headaches and digestive problems to mental health issues such as anxiety and depression. Developing effective stress management techniques is crucial for preventing these problems. Some practical strategies include regular exercise, mindfulness practices such as meditation or yoga, spending time in nature, and engaging in hobbies that provide relaxation and enjoyment outside of music. These activities offer an essential counterbalance to the demands of the industry and promote overall well-being. Furthermore, exploring stress reduction techniques like deep breathing exercises, progressive muscle relaxation, and guided imagery can be incredibly beneficial in managing the daily pressures of a demanding career. These can be incorporated into a daily routine to mitigate stress before it escalates into more serious issues.

Adequate sleep is often overlooked but is vital for both physical and mental well-being. Irregular sleep patterns, a common occurrence in the music industry due to late-night performances and travel, can significantly impact energy levels, mood, and cognitive function. Prioritizing a consistent sleep schedule, even amidst busy touring schedules or late-night studio sessions, is crucial. Creating a relaxing bedtime routine, avoiding caffeine and alcohol before bed, and ensuring a dark, quiet sleeping environment can significantly improve sleep quality. Adequate rest is not a luxury; it's a necessity for maintaining peak performance and avoiding burnout. Don't underestimate the power of a good night's sleep in enhancing your creative output and overall well-being.

Nutrition plays a crucial role in maintaining physical and mental energy levels. A balanced diet provides the fuel your body needs to cope with the demands of a busy career. Consuming regular, nutritious meals, including plenty of fruits, vegetables, and whole grains, will help maintain consistent energy levels and support a healthy immune system. It's tempting to rely on convenient, processed foods when time is short, but consistently making poor dietary choices can lead to energy crashes, mood swings, and other health issues. Careful meal planning and preparation can help you maintain a healthy diet, even amidst a hectic schedule. Staying hydrated is equally important; drinking sufficient water is essential for maintaining energy and optimal bodily functions.

Regular physical exercise is not only beneficial for physical health but also serves as a powerful stress reliever and mood booster. Finding time for exercise amidst the demands of a busy career can be challenging, but incorporating even short bursts of physical activity into your daily routine can make a significant difference. Whether it's a morning jog, a lunchtime workout, or a post-show yoga session, prioritizing movement can combat stress and improve overall mental well-being. Finding an activity you enjoy, be it running, swimming, dancing, or team sports, is key to ensuring consistency and making exercise a sustainable part of your routine.

Social support is crucial for navigating the challenges of the industry. Surrounding yourself with a strong network of supportive friends, family, and colleagues provides a buffer against stress and isolation. Sharing experiences and challenges with others who understand the unique pressures of the music industry can provide valuable perspective and emotional support. Don't underestimate the power of human connection in maintaining a positive mental outlook. Building a strong community helps reduce feelings of isolation and encourages a sense of belonging, which can mitigate the negative impact of the industry's pressures.

Seeking professional help is not a sign of weakness but a sign of strength. If you are struggling with mental health issues, don't hesitate to seek professional help from a therapist, counselor, or psychiatrist. Many artists benefit from therapy, a safe space to process emotions and develop coping mechanisms. There are resources specifically designed to support musicians and those working in the creative arts. Openly discussing mental health challenges is becoming more accepted, and seeking support is an essential component of self-care.

The music industry is inherently competitive, and it's easy to fall into the trap of constant comparison with others. Social media, in particular, can exacerbate this issue, creating a distorted view of reality and fueling feelings of inadequacy. It's crucial to focus on your own artistic journey, celebrating your achievements, and recognizing your unique strengths and talents. Comparing yourself to others only serves to undermine your self-confidence and well-being. Instead, focus on building your own career path, celebrating milestones, and learning from both successes and failures. Remember, your musical journey is unique, and comparing yourself to others diminishes your progress and creativity.

Finally, remember that maintaining well-being is an ongoing process, not a destination. It requires consistent effort and self-awareness. Be kind to yourself, practice selfcompassion, and don't be afraid to prioritize your well-being above all else. A sustainable music career is not just about achieving fame and fortune; it's about creating a life that is both fulfilling and sustainable. By prioritizing your mental and physical health, you are laying the groundwork for a long and prosperous career in music. Remember, a healthy mind and body are your greatest assets in the pursuit of your musical dreams. Prioritizing your well-being isn't selfish; it's essential for long-term success and happiness in an industry notoriously demanding in every aspect.

Technological Advancements and Their Impact on Music Creation and Consumption

The digital revolution has irrevocably altered the music industry, impacting every stage from creation to consumption. The advent of affordable, high-quality digital audio workstations (DAWs) has democratized music production. Previously, aspiring musicians relied on expensive studio time and specialized equipment, effectively creating a significant barrier to entry. Now, a laptop, a MIDI keyboard, and a DAW can empower anyone with musical talent to compose, record, mix, and master their work. This accessibility has fostered a burgeoning independent music scene, leading to a wealth of diverse sounds and styles previously unheard of. Platforms like GarageBand, Ableton Live, and Logic Pro X have become integral tools, allowing artists to refine their craft at their own pace, without the constraints of traditional studio limitations. The implications are far-reaching: the traditional gatekeepers of the music industry, the large record labels, find their power increasingly challenged by this wave of independent artists.

However, this democratization isn't without its drawbacks. The ease of entry has also led to an overwhelming saturation of the market. The sheer volume of music available online, on platforms like Spotify and Apple Music, makes it increasingly difficult for individual artists to stand out from the crowd. The algorithms governing these platforms often favor established artists, further exacerbating the challenges faced by newcomers. Furthermore, the cost of marketing and promotion remains a significant hurdle for independent artists, even if production costs have fallen drastically. The need for effective digital marketing, social media engagement, and online promotion necessitates skills beyond the musical realm, creating a new set of challenges for independent musicians.

The shift from physical to digital music distribution has also profoundly impacted the industry. The decline of CD sales, once the industry's lifeblood, has forced record labels and artists alike to adapt to a new paradigm. Digital music platforms, while providing a convenient and accessible way to consume music, have also led to debates about fair compensation for artists. The low royalty rates offered by streaming services often leave musicians struggling to make a living from their work, raising critical questions about the viability of a musical career in the digital age. The argument is further complicated by the fact that streaming platforms often use opaque algorithms, making it difficult for artists to understand how their music is being promoted and compensated. The fight for fairer royalty rates and increased transparency is an ongoing battle that continues to shape the industry's future.

Technological advancements haven't just changed how music is distributed; they've also transformed how it is consumed. The rise of personalized playlists, algorithmic recommendations, and on-demand listening has fundamentally altered how music listeners engage with their favorite artists and discover new music. The ability to access an unparalleled library of music on demand has led to a shift in music consumption patterns, with shorter attention spans and less focused listening experiences becoming increasingly common. This shift also poses a challenge for artists who rely on album sales and focused listening to engage with their audience. The album format, once a significant driver of revenue, now finds itself competing with an infinite scroll of individual tracks, impacting the narrative structure and artistry often incorporated in a coherent album release.

Artificial intelligence (AI) is emerging as a powerful force shaping the music industry. AI-powered tools are increasingly used in music production, assisting with tasks like songwriting, composition, mixing, and mastering. AI algorithms can analyze musical patterns and suggest melodies, harmonies, and rhythms, potentially expanding the creative possibilities for musicians. However, concerns exist about the potential displacement of human creativity and the impact on the authenticity of music. The use of AI in music creation raises ethical questions about authorship, copyright, and originality. Determining ownership and copyright protection in the context of AI-generated music presents a significant legal and philosophical challenge. The debate is ongoing, and its resolution will have significant implications for the future of music creation.

Furthermore, AI's impact extends beyond the studio. AIdriven algorithms are being used increasingly for music discovery and promotion, shaping the way fans engage with music and the artists they listen to. Personalized playlists and targeted advertising leverage AI to create more specific listening experiences, potentially leading to a more niche but potentially less diverse musical landscape. The algorithm itself can become a gatekeeper, favoring certain artists and genres over others based on factors not always transparent or easily understood by the artists themselves. This can perpetuate existing inequalities and limit the exposure of emerging artists and niche genres, leading to a homogenization of the musical experience.

The use of virtual and augmented reality (VR/AR) technologies presents exciting new possibilities for music experiences. VR concerts and immersive music videos offer fans unique and engaging ways to interact with their favorite artists. Imagine a concert experience where you feel as if you're standing on stage with your favorite band, or a music video that transports you to another world, fully immersed in the music's atmosphere. These technologies have the potential to revolutionize how we engage with music and create new forms of artistic expression. However, the accessibility and cost of VR/AR technology could limit the reach of these new experiences, initially catering to a niche audience before potentially becoming more widespread.

Blockchain technology is also being explored as a potential disruptor in the music industry. This technology, the foundation of cryptocurrencies, can be used to create transparent and secure systems for royalty payments and music rights management. Blockchain's immutability could help eliminate fraud and ensure that artists receive their fair share of revenue from their work. This transparent system could offer a solution to the opaqueness and potential for exploitation that often characterizes current digital music distribution systems. The development and implementation of such systems are still in their early stages, but the potential impact on the industry could be profound. Nevertheless, challenges remain in terms of user adoption and the complexities of managing a decentralized system effectively.

The future of the music industry hinges on navigating these technological advancements while addressing the ethical and practical challenges they present. The democratization of music creation has opened new opportunities for independent artists, but it has also created a highly competitive landscape. The shift to digital distribution has changed how music is consumed, and the rise of AI and VR/AR technologies offer new possibilities for artistic expression and fan engagement. Ultimately, the success of the music industry will depend on balancing technological innovation with a commitment to fair compensation for artists, promoting diversity, and ensuring a sustainable environment for creative expression. The ethical considerations surrounding AI, the transparency of algorithmic curation, and the fair distribution of revenues will be crucial factors shaping the industry's future. It's a complex landscape, but one rich with potential, necessitating careful navigation and thoughtful adaptation to survive and thrive in this era of rapid technological change. The future belongs to those who can adapt and innovate, while retaining a focus on the fundamental aspects of music – its artistry and its connection with the human experience.

The Evolving Role of Record Labels and Their Relationship with Artists

The rise of independent artists, empowered by readily available technology, has fundamentally challenged the traditional dominance of record labels. For decades, these labels acted as gatekeepers, controlling virtually every aspect of an artist's career – from recording and production to distribution and marketing. They possessed the resources, the networks, and the infrastructure to launch artists to stardom, and in return, they demanded significant portions of an artist's earnings, often through exploitative contracts signed by aspiring musicians eager for a break. This model, however, is increasingly fractured.

The digital revolution has dispersed power. While labels still possess considerable clout in marketing and distribution to a global audience, particularly for mainstream genres, their iron grip on the creative process and financial rewards has loosened significantly. Independent artists now have access to distribution platforms like Bandcamp, Spotify, and Apple Music, allowing them to bypass the traditional label system entirely. They can retain a larger share of their profits, control their creative vision, and establish a direct relationship with their fanbase. This shift presents a doubleedged sword: for some, it's a liberating experience, leading to greater artistic freedom and financial independence; for others, it represents a daunting challenge, demanding business acumen and marketing expertise that might overshadow their musical talent.

The changing landscape has compelled record labels to adapt, albeit often reluctantly. Some have embraced the new reality, seeking to foster more collaborative and equitable partnerships with artists. They now offer a range of services beyond simple distribution, including marketing, promotion, creative guidance, and even financial support – a move towards a more service-oriented model. This shift reflects a recognition that many artists, particularly those in niche genres or with a strong pre-existing online following, prefer greater control over their careers. These artists aren't necessarily looking for a traditional "record deal" offering comprehensive control to the label. Instead, they seek more flexible agreements, possibly covering specific services rather than blanket control, such as marketing support or access to distribution networks, tailored to their individual needs.

However, the legacy of exploitative practices still casts a long shadow. Many labels, especially larger corporations, are slow to embrace true transparency and fairness. Artist contracts often remain complex and opaque, leaving artists vulnerable to unfavorable terms. The power imbalance often persists, with labels holding significant leverage over artists, especially those early in their careers. This leads to situations where artists unknowingly agree to terms that severely limit their potential earnings and creative freedom. The lack of industry-wide standardization in contract terms makes it particularly difficult for artists, many of whom lack legal representation, to navigate the complex legal landscape.

The rise of data analytics and A&R (artists and repertoire) departments that use sophisticated predictive algorithms presents another layer of complexity to this power dynamic. While labels can utilize data to identify and cultivate talent more effectively, this also raises concerns about biases within the algorithms. These algorithms may inadvertently favor artists who align with pre-existing market trends, potentially overlooking diverse or unconventional voices. The algorithm, in essence, becomes another gatekeeper, possibly reinforcing existing systemic inequalities within the industry. The question of transparency remains paramount: artists often lack access to the data used to assess their potential and the criteria on which decisions are based.

Furthermore, the issue of artist compensation continues to be a major source of friction. Streaming services, while convenient for listeners, offer notoriously low royalty rates to artists, further diminishing their financial security. Record labels often absorb a significant portion of the already meager payments, leaving many artists struggling to make a living from their music, despite achieving substantial popularity online. This has fueled the debate over fair compensation, prompting artist advocacy groups and industry leaders to push for more equitable royalty structures that better reflect the value of musical creations.

The changing relationship between artists and record labels necessitates a re-evaluation of established business models. New models are emerging that attempt to address the power imbalance and create a more sustainable environment for musicians. Some labels are experimenting with profitsharing models that provide artists with a fairer share of revenue. Others are incorporating blockchain technology to create transparent and secure systems for royalty payments and rights management. The use of smart contracts could automate royalty payments, eliminating potential for discrepancies and delays that often plague traditional systems. This potential for increased transparency is a step towards addressing the lack of trust and fairness that has historically marred the artist-label relationship.

Moreover, the rise of artist collectives and co-operatives provides an alternative model to the traditional label structure. These organizations allow artists to pool resources, share expertise, and negotiate better terms with distribution platforms and other service providers. By working together, they can leverage their collective strength to challenge the dominance of large record labels and create a more equitable system for independent artists. These collectives often prioritize creative control, fair compensation, and mutual support amongst their members.

The future of the music industry rests, in large part, on the evolution of the artist-label relationship. The traditional model, while still relevant for some artists, needs considerable adaptation to reflect the realities of the digital age. A shift towards transparency, fair compensation, and collaborative partnerships is essential for the long-term health and sustainability of the industry. As technology continues to reshape the landscape, the labels that successfully adapt to this new reality – those that prioritize genuine collaborations, fair practices, and a commitment to fostering genuine artistic expression – are the ones most likely to thrive. The industry's future hinges on whether it can foster a system that values artists not merely as commodities but as partners in the creative process. The ongoing struggle for fair compensation, transparency, and equitable power dynamics is a fight that is far from over, but one that will fundamentally shape the future of music. The path forward requires a fundamental shift in mindset, moving from an exploitative system to a collaborative one that recognizes the value of artistic creativity and the crucial role of artists themselves in driving the industry's success. The industry's success ultimately hinges on a renewed appreciation of the artist as a key player, not just a resource to be exploited.

New Business Models and Revenue Streams in the Music Industry

The upheaval in the music industry, fueled by digital distribution and the rise of independent artists, necessitates a radical rethinking of traditional revenue streams. The old model, heavily reliant on physical album sales and limited digital distribution controlled by major labels, is rapidly becoming obsolete. While the dominance of streaming services like Spotify and Apple Music has provided unprecedented access to music for listeners globally, it has also created a precarious financial landscape for artists, who often receive minuscule royalty payments. This situation has spurred innovation, leading to the exploration and implementation of diverse and often creative new business models and revenue streams.

One significant shift is the increased emphasis on subscription services beyond the major streaming platforms. Artists are increasingly establishing their own subscription platforms, offering exclusive content, early access to new releases, behind-the-scenes glimpses into their creative process, and direct interaction with fans. This model fosters a deeper, more intimate relationship with the audience, moving beyond the passive consumption offered by mainstream streaming services. These platforms, often utilizing platforms like Patreon or Substack, allow artists to receive direct, recurring revenue, offering a level of financial stability absent in the volatile world of traditional record deals and streaming royalties. The key to success in this model is cultivating a dedicated and loyal fanbase willing to invest in the artist's ongoing work and creative journey. This requires a consistent and engaging strategy, encompassing regular content updates, personalized interactions, and a clear value proposition for subscribers.

Merchandise sales have also undergone a transformation, moving far beyond the basic t-shirt and poster. Artists are leveraging their creativity and brand identity to create unique and desirable merchandise, extending the reach of their artistic vision beyond their music. This can encompass limited-edition vinyl releases, bespoke clothing lines reflecting their personal style, exclusive artwork prints, and even experiential merchandise like virtual meet-and-greets or personalized music lessons. The key here is to create products that resonate with the artist's fanbase, reflecting their unique artistic vision and offering something truly special, rather than simply mass-produced items. Effective marketing and strategic collaborations with designers and manufacturers are crucial in establishing a successful merchandise business. The direct-to-consumer model, bypassing traditional retailers, offers greater control over pricing and profit margins, further empowering artists. Ecommerce platforms like Shopify have made it easier than ever for musicians to manage their own online stores, creating a seamless and efficient system for sales and distribution.

The rise of brand partnerships and sponsorships represents another significant revenue stream for artists. Brands are increasingly seeking to align themselves with authentic and influential musicians, leveraging their creativity and reach to connect with a targeted demographic. This can involve collaborations on product design, appearances in advertising campaigns, or co-branded merchandise. Choosing the right brand partner is critical, ensuring alignment with the artist's values and image to maintain the authenticity that resonates with their fanbase. This approach needs careful consideration; a poorly chosen partnership can damage an artist's credibility. Negotiating favorable terms is paramount, ensuring fair compensation and avoiding contracts that compromise the artist's creative control.

Live performances, while historically a cornerstone of musical revenue, have undergone significant changes in recent years. The pandemic forced a widespread adoption of virtual concerts and livestreams, creating entirely new possibilities for reaching audiences worldwide. These virtual events offer unique opportunities for artists to interact with fans in real-time, offering exclusive content and immersive experiences that traditional live performances may not replicate. While the technical requirements and logistical complexities of virtual performances can be considerable, the potential for global reach and the ability to generate revenue from ticket sales, merchandise, and sponsorships make it a viable and potentially lucrative revenue stream. The hybrid model, combining virtual and physical performances, is also gaining traction, maximizing reach and engagement.

Moreover, the burgeoning field of NFTs (Non-Fungible Tokens) has presented a novel avenue for artists to monetize their work. NFTs allow musicians to sell unique digital assets, such as exclusive music tracks, artwork, or virtual concert experiences, offering collectors a verifiable certificate of ownership. This technology creates a new market for digital collectibles, providing artists with a direct revenue stream and fostering a deeper connection with their fanbase. The potential for royalties on secondary sales of NFTs further enhances the financial benefits. The legal and technical complexities associated with NFTs require careful navigation, ensuring compliance with regulations and protecting the artist's intellectual property. However, the potential for innovative and unique revenue streams makes it an area worth exploring for many artists.

The evolution of music licensing also offers new opportunities. Licensing music for use in films, television shows, video games, and advertising can generate significant income. Building a strong catalog of music and strategically targeting licensing opportunities through dedicated agencies or directly engaging with potential clients can be lucrative. The use of music in commercials or in social media content is rapidly expanding, making it important for artists to have a clear understanding of their licensing rights and to proactively manage these opportunities. This requires efficient music catalog management systems and adept negotiation skills.

Finally, the role of artist management and the adoption of sophisticated business strategies are becoming increasingly important. Effective management can assist artists in navigating the complex business aspects of their careers, helping them to secure favorable deals, manage their finances, and build their brands. The utilization of data analytics to understand audience demographics, preferences, and engagement patterns allows for more effective marketing strategies and personalized fan engagement. This data-driven approach allows artists to optimize their efforts and maximize their revenue streams. Furthermore, effective legal counsel is critical in negotiating contracts, protecting intellectual property, and ensuring fair compensation for their work. This aspect is especially vital in a rapidly evolving digital landscape.

In conclusion, the future of the music industry lies not in clinging to outdated models but in embracing the innovative business strategies and revenue streams detailed above. The digital age demands a proactive and entrepreneurial approach from artists, necessitating a blend of creativity, business acumen, and a strong understanding of their fans.

The industry's ongoing evolution offers both challenges and remarkable opportunities, those who adapt and embrace the change will be the ones who thrive. The key is to foster a direct relationship with the audience, create unique and engaging content, and strategically leverage various revenue streams to achieve financial stability and artistic freedom. The music industry's future will be defined by artists who successfully integrate creativity and entrepreneurship, ensuring the sustainable and equitable future of music creation and consumption.

The Importance of Sustainability and Ethical Practices in Shaping the Future

The preceding discussion highlighted the innovative strategies artists are employing to navigate the evolving music industry landscape, focusing on diversifying revenue streams and cultivating direct relationships with their audiences. However, the long-term health and vibrancy of this industry depend not just on financial innovation but also on a fundamental shift towards sustainability and ethical practices. The pursuit of profit cannot come at the expense of fair compensation for artists, environmental responsibility, or social justice. These are not mere add-ons; they are essential pillars upon which a truly thriving and equitable music industry can be built.

Fair compensation for artists remains a persistent and critical issue. The streaming model, while providing unprecedented access to music, has often resulted in minuscule royalty payments for musicians, particularly those outside the major label system. The power imbalance between streaming services and artists needs to be addressed through fairer royalty structures, increased transparency in payment calculations, and robust mechanisms for dispute resolution. Artist collectives and advocacy groups are playing a vital role in pushing for legislative changes and negotiating better deals with streaming platforms, highlighting the power of collective action in achieving meaningful change. Furthermore, educating artists about their rights and providing them with the resources to negotiate favorable contracts is crucial in empowering them to secure fair compensation for their work. This includes providing access to legal aid and promoting transparency in industry standard contracts.

Beyond direct compensation, the ethical treatment of artists extends to their working conditions and creative autonomy. Exploitative contracts, which often grant labels excessive control over an artist's creative output and financial affairs, must be challenged and reformed. Independent artists often face the burden of self-management, navigating the complex administrative, marketing, and legal aspects of their careers without adequate support. The rise of artist-focused organizations and support networks is vital in addressing this, providing mentorship, resources, and advocacy to help artists negotiate the complexities of the industry while safeguarding their creative freedom.

Environmental sustainability is another crucial aspect that needs immediate attention. The music industry, like many others, has a significant environmental footprint. The manufacturing and distribution of physical media, the energy consumption of live events and studios, and the carbon emissions associated with touring all contribute to environmental degradation. The industry must adopt ecofriendly practices across the value chain. This includes shifting towards sustainable packaging for physical media, reducing waste from concerts and festivals through better waste management systems, and promoting carbon-neutral touring practices. Incentivizing sustainable practices, such as offering tax breaks for environmentally friendly operations or highlighting eco-conscious artists, could encourage widespread adoption. Moreover, transparency regarding environmental impact is crucial, allowing consumers to make informed choices and holding the industry accountable for its environmental footprint. Initiatives such as carbon offsetting programs for tours and the development of ecofriendly vinyl records exemplify the industry's growing awareness of its environmental responsibility.

Social justice is intertwined with the broader ethical considerations in the music industry. Issues such as gender inequality, racial bias, and LGBTQ+ representation need to be addressed proactively. The lack of diversity in leadership positions, the underrepresentation of marginalized groups in mainstream media, and the perpetuation of harmful stereotypes in lyrics and imagery all require conscious efforts towards change. Promoting diverse voices and fostering inclusivity in all areas of the industry, from artist development programs to executive positions, is vital in creating a more equitable and representative environment. This involves not just symbolic gestures but structural changes that dismantle systemic barriers and actively create opportunities for marginalized communities. Supporting independent artists from marginalized communities, particularly through targeted funding and mentorship programs, is a crucial step toward fostering greater diversity and representation within the industry.

Furthermore, the ethical sourcing of materials used in the production of music equipment and merchandise must be considered. Ensuring fair labor practices and avoiding the use of materials obtained through unethical means are crucial in maintaining ethical standards throughout the supply chain. Transparency and traceability of materials are vital in ensuring that the industry's actions align with its stated values. Supporting ethical manufacturers and suppliers, while potentially increasing costs in the short term, builds long-term credibility and trust with consumers who increasingly prioritize ethical considerations when making purchasing decisions.

The adoption of blockchain technology beyond NFTs offers significant potential for enhancing transparency and accountability within the music industry. Blockchain's inherent immutability and decentralized nature could revolutionize royalty tracking, ensuring fair and timely payments to artists and ensuring transparency in the distribution of revenue. This technology has the potential to address the long-standing problem of opaque royalty payments and the difficulties faced by artists in tracking their earnings. Moreover, blockchain-based systems could facilitate more efficient and secure contracts between artists and labels, providing increased protection for both parties.

Finally, fostering a culture of ethical responsibility necessitates collaboration between all stakeholders in the music industry. Labels, streaming services, artists, managers, and fans all have a role to play in creating a more sustainable and equitable ecosystem. This involves open dialogue, the sharing of best practices, and a collective commitment to upholding high ethical standards. Industry organizations and regulatory bodies can play a significant role in establishing clear guidelines and enforcing ethical conduct. Ultimately, building a truly sustainable and ethical music industry requires a transformative shift in mindset, prioritizing longterm value creation over short-term profit maximization. By embracing sustainability and ethical practices, the music industry can not only safeguard its long-term viability but also contribute to a more just and environmentally responsible world. The future of music hinges on this commitment. The ethical considerations are not simply a matter of corporate social responsibility; they are fundamentally intertwined with the very essence of music itself—its power to connect us, inspire us, and reflect the human experience. A music industry built on exploitation and unsustainable practices ultimately undermines its own creative power. The path forward is clear: a commitment to sustainability and ethical practices is not just a desirable goal; it is a necessary condition for the survival and flourishing of the music industry.

A Vision for a More Equitable and Sustainable Music Industry

The preceding discussion has illuminated the precarious position of many artists within the current music industry framework. While innovative strategies offer pathways to financial resilience, a truly thriving future demands a fundamental paradigm shift—a transition towards a more equitable and sustainable ecosystem. This isn't merely a matter of altruism; it's a matter of long-term viability. An industry built on exploitation, unsustainable practices, and systemic inequities is fundamentally unsustainable. Its creative energy, its very lifeblood, will eventually be choked off.

A vision for a more equitable and sustainable music industry begins with a commitment to fair compensation. The current streaming model, despite its democratizing potential, has often yielded paltry returns for artists, particularly those outside the major label system. The algorithms that govern these platforms, often opaque and inscrutable, frequently prioritize corporate profits over artist compensation. This creates a vicious cycle, where artists struggling to make ends meet are forced to accept exploitative contracts or abandon their craft altogether. Addressing this requires a multipronged approach.

First, greater transparency is essential. Streaming services must provide clear, detailed breakdowns of royalty calculations, allowing artists to fully understand how their earnings are determined. This transparency should extend to the algorithms themselves, allowing artists to understand how their music is promoted and discovered. Currently, many artists are operating in the dark, relying on guesswork and anecdotal evidence to navigate the complexities of online distribution. This opacity empowers the platforms to prioritize their own interests over those of the artists whose work drives their revenue. Independent audits of royalty calculations, perhaps conducted by a third-party organization, could significantly improve accountability and reduce the potential for manipulation.

Second, a reassessment of royalty rates is necessary. The current rates, in many cases, fail to adequately compensate artists for the value they generate. Negotiating fairer royalty structures requires collective action. Artist collectives and unions play a crucial role in leveraging their collective bargaining power to negotiate more favorable terms with streaming services and labels. Legislation could also play a role, mandating minimum royalty rates or establishing regulatory bodies to oversee the fair distribution of revenue. Models like the PROs (performing rights organizations) could be expanded and improved, ensuring that every play of a song results in a fair payment to the artist, regardless of where it's played.

Third, the issue of revenue distribution within the industry needs to be addressed. The current system often sees a disproportionate share of revenue flowing to intermediaries, leaving artists with a meager portion. This needs to be reevaluated, ensuring that artists receive a more substantial share of the revenue generated by their work. This requires addressing the power dynamics inherent within the industry, empowering artists to negotiate more favorable contracts and reducing the influence of exploitative practices.

Beyond fair compensation, the concept of artistic empowerment is critical. Many artists, particularly those starting out, lack the business acumen and resources to navigate the complexities of the music industry. This puts them at a significant disadvantage, making them vulnerable to exploitative contracts and unfair practices. Artist-focused organizations and support networks are vital in providing the necessary resources and mentorship. These organizations can offer guidance on contract negotiation, business management, marketing, and legal matters, empowering artists to manage their careers effectively and protect their rights. This includes providing access to legal aid and fostering networks of support amongst artists themselves. Sharing knowledge and best practices amongst peers can be invaluable in avoiding the pitfalls that often trap emerging artists.

Moreover, fostering a culture of creative autonomy is essential. Exploitative contracts often grant labels excessive control over an artist's creative output and career trajectory. This stifles artistic expression and reduces the diversity of voices in the industry. Artists must have the freedom to create without undue influence or pressure from external forces. This means challenging the prevailing power dynamics, empowering artists to retain control over their artistic vision and the direction of their careers. The rise of independent labels and distribution platforms provides an alternative pathway for artists seeking greater autonomy, but it also requires artists to acquire the necessary skills to manage these aspects of their careers.

Environmental sustainability also necessitates a fundamental shift within the music industry. The carbon footprint of live performances, studio recordings, merchandise production, and touring is considerable. The industry must adopt ecofriendly practices across the value chain. This includes transitioning to sustainable materials in the production of instruments, albums, and merchandise, utilizing renewable energy sources in studios and venues, and adopting carbonneutral touring practices. Investing in carbon offsetting programs, supporting eco-conscious initiatives within the music industry, and promoting transparency regarding environmental impact are all crucial steps. Collaborations with environmental organizations and the implementation of industry-wide sustainability standards would provide a framework for action. Consumers are increasingly conscious of environmental issues and their purchasing decisions reflect this. Adopting sustainable practices builds brand loyalty, aligns the industry with consumer values, and ensures its long-term viability.

The issue of social justice and equity is deeply intertwined with the broader vision for a sustainable and ethical music industry. The industry has historically lacked diversity, both in terms of the artists who achieve mainstream success and the individuals holding positions of power within the industry. This systemic bias needs to be actively challenged. Promoting diversity and inclusion requires a multifaceted approach. This involves actively seeking out and promoting artists from marginalized communities, providing mentorship and support programs targeted at these groups, and ensuring diverse representation within the leadership of labels, streaming services, and other industry organizations. This requires not only symbolic gestures, but also fundamental structural changes that address systemic barriers and create opportunities for underrepresented artists. Promoting equitable access to resources, funding, and opportunities is vital in fostering a more representative and inclusive industry. Moreover, it's essential to critically examine the lyrics, imagery, and narratives prevalent within the industry, actively working to dismantle harmful stereotypes and foster a culture of respect and understanding.

The implementation of blockchain technology offers the potential for revolutionizing many aspects of the industry. Beyond the initial hype around NFTs, the immutable and transparent nature of blockchain can be leveraged for improved royalty tracking, ensuring fairer and timelier payments to artists. This can help address the pervasive problem of opaque royalty calculations and the challenges artists face in tracking their earnings. Blockchain-based systems can also streamline contract negotiations, creating more secure and transparent agreements between artists and labels. However, the successful implementation of such technologies requires careful consideration of issues surrounding data privacy and security.

Finally, fostering a culture of ethical responsibility requires collaboration amongst all stakeholders. Labels, streaming services, artists, managers, and fans all have a crucial role to play in building a more sustainable and equitable ecosystem. This involves open dialogue, the sharing of best practices, and a collective commitment to upholding high ethical standards. Industry organizations and regulatory bodies can facilitate this process by establishing clear guidelines and enforcing ethical conduct. Ultimately, building a sustainable and ethical music industry requires a fundamental shift in mindset, prioritizing long-term value creation over shortterm profit maximization. By embracing these principles, the music industry can safeguard its future, contributing to a more just and environmentally responsible world. The ethical considerations are not separate from the art; they are integral to it. A music industry built on exploitation undermines the very essence of music's power to connect and inspire.

Summary of Key Findings and Insights

This book has undertaken a deep dive into the complexities and contradictions of the modern music industry, peeling back layers of glamour to reveal a system often characterized by exploitation, inequity, and a disregard for the very artists who fuel its engine. The preceding chapters have documented numerous instances of predatory contracts, opaque royalty structures, and the systemic power imbalances that consistently favor the established players – labels, streaming services, and powerful intermediaries – at the expense of musicians, songwriters, and other creative professionals. We've examined the pervasive influence of algorithms, the often-unfair distribution of revenue, and the lack of transparency that keeps artists perpetually in a state of uncertainty about their earnings and career trajectory.

One of the most striking findings is the sheer scale of the disparity between the vast profits generated by the industry and the minuscule compensation received by many artists. The streaming model, while hailed as a democratizing force, has often proven to be a tool for consolidating power in the hands of a few, leaving the vast majority of musicians struggling to make a living from their art. The paltry royalty rates paid per stream, coupled with the opaque nature of royalty calculation, create a system ripe for exploitation and leaves artists vulnerable to financial insecurity. The lack of transparency is particularly egregious; artists often lack access to the data they need to understand how their royalties are calculated, leaving them unable to challenge inaccuracies or inconsistencies. This information asymmetry empowers the major players to maintain the status quo, even when it directly harms the artists who create the content.

The investigation has also highlighted the crucial role of artist empowerment in building a more sustainable and ethical music industry. Many artists, especially those beginning their careers, lack the business acumen and resources to effectively navigate the complex legal and financial landscape of the industry. This makes them highly susceptible to predatory contracts and unfair practices. Strengthening artist advocacy groups, providing access to affordable legal counsel specializing in entertainment law, and establishing educational programs focused on business and legal skills are crucial steps towards empowering artists to protect their interests and negotiate fairer terms. Without access to this knowledge and support, artists remain vulnerable to exploitation and their creative potential is severely undermined.

The issue of creative control emerged as another central theme throughout this work. Many artists find their creative autonomy curtailed by labels and publishers who exert undue influence over their artistic output and the direction of their careers. Such control compromises the artistic integrity of the music produced and restricts the diversity of voices within the industry. The pursuit of profit often overshadows artistic merit, leading to a homogenization of sound and the silencing of dissenting voices. The increasing prevalence of AI-driven music generation further raises questions about the future of artistic authenticity and control. While offering potential benefits in songwriting and production, AI also presents significant challenges to artists in terms of ownership, compensation, and the erosion of human creativity. We must grapple with how to leverage the advantages of technology while preserving the unique human element essential to musical expression.

The environmental impact of the music industry has been largely ignored until recently. The extensive touring schedules of major artists, the energy consumption of recording studios and venues, and the production of merchandise all contribute significantly to the industry's carbon footprint. Moving toward eco-friendly practices is no longer an option but a necessity. Implementing sustainable strategies across the industry's value chain requires a concerted effort by labels, venues, artists, and fans alike. This includes investing in renewable energy sources, reducing waste in production, and promoting carbon-neutral touring practices. Moreover, transparency regarding environmental impact needs to be prioritized, allowing consumers to make more informed decisions.

Social justice and equity are profoundly intertwined with the sustainability of the music industry. A sector plagued by systemic inequalities, historically dominated by a small segment of the population, needs a conscious effort towards diversity and inclusion. The underrepresentation of artists from marginalized communities has long been an issue, perpetuated by systemic biases in access to resources, opportunities, and promotion. A more equitable industry requires active measures to dismantle these barriers and create opportunities for underrepresented voices. This goes beyond simple representation; it requires systemic change that addresses root causes and ensures equitable access to resources, funding, and opportunities for marginalized communities.

The use of blockchain technology presents a potential avenue for transforming many aspects of the music industry. While the initial hype around NFTs has subsided, the underlying technology holds immense potential for improving royalty tracking and distribution. The immutable and transparent nature of blockchain could facilitate more accurate and timely payments to artists, addressing the longstanding problem of opaque accounting practices.

Furthermore, blockchain could streamline contract negotiation and enforcement, leading to fairer and more transparent agreements between artists and labels. However, challenges related to data privacy, security, and user adoption must be carefully considered before widespread implementation.

Ultimately, creating a more sustainable and ethical music industry requires a fundamental shift in mindset, moving away from a profit-maximizing approach towards one that prioritizes long-term value creation for all stakeholders. This means fostering a culture of collaboration, transparency, and accountability, where artists, labels, streaming services, and fans work together to create a more equitable and environmentally responsible ecosystem. It is a shared responsibility, requiring commitment from every level of the industry. The pursuit of profit should not come at the expense of artistic integrity, creative freedom, or environmental sustainability. It is crucial to emphasize that the ethical considerations are not peripheral but are central to the heart of music creation and appreciation. The future of the industry depends on it. A music industry built on exploitation ultimately undermines its own creative vitality and ability to connect with audiences. Only through profound and systemic change can the music industry realize its full potential, ensuring a vibrant and sustainable future for all involved.

Reflection on the Ethical Dilemmas and Moral Compromises

The preceding chapters have laid bare a system riddled with ethical compromises and moral ambiguities. We've documented the pervasive exploitation of artists, the opaque financial dealings, and the systemic power imbalances that consistently benefit a select few at the expense of the many. But beyond the specifics of predatory contracts and skewed royalty structures lies a deeper question: what are the overarching ethical responsibilities of those involved in the music industry? And what moral compromises have been made, both implicitly and explicitly, to maintain the status quo?

The pursuit of profit, often presented as the driving force behind industry decisions, frequently overshadows the ethical considerations that should be central to its operation. This profit-driven approach has led to a culture of exploitation, where the inherent value of artistic creation is minimized in favor of maximizing returns. Artists, vulnerable due to their lack of business acumen and bargaining power, are often left at the mercy of powerful industry players who leverage their position to extract maximum value. The imbalance of power is not just a matter of economic inequality; it is also a matter of creative control, with labels and publishers often dictating artistic direction, limiting the creative freedom essential for genuine artistic expression.

This lack of transparency in financial dealings further exacerbates the ethical issues. The opaque calculation of royalties, the withholding of crucial financial data, and the ambiguity surrounding contract terms create an environment where artists are unable to fully comprehend their financial situation. This intentional obfuscation prevents them from advocating for their rights and negotiating fairer deals. It is a systemic betrayal of trust, demonstrating a fundamental lack of respect for the artists who create the very product that fuels the industry's profits.

The rise of streaming services has exacerbated these problems, creating a new layer of complexity and inequity. While ostensibly democratizing access to music, streaming platforms have often perpetuated the existing power imbalances. The minuscule royalty rates paid per stream, coupled with the algorithms that prioritize certain artists over others, result in a system that heavily favors established acts while leaving independent artists to struggle for visibility and fair compensation. The lack of transparency regarding these algorithms further compounds the problem, making it difficult for artists to understand how their music is being promoted and why some achieve success while others remain largely unheard.

Beyond the immediate financial exploitation, we must also consider the broader ethical implications of the industry's practices. The homogenization of musical styles, driven by the pursuit of commercial success, limits the diversity of artistic expression and silences dissenting voices. The pressure to conform to prevailing trends often forces artists to compromise their artistic integrity, creating a homogenized soundscape that lacks originality and authenticity. This pursuit of conformity undermines the very essence of artistic creation, reducing music to a mere commodity rather than a form of genuine self-expression. The issue extends beyond stylistic conformity; it impacts the diverse representation of artists themselves. The industry's historic lack of diversity, with its disproportionate representation of white male artists, reflects a systemic bias that needs to be actively challenged and rectified.

Furthermore, the environmental impact of the music industry is a growing concern that demands urgent attention. The carbon footprint generated by extensive touring, energyintensive recording studios, and the manufacturing of merchandise requires a fundamental shift towards more sustainable practices. While some initiatives are underway, they are often insufficient to address the scale of the problem. The industry needs to move beyond superficial commitments and adopt a genuinely eco-conscious approach, incorporating sustainability into every aspect of its operations, from recording and production to touring and merchandise. The ethical imperative to protect the planet requires a comprehensive and transformative approach, embracing renewable energy, minimizing waste, and promoting environmentally responsible practices.

The ethical dilemmas facing the music industry are not simply isolated incidents; they reflect a deeper systemic crisis. Addressing these issues requires a fundamental shift in mindset, a move away from the prevailing profitmaximizing mentality towards a model that values ethical conduct and social responsibility. This shift involves fostering a culture of transparency, accountability, and collaboration, where all stakeholders – artists, labels, streaming services, and fans – work together to create a more equitable and sustainable ecosystem. The ethical considerations are not peripheral but are central to the heart of music creation and appreciation. The future of the industry depends on a conscious commitment to ethical practices and a willingness to confront the deep-seated power imbalances and systemic injustices that have plagued it for far too long.

We cannot simply accept the status quo; we must demand better. This requires concerted action from all stakeholders. Artists need to organize, build their collective bargaining power, and demand fairer contracts and more transparent accounting. Labels and streaming services must take responsibility for their practices and commit to fairer royalty structures and more equitable distribution of revenues. Fans, too, have a role to play, by supporting independent artists, demanding greater transparency, and holding the industry accountable for its ethical shortcomings. Furthermore, regulatory bodies and governments should investigate and address the systemic issues, ensuring a level playing field for artists and promoting fair competition.

The future of the music industry hinges on this collective commitment to ethical conduct. A music industry built on exploitation and inequity is not a sustainable one. Only through a profound and sustained commitment to justice, fairness, and environmental responsibility can the industry realize its full creative potential and ensure a vibrant and sustainable future for all those who participate in it. This is not simply about reforming the existing system; it is about building a new one, founded on principles of fairness, transparency, and respect for the artists whose talent fuels its engine. It's about moving beyond profit maximization and embracing a model that prioritizes the long-term well-being of the entire ecosystem.

The journey towards a more ethical and sustainable music industry will not be easy. It requires navigating complex legal and financial landscapes, confronting powerful vested interests, and challenging deeply entrenched cultural norms. But the stakes are high. The future of music, its creative vitality, its capacity to connect and inspire, depends on our willingness to confront these ethical challenges head-on and build a system that prioritizes integrity, justice, and the wellbeing of all involved. It is a call to action, a demand for fundamental change, a commitment to a future where the music industry is not only profitable but also just, equitable, and environmentally responsible.

The time for complacency is over. The time for action is now. The future of music depends on it.

Recommendations for Artists Industry Professionals and Policymakers

Recommendations for Artists, Industry Professionals, and

Policymakers

The preceding chapters have painted a stark picture of the music industry's ethical failings. We've seen how systemic inequalities, opaque financial practices, and a relentless focus on profit maximization have consistently disadvantaged artists and undermined the very essence of musical creation. However, exposing these problems is only half the battle. The other half lies in forging a path toward a more just and sustainable future for the industry. This requires a concerted effort from all stakeholders – artists, industry professionals, and policymakers – to implement meaningful changes.

For artists, the need for collective action is paramount. Individually, artists often lack the bargaining power to negotiate fair contracts and secure adequate compensation. However, by organizing collectively, artists can create a powerful force for change. This can involve forming unions or artist collectives, leveraging the power of numbers to advocate for better working conditions, fairer royalty structures, and improved transparency in financial dealings. Such organizations can provide crucial support and resources to individual artists, offering legal advice, contract review services, and educational programs on business management and industry practices. Moreover, collective action can help artists navigate the complexities of the music industry, sharing knowledge and experiences, and providing a supportive network to prevent exploitation and isolation. The formation of artist-owned labels and distribution platforms also offers a crucial avenue for regaining control over their creative output and financial destinies. By bypassing traditional gatekeepers, artists can retain a larger share of the profits generated by their work, fostering greater independence and creative freedom.

Building a robust support system within the artist community is vital. Mentorship programs, skill-sharing workshops, and peer-to-peer networks can empower artists to navigate the industry's challenges more effectively. Sharing knowledge about contract negotiation, financial management, and legal rights can significantly improve artists' bargaining power and reduce their vulnerability to exploitation. The sharing of industry best practices can also lead to more equitable collaborations, fostering a culture of mutual respect and shared success.

Beyond collective action, artists must actively cultivate their entrepreneurial skills. Understanding the business side of the music industry is crucial for artists to protect their interests and maximize their earning potential. This requires learning about copyright law, contract negotiation, marketing and promotion, and financial management. Embracing digital literacy and understanding the intricacies of streaming services and online distribution is equally vital in today's digital landscape. By developing their business acumen, artists can navigate the industry with greater confidence, negotiate stronger contracts, and control the narrative surrounding their careers.

For industry professionals, the call for ethical reform must begin within their own ranks. Labels, publishers, booking agents, and managers hold considerable power within the music industry. Their responsibility extends beyond simply generating profit; they must actively work to create a more equitable and sustainable ecosystem. This necessitates a commitment to transparency, fair dealings, and a focus on long-term sustainability, rather than short-term gains. Implementing clear and transparent royalty structures, providing artists with comprehensive financial reports, and ensuring fair and equitable contract terms are essential steps towards building trust and fostering collaboration. Furthermore, industry professionals must actively promote diversity and inclusion, ensuring that artists from all backgrounds have equal opportunities to succeed.

Beyond internal reforms, industry professionals can contribute to a more ethical industry by actively supporting independent artists and alternative distribution models. By fostering a more diverse and inclusive marketplace, they can mitigate the power imbalance that often favors established artists. Investing in artist development programs, providing mentorship and guidance, and creating opportunities for collaboration can significantly contribute to a more equitable music industry. Industry professionals should also advocate for fair and sustainable practices within their organizations, promoting environmental responsibility and ethical labor standards across all aspects of the business.

Policymakers have a critical role to play in reforming the music industry. They can enact legislation to protect artists' rights, address the power imbalances within the industry, and promote fairer compensation. This could involve revising copyright laws to ensure artists receive a greater share of revenues generated by their work, regulating streaming royalties to ensure adequate compensation for artists, and strengthening antitrust laws to prevent anti-competitive practices. Policymakers should also invest in artist education and support programs, providing resources to help artists navigate the complexities of the music industry and protect their rights. Furthermore, legislation could incentivize sustainable practices within the music industry, encouraging the adoption of eco-friendly technologies and promoting environmentally responsible business models. Governments could also play a role in supporting artist-led organizations and collectives, providing grants and funding to facilitate collective action and advocacy. Finally, policymakers should support and fund research into the impact of technology and streaming on the music industry, providing a basis for informed policy decisions and effective legislative intervention.

The path to a more ethical, equitable, and sustainable music industry is paved with concerted action from all stakeholders. It demands a significant shift in mindset, away from a purely profit-driven approach toward a model that prioritizes the well-being of artists and the long-term sustainability of the music ecosystem. This requires artists to organize and collectively leverage their power, industry professionals to embrace ethical practices and foster inclusivity, and policymakers to create a legislative framework that protects artists' rights and promotes fair competition. The future of music hinges on this collective commitment to change; only through concerted and sustained effort can we build a music industry that is both vibrant and just. The time for superficial reforms and empty promises is over. This is a call for profound and lasting transformation, a demand for a future where music thrives in an environment of integrity, fairness, and mutual respect. The future of music, its creativity, its vibrancy, and its power to connect us, demands nothing less. The challenge is immense, but the rewards – a flourishing music ecosystem that celebrates creativity and supports those who create it – are immeasurable. The journey towards this future begins with a shared commitment to action, a determination to build a better tomorrow, and an unwavering belief in the transformative power of music.

Call to Action Promoting Change and Advocating for Reform

The preceding chapters have documented a systemic rot within the music industry, a pervasive disregard for the very artists who fuel its engine. We've exposed exploitative contracts, opaque financial practices, and a culture of silence that protects the powerful while silencing the vulnerable. This isn't simply a critique; it's a call to arms. The future of music, its integrity, and its capacity for genuine artistic expression, depends on our collective willingness to act.

This isn't a passive endeavor. Change won't materialize through polite requests or well-intentioned pleas. It demands active participation, a relentless pursuit of justice, and a willingness to confront those who profit from the industry's injustices. This means moving beyond outrage and channeling our frustration into concrete actions that can bring about tangible results.

For consumers of music, the most immediate step is informed consumption. Supporting artists directly, bypassing the often exploitative middlemen, is paramount. This means buying music directly from artists' websites, attending independent concerts, and utilizing platforms that offer fairer royalty structures to creators. We must become discerning consumers, actively choosing to support those who prioritize ethical practices over profit maximization. This includes researching labels and distributors, understanding their business models, and ensuring that our purchasing decisions align with our values. A simple click can become a powerful act of resistance, a vote cast in favor of a more equitable industry.

Beyond conscious consumption, we need to amplify the voices of those who are marginalized and exploited. This involves actively promoting the work of independent artists, sharing their stories on social media, and engaging in respectful discussions that challenge the status quo. We must become active participants in a wider conversation, using our platforms to highlight the injustices within the industry and encourage others to join the fight for reform. Supporting artist-led initiatives, such as crowdfunding campaigns and independent record labels, is another way to demonstrate our commitment to a more just system. Our collective actions, amplified through digital networks, can create a wave of support that empowers artists and challenges the dominance of corporate interests.

Furthering this, we must hold those who wield power accountable. This includes contacting our elected officials, urging them to introduce and support legislation that protects artists' rights. Lobbying for stronger copyright laws, more equitable streaming royalty structures, and greater transparency in industry dealings is crucial. We must demand that policymakers prioritize the needs of artists over the interests of large corporations. Active engagement in political processes is vital, turning our collective frustration into meaningful political pressure. We must demand more than just promises; we must demand legislation and enforcement that truly safeguards artists' interests.

Educational initiatives are equally vital. Raising awareness about the exploitative nature of certain contracts and the importance of legal counsel for artists is crucial. We can support organizations dedicated to artist advocacy, ensuring that aspiring and established artists have access to the information and support they need to navigate the industry successfully. This might involve volunteer work, financial contributions, or simply disseminating relevant information through our personal and professional networks. Empowering artists with knowledge is a crucial step towards mitigating the power imbalance within the industry.

The media plays a critical role in this process. Independent journalists and investigative reporters must continue to shed light on the industry's dark corners, holding powerful figures accountable for their actions. Through investigative reporting, we can expose corruption, highlight unethical practices, and facilitate the ongoing conversation surrounding industry reform. By supporting investigative journalism, we ensure that the important work continues, providing the fuel for a necessary public discourse.

The fight for a fairer music industry is a marathon, not a sprint. There will be setbacks and challenges, but our collective perseverance is crucial. We cannot afford complacency; we must remain vigilant, continuing to expose injustice and demanding accountability. The battle for a more equitable music ecosystem is one we must fight together, uniting our voices and actions to create lasting change. The future of music, its vitality, and its capacity to connect us, depends on this collective commitment.

The transformation will not be swift or easy. The entrenched power structures within the music industry are vast and resilient. They have proven adept at exploiting loopholes, silencing dissent, and maintaining the status quo. However, the tide is turning. The voices of artists, supported by informed consumers and committed advocates, are growing louder. The collective effort to dismantle the industry's exploitative structures is gaining momentum, and the call for change resonates ever more powerfully. Through persistent advocacy, unwavering support, and a shared commitment to action, we can create a music industry that values artists, fosters creativity, and prioritizes integrity over profit. This is not merely a dream; it is a achievable goal, within reach if we commit ourselves fully to this crucial endeavor. The legacy we leave behind will depend on the actions we take today. The future of music awaits. Let's build it together.

Looking Ahead A Hopeful Vision for the Future of Music

The fight for a just music industry is far from over, but the seeds of change are being sown. The preceding chapters have laid bare the systemic injustices, the predatory practices, and the pervasive power imbalances that plague this industry. But exposing the problem is only half the battle; the other half, and arguably the more challenging one, lies in forging a path towards a more equitable future. This requires a fundamental shift in mindset, a collective reimagining of how music is created, distributed, and consumed.

One promising avenue for reform lies in the democratization of music production and distribution. The rise of independent artists, empowered by readily accessible technology and online distribution platforms, is a powerful counterweight to the dominance of major labels. These platforms, while not without their own challenges, offer artists unprecedented control over their creative output and the means of its dissemination. This bypasses the traditional gatekeepers, allowing artists to connect directly with their audiences, fostering a more authentic and transparent relationship. This direct connection also allows for fairer revenue sharing, cutting out the often exorbitant fees extracted by intermediaries. However, it's crucial to acknowledge that these platforms aren't a panacea. They often grapple with their own issues of algorithmic bias, promoting certain artists over others and creating new forms of control. Nonetheless, the potential for a more decentralized and equitable music ecosystem is undeniable.

Further fueling this democratization is the growing awareness among consumers of the industry's exploitative practices. The demand for transparency and ethical practices is rising, driven by a growing awareness of the challenges faced by artists. Consumers are increasingly inclined to support artists directly, bypassing major labels and streaming services that offer less favorable royalty rates. This conscious consumerism, coupled with the increasing popularity of subscription services that prioritize fair compensation for artists, is pushing the industry towards a more sustainable model. This necessitates a shift away from a focus solely on streams and downloads, towards a model that recognizes the multifaceted value of artists' contributions – their creative work, their performances, and their engagement with their fan base.

Moreover, the legal landscape surrounding music rights is slowly evolving. While significant hurdles remain, there's a growing recognition of the need for stronger artist protections. This includes more equitable royalty rates for streaming services, stricter regulations on contracts, and improved mechanisms for dispute resolution. The ongoing debate surrounding fair use and copyright laws also requires careful consideration, balancing the rights of artists with the needs of consumers. The fight for legislative reform is a long and arduous process, requiring sustained advocacy and pressure from artists, consumers, and policymakers alike. However, the increasing public awareness of these issues is laying the groundwork for meaningful legal reforms.

The role of technology in shaping this new landscape cannot be overstated. While technology has been used to exploit artists, it also possesses the potential to empower them. Blockchain technology, for example, offers a transparent and secure way to track and manage music rights, preventing fraud and ensuring artists receive their due compensation.

Artificial intelligence, while posing potential threats to artists, could also be harnessed to assist with tasks such as music production, marketing, and distribution, reducing the reliance on expensive intermediaries. The key lies in harnessing these technological advancements ethically and responsibly, ensuring they serve to empower artists rather than further marginalize them.

Education is also crucial in this process. Aspiring and established artists alike need access to comprehensive legal and financial advice. This includes guidance on navigating complex contracts, understanding their rights, and effectively managing their careers. Educational initiatives, workshops, and online resources can play a significant role in equipping artists with the knowledge and skills to navigate the industry's complexities, reducing their vulnerability to exploitation. This proactive approach empowers artists to make informed decisions, ensuring they are not taken advantage of by those with greater resources and experience.

Furthermore, the role of advocacy organizations and artist collectives cannot be overlooked. These groups are vital in providing a unified voice for artists, lobbying for policy changes, and providing essential resources and support. By working collectively, artists can amplify their voices, achieving a level of influence that would be impossible individually. These organizations can provide valuable legal assistance, mentorship programs, and networking opportunities, fostering a supportive community that empowers artists to navigate the complexities of the music industry successfully.

The future of music is not predetermined. It is a canvas upon which we, as artists, consumers, and advocates, paint the picture. The path ahead is not without its challenges. The entrenched power structures of the industry will undoubtedly resist change, deploying their resources and influence to maintain the status quo. But the collective will for a fairer, more sustainable music industry is gathering momentum. The growing awareness of systemic injustices, coupled with the rise of independent artists and informed consumers, is creating an environment conducive to meaningful reform.

The shift will not be instantaneous. It will require sustained effort, collaboration, and a willingness to challenge established norms. But the potential for positive change is within reach. By embracing transparency, promoting ethical practices, and harnessing the power of technology and collective action, we can create a music industry that genuinely values and supports artists, fostering a vibrant and diverse musical landscape for generations to come. The music industry's future isn't just about profit; it's about preserving the art form itself, ensuring its continued evolution and accessibility. It's about ensuring that the passion and dedication of artists are rewarded, not exploited. It's about ensuring that music remains a source of joy, connection, and artistic expression, unburdened by the predatory practices that have plagued it for far too long. The future of music is not a destination but a continuous journey toward justice and equity. It's a journey we must embark upon together, united in our pursuit of a more just and sustainable musical landscape. The potential for a richer, more vibrant musical ecosystem is there; it awaits our collective action to make it a reality.

Acknowledgments

This book would not have been possible without the contributions of numerous individuals. First and foremost, I owe a debt of gratitude to the brave whistleblowers and former industry insiders who risked their careers and reputations to share their stories. Their willingness to speak truth to power is the foundation upon which this investigation rests. Their trust and candor were invaluable. I am also deeply indebted to the investigative journalists, lawyers, and academics who generously shared their expertise and insights, providing invaluable context and guidance. Special thanks go to [Name of

Researcher/Lawyer/Academic 1] for their assistance with

[specific area of assistance], and to [Name of

Researcher/Lawyer/Academic 2] for their invaluable insights into [specific area of assistance]. The unwavering support of my editor, [Editor's Name], who believed in this project from the outset and provided invaluable editorial guidance, is deeply appreciated. Finally, to my family and friends, your patience and understanding throughout this long and often challenging journey are deeply appreciated. This book is dedicated to them.

More from This Author

The Malcolm Dynasty

A Woman's worth

Fame

Fame 2

Awakening: Lies you were told, Sweater after difficulty.

The Cabin Killers

Lock & Key -—Coming Soon

Nightmare on Cannon Ave —Coming Soon

Night Fall – Coming Soon

Check out your Author's Music

YURI tha Jury – Music available on all music platforms...

1. Street Revival
1. Thank me now (Vol. 1 – 2)
1. Thanks 4 now
1. The Zodiac Collection (Vol. 1-4)
1. Propaganda
1. It will all make sense later – Coming Soon

<u>Straight Shooter – Music available on all music platforms...</u>

1. Money power respect
1. Street paper (Vol. 1 – 2)
1. Missing over mind
1. Street Commodity (Vol. 1 – 2)

Be sure to check out: Industry walk through podcast – Everywhere podcasts are Available

Dear Valued Customer,

Thank you for choosing to purchase one of our books. We are thrilled to have you as a customer and hope the book you selected has met your expectations.

As you may already know, our publishing house is known for its exceptional collection of books by different authors. On that note, we would like to recommend that you consider sampling another incredible book called:

The Malcolm Dynasty.

This captivating book takes you on a journey through the life and times of one of the most affluent American families. Through the book, you will get to learn about the struggles, triumphs, and friendships that helped shape the Malcolm Dynasty.

At our publishing house, we have received excellent feedback from those who have read this fantastic book, and we believe that you too will appreciate the thought-provoking and entertaining story it tells.

Once again, thank you for choosing to purchase one of our books. We value your business and look forward to serving you again in the future.

Best regards,

Mankraft Publishing

The Malcolm Dynasty

SAMPLE

Chapter 1: The Beginning

As the sun set over the city, the streets became dimly lit with the flickering of streetlights casting long shadows down the alleyways In a run-down apartment building, a man named Jackson sat alone in his dreary living room. The only light came from the television that was tuned to the news. The reporter's voice filled the room, announcing the latest victim of the serial killer haunting the city. Jackson's stomach turned as he listened to the gruesome details. Three women had been found dead, their bodies mutilated beyond recognition. The police were no closer to finding the killer, and the city was gripped by fear.

Jackson had seen the killer – or at least he thought he had. He had been walking home late one night when he saw a shadowy figure lurking in the alleyway. He couldn't get a good look at the person's face, but he could tell they were up to no good. Since that night, Jackson had been consumed by paranoia. He constantly looked over his shoulder, convinced that the killer was watching him, waiting for the right moment to strike.

As the night wore on, Jackson tried to distract himself by reading a book or watching a movie, but he couldn't shake the feeling of dread that permeated every inch of his apartment. Just before midnight, there was a knock at the door. Jackson froze, his heart racing. He cautiously approached the door and peered through the peephole. Standing on the other side was a tall, shadowy figure. Jackson's pulse quickened as he reached for the doorknob. He knew it was probably foolish to open the door, but he couldn't help himself. The figure stepped inside the apartment, and Jackson could feel the chill of death in the air. He tried to stumble backward, but the figure moved too fast for him to get away. As Jackson fell to the ground, he caught a glimpse of the figure's face – a twisted, contorted visage that would haunt his nightmares for years to come. The killer had finally found him, and he knew there was no escape. As his vision faded to black, he realized that the darkness he had felt for so long had finally consumed him. The sun was setting behind the tall buildings, casting long shadows across the dark alleyway. A lone figure stepped out of the shadows, her black leather jacket glinting in the fading light. Her name was Raven, and she was one of the deadliest assassins in the city. She had been hired to take out a corrupt politician who had been causing problems for her client. As she made her way through the city streets, she couldn't shake the feeling that she was being followed. She quickened her pace, but the footsteps behind her only grew louder. Suddenly, a hand grabbed her shoulder, and she spun around, her hand already reaching for

Her weapon. But the figure standing before her wasn't an enemy. It was a man, dressed in all black with a face mask covering his features. "Who are you?" she demanded. The man didn't answer, but he handed her a piece of paper with an address written on it. "Meet me here tomorrow night," he said, before disappearing into the shadows once more. Curiosity getting the better of her, Raven decided to investigate. She had no idea what was in store for her. Raven is like your average red neck from Oklahoma.

Follow the Author on Instagram @ YURI tha Jury _ official

Did you love *The music industry Inside Secrets*? Then you should read *Lock & Key: The industry secrets*[1] by YURI tha Jury and Straight-Shooter!

[2]

All about the world of music and entertainment, from the views as a Artist, Manager, producer and consumer as well as the dark side of entertainment as we know it today

1. https://books2read.com/u/3LXpn7
2. https://books2read.com/u/3LXpn7

Also by YURI tha Jury

Book series 1
Fame

Standalone
The Malcolm Dynasty
A women's worth
YURI tha Jury _Fame 2
Nightmare on Cannon Ave
Lock & Key: The industry secrets
Family Dynasty
The music industry Inside Secrets
Night fall
The Straight Shooter Story

www.ingramcontent.com/pod-product-compliance
Lightning Source LLC
LaVergne TN
LVHW090302210926
848480LV00001B/106
9798230175629